THE AVANT GARDE OF WESTERN CIV

THE AVANT GARDE OF WESTERN CIV

A MEMOIR

DAVID HOLDRIDGE

PRESS AMERICANA
Los Angeles   Hollywood

PRESS AMERICANA

americanpopularculture.com

Cover Art and Metro: Sara Walker

Kolera Sketch: Jhon Charles

Map: Anne Patrice Swanson

Library of Congress Cataloging-in-Publication Data

Names: Holdridge, David, author.
Title: The avant garde of Western civ : a memoir / David Holdridge.
Description: Los Angeles : Press Americana, [2017]
Identifiers: LCCN 2016051484 | ISBN 9780996777919
Subjects: LCSH: Holdridge, David. | Holdridge, David--Travel. |
Humanitarian
assistance, American--Middle East--History. | War relief--Middle
East--History. | Non-governmental organizations--Employees--
Biography. |
Americans--Middle East--Biography. | Vietnam War,
1961-1975--Veterans--United States--Biography. | Middle East--Politics
and
government--1979- | Middle East--Relations--United States. | United
States--Relations--Middle East.
Classification: LCC HV590 .H76 2017 | DDC 363.34/9857092 [B] --dc23
LC record available at https://lccn.loc.gov/2016051484

For that "unsuspecting faith,"
lying beside me at 27 Rue Buffault

Contents

PREFACE

Chelsea Naval Hospital, 1970

Things didn't go anywhere in neuropsychiatric. They rolled me out and down the elevator every week or two to the basement to probe the ganglion with a needle. Face up, I watched them push the needle through my neck until it reached the spine. The results continued to be hopeless. In the time between, I sailed on drugs. Except for another Big Nurse who threw away wet towels and snapped open shades, the others left me alone, wrapped in damp cloth in a dark room. Eventually, they took the casts off my right leg and left arm. While there was some regeneration – except of course in the dead right arm – it didn't matter anymore. The pain in the left palm and the prospect of it had completely crippled me.

I passed the time in my way. After the shot, I had learned how to push the stylus with my thumb into the groove on my portable record player and whereby be, for the most part, asleep but conscious enough that I could affect my dreams. Their direction, pace, and detail. Modulating the weather. Painting tragic circumstances. Killing enemies. A face was beatified. A woman's kindness prevailed...while the strains of the music sifted through my mind. The towels dried, and I slept on, unaware of their dryness. The I.V. was changed, and I slept on. I took the prescribed cc's from one shot to the next. The bed sores multiplied and grew in circumference. From rashes to bloody pulp. They had given up on trying to get me to walk. They said they had others who needed their time. Change the solutions, wet the towels, Demerol, remove the bedpan, clean up my mess. As with the music, I served myself in other ways. I used the fingers on my good hand to crabwalk across the sheets to get the pack of cigarettes, the pieces of food on the tray, the lighter, the tissues. At night, I was happiest. I stayed awake and smoked, my resting hand just under my chin, my forefingers lifting the butt an inch for a drag, staring beneath the window shade at the Chelsea Bridge as the distant trucks moved through the trestles under the lights. I blew the ashes down the covers and flicked the butt on the floor.

I was not crazy as many thought.

"He'll be well when he wants to be well," they had told my parents when they drove up to visit. My father, unable to look at me; my mother, set to nursing the wounded. I was not crazy. My mind had it all.

They called it causalgia. The sympathetic and the parasympathetic were somehow fused, and I physically could no longer tolerate discordant sound, dryness or bright light, all of which created an unbearable searing pain in my left palm, soothed only by those shots within a very still world of both dark and wet. Beyond that, there was Big Nurse and the weekly practice on my neck in the dungeon that would, I knew, soon enough drive me crazy.

Finally, after months, they gave up. They gave me a refillable prescription for lesser drugs and a permanent transfer out. Permanently disabled, I was called. Pensioned out, honorably.

Suffield, 1970

They had laid me across the back seat of the Ford, swaddled in the wet compresses. My father's attempt had followed. "David, just so I understand, how does the water help?" Silence. "I mean what would happen without it?" I didn't bother answering. They had a war hero on their hands. So back off with the things will be OK routine. My mother looked at Henry to drop it and pulled out another washcloth from the bucket she had put between her legs in the well of the car.

After some more words, they agreed to set up a bed for me in the basement. It had always been dank. The cement sweated. The floor was beneath the water table. There was one old cobwebby window at ground level, which, when I reclined, gave me a glimpse of the sky and whenever the wind blew, of a branch of the old cottonwood. There wasn't much else. My old set of barbells, the furnace, the oil tank. My mother brought down a side table for my portable record player, and a waste paper basket. There was a tap and a bucket where I soaked my towels. I could limp to a sump hole for a piss and shit in another bucket. Three times a day she brought down cut-up food. Once a week she took the sheets. She informed me of visitors and callers and dutifully sent them away.

With time, she helped me to lift the hatch at night and take a couple of steps in the backyard. Barefoot in the cold grass, ragged in my blue hospital bottoms, I took my first steps in months...with my grandfather's mahogany cane no less. Except for an occasional bark or the light coming off a full moon on a cloudless night, it was painless. By later in the year, I even took to longer distances. The sores retracted. My mother was pleased with the progress. There were traces of something else on the bone beside skin and gristle. The bucket could be taken away; I shat in the woods. With the first snows, I was forced to wear slick black rubbers on my feet and drape my old school coat over me.

Days were different. Darvon, even several, is not Demerol. I got my mother to bring down jug wine and washed them down. She disapproved, yet this routine kept me afloat until nightfall. Henry said he hoped she knew what she was doing. I heard his car pull in each evening. He'd stick his head down the stairwell and ask me how things were. I answered, "OK." "Any chance of you joining us tonight, David? It'd sure mean a lot to us." My palm burned at the thought. Silence. "If there's anything you need, call us, won't you, David?" Silence. "Won't you David?" A tinge of anger in the voice. "Yes," I answered. The door closed. Sister Roo visited once, but I closed the door there, too. "I told you mom, no visitors. It's not their bloodline that causes burning. It's their noise. Is Roo noiseless?" My sister had brought a friend from California. They were sitting out where I walked at night. In Moroccan leather hats and lumberjack shirts, their hair braided in cornrows.

I didn't come up for Christmas, and there was nothing I could use anyway. I got a little drunker than usual and played Adeste Fideles on my portable. A couple of weeks later mom and I moved my bed closer to the furnace, and I lost my occasional glimpse of the day entirely. I spent the rest of the winter and spring like that. Now running – even in the snow – building my strength, actually putting a clock on myself as I ran, right arm still dangling dead as polio Clem, through the forest to the field where Dickie and I had made a sort of love in our underground tunnels and back again. Down to the frozen swimming hole at Stony Brook where fifteen years earlier we had danced around with flowers in our pee holes. Usually out by midnight, I was back before the first car lights came down the road. I didn't think beyond that. There was no one. There was no one looking for me. My father had suffered as much as he could. His only boy, in his prime, living like a mole. A dark story alongside all the sales talk. Swanie was nursing her child. Roo had her life. I had my woman in my mind who came as she was imagined and of course the faces of the dead soldiers hanging there.

In summer, my mother effected another breakthrough. Almost on the anniversary of my seclusion in the basement. I had had my hands in the water pail gripping onto a towel when she had slipped on the last stair and the tray of lunch had gone clattering onto the cement. I had spun my head over my shoulder ready to take the inevitable burn. It never came. While she was bent over picking up the pieces and calling herself clumsy, she had unconsciously happened on a great discovery. I could handle noises, and presumably light, if I – my hands I mean – were in water, in contrast – and this was the discovery – to only being wet. I told her to scrape her shoes on the stairs. Nothing. Not the slightest burn. Asked her to turn on the lights...to rub her dry hands on her dress. Dry on dry, in glaring light. The worst. I looked down at my hands magnified in the water, one apparently doused, the other hanging by a nearly dead line from my shoulder. I turned the palms up underwater. There was no pain.

In the beginning, I was tentative. I went out at twilight, my mother holding a pail of water with my hands in it. My father stood off to the side offering encouragement for the first steps in daylight, albeit somewhat complicated by the accessory. Roo was phoned and given the good news.

My father prevailed. The pool they bought was a temporary model. A Kool Pool it was called. A plastic tub four feet deep and fourteen feet across. "Don't be ridiculous, Swanie. We are not spending ten thousand dollars on an in-ground pool for something that could be over tomorrow. Sometimes you amaze me. Is that what you want...the boy to spend his life as a reptile?"

Of course she didn't, she said. "Sometimes Henry, you can be so cheap."

Now my life was topsy-turvy. In the blaze of the day with lawnmowers humming and children screaming, there I was lolling like an alligator, in my pool, feeling none of it. My metal head plate, part of the earlier desecration of my body by shrapnel, warming like a pan. The corpus shriveled like a pink prune, the sun burning my maze of scars scarlet.

Neighbors stopped by to converse. My father brought Rotarians by. I was interviewed for the local paper. Always with my hands way beneath the surface. Otherwise, I stared over the edge, took in the world at peace, and when I had had enough, dropped down under the water and pushed off across my pool, my hands fluttering like fins behind me. This was late June. By August, I was propelling myself from both elbows down. The nerves definitely regenerating as the doctor Henry had brought poolside, pronounced. Life crept up to my shoulders. Muscle reappeared on the arm bones. And on one dramatic day, I took my better arm out for a stroke. Dragged it along the surface and let it sink down. Late into the night one became several, my body rolled in the rhythm of the crawl. Progress was swift. I pulled myself across. Back and forth in fourteen foot laps. Then no legs and finally by the cool days of autumn, weights tied to the ankles. Emerging, at the end of the day, over the side in the dark. Purple and shriveled. And soon back under the light in the basement with my hands in the pail, my body now becoming a faded pink jigsaw. Now with the flush of health on the face. Unkempt hair. I took the vanity of tailoring the beard. But not much more. Once I had overheard that Roo was looking for a solution. From November to April, I reverted to running at night.

Only once in the second year, and that for my father's sake, did I let myself be taken out. Someone from the town. One of my former enemies from school, now a born again Christian. I took a lot of Darvon and a couple of quarts of wine and soaked my socks and gloves beforehand. I had donned sunglasses. I looked like a myth. There I was in the shadows at a corner table, overwhelmed by the glamour of the bar, alternately pouring water into my shoes and gloves. Girls had never been talked to as such. Someone with a live coal in his hand putting words to

them fearlessly. Throwing back glasses of whiskey without a
wince. Dousing the dry in his shoes with table water. And they
can tell when it's real. No theatre by the piano at Saratoga from
me this time. Those glossy lips, the creamy skin, the sweeping
lashes were getting more passion off him than they'd get in a
lifetime. Nothing to do with legs in the air and a dick like a
piston. A brilliant residue of war inches from their lips. Others,
boyfriends, tugged at them even as they looked back to stay with
me. The bar was closing. I put the rest of the water in my gloves
and was driven home.

The Christian didn't call again, and anyway there was no
future to the incident. How would the unprecedented passion
hold up when they pulled the shirt apart onto a crisscross of
scars, onto the black specks of shrapnel, now a year later rising
to the surface? A lover who did them in his basement on wet
sheets? Whose last such remembrance was the pocked orderly
washing his dick, interminably, while he thrashed about,
strapped to his gurney.

Asylum Hill, 1971

One night in April, my dad waited for me to come out and run.
He sat on the stump of the willow perfectly still, as the whole
family now knew how to do, save those hours when I was in
water. There was a specialist. A Doctor Benjamin Whitcomb. He
would see me. Roo would drive me there. I'd see him at his
home tomorrow night. I said I thought I could stay as I was. Why
confuse it?

So for the last time, I prepared to go out. To an old Tudor
home on Asylum in Hartford. I was led into the main room.
Tapestries and hardwood. A great stone fireplace. I sat, Roo still,
the sock drying, licking the palms of my gloves. I would ask him
to cut it off. A white-haired Yankee. The healer. He talked to me
before the fire. I described the pain. What had been done before
Chelsea. "Could you take one of the gloves off?" He saw me
shaking. Inside I was chanting. Madly, blinking my eyes. The
doctor held my hand, and with his other, he reached up to a table
lamp. I chanted louder and looked past him. He pulled the
switch, and I could go no further. I yanked back my hand into

my crotch and doubled up. The nonsense burst out. Do dah, Do dah, Do dah, La, La, La, La, La...

Roo took me to the bathroom where she filled the sink over my hands and soaked the gloves. Later, she took me out, and we met the doctor on a path through the front lawn. He told Roo to check me in, the next day. He'd operate the day after.

"Can you fix it, doctor?" I asked.

"I think so," he said.

PART ONE

CHAPTER 1

Desert Shield and Desert Storm, 1990–1991

The specter of Palestinians dancing on their roofs in East
Jerusalem as Saddam's scuds came in was enough to silence any
further debate on the matter. And so most mainstream overseas
charities – also known as humanitarian agencies or NGOs (Non-
Governmental Organizations) – such as mine got reduced to
platitudes about peace. Once again, it seemed that Christian
teachings had fallen victim to the politics of the water below.
Very much below, if you consider their complicity in the
keeping of Secretary Baker's promise to send Iraq back to the
dark ages, should it not capitulate.

That, seen against those Quaker Friends lining Baltimore's
Charles Street, not far from my headquarters, was infuriating.
Yes, the juxtaposition of the Friends with candles – subjecting
themselves to popular taunts – with that of the Supreme Council
of American Catholics as it got set to endorse Desert Storm as
Jus Bellum Iustum was stark.

For me, it was a tough adjustment to make – to look away
from the descent of Africa where I had been working – and now
to focus on the trials of populations most usually accustomed to
a modicum of comfort. I had not even discussed the possibility
of a choice for my colleague Joe at the time of the Baker
ultimatums, when those first refugees had begun to come down
the road from Baghdad to Amman. He had willingly dispatched
himself from his seat in Cairo to help insert the agency into
caring for those migrants.

Here in Amman, it was not some forgotten tragedy like
Southern Sudan. Here, you needed sharp elbows and a knack for
marketing. Yes, indeed, these were souls seeking refuge. But, for
the most part, they were not Iraqis. These were Egyptian,
Vietnamese, Filipinos, and Sudanese. They were the guest
workers paid from Iraqi oil, now unwilling to get caught in the
hi-tech maelstrom to come.

No, I asserted, before these pyrotechnics, there would be no slow death march...following the corpses to the Ethiopian border. No, here they came down the road in big sedans, paid for by a fire sale of those assets, which were immovable. It took getting used to. No swollen bellies and no dead babies still cradled in the mother's arms. No, here it was a quick transit to planes or ferries taking them back home where they would wait out the war. Joe knew the game. Perhaps better than anyone. The game being a situation so highly publicized in the West that no board of a major charity would allow itself to be absent, notwithstanding that by being present it would be putting itself in a situation where oftentimes the assistance suffocates the recipients.

Joe knew. Get visible, get visible quick, and get the press there. This calamity, which now had America at the edge of war, needed an NGO billboard in the midst of it. Light on the ground. Big before media.

"Dry packs," Joe said.

"Go on," I replied.

"We set up right on the road; all in Catholic Relief Services T-shirts and insignia. We give them a plastic package of fruit and crackers and drink...sort of to hold them till they can reach the ferry in Aqaba or catch the charter out of Amman."

And so Joe had gotten us visible and seemingly pertinent. Money, once again, was flowing into HQ from our domestic constituency; mostly, I was sure, from those same citizens who had cruised by the Friends on Charles in Baltimore that night.

This boost to revenues would do for HQ, but it would not do for Joe and me. It was not why I had been given my head. Inexorably, America was preparing for war. There was no doubt anywhere about the American led coalition securing victory. The only debate got to the issue of whether America would accept any casualties. The post-Vietnam syndrome they called it. Make victory quick and bloodless, or Americans will lose interest. In other words, no body bags. As events conspired, Joe and I, from our respective locations, had not had to wait long, looking down the road out there with our dry packs.

The incandescence, as seen from the roof of the Al Rasheed Hotel on the banks of the Tigris, transfixed a hundred million viewers. Afterwards, it was what you would expect of us. Get into Baghdad fast...before Desert Storm was spent. Get in and then from that base provide the Iraqi mothers and fathers, the children, the grandparents with another, albeit mostly symbolic, view of America. Get in there and help the survivors get food and medicine. Make the distinction to Americans, not allowed by the war machine, between Saddam and the victims.

"Perfectly what you would expect," I had written in my diary. "Joe, as that piece of paper settling to earth...one day eventually, au hasard, to blacken and curl in a fire. And me, his boss, under grey skies, gunpowder in the air, all Tennyson, despite what had befallen me in Vietnam."

We left according to script. That same adrenaline flow that went through you whenever you crossed that line into terra incognita. A four-wheel drive, a Jordanian driver, Joe and I, now leaving the outskirts of Amman at 9pm and bound for Baghdad. "Thirteen hours," I said to Joe, "if we get through."

But, as I said, Joe didn't know about these details. He just knew this is what he did. And, soon enough, his eyes had closed and his legs had curled up, while I, as ever, in search of incandescence, was as wide-eyed as the deer in the headlights and wouldn't have been able to miss a second.

At times like this, there is an otherworldly quiet in the car — just some occasional sounds from Joe as he turned in his sleep. The lights on the dash. The road is unrelieved, a straight hard surface across the bleak Hamada. The silhouette of a dog howling at the moon. And you are alone. There is no traffic but you. It was what I had done before in South Lebanon and would do again in Belgrade. It was the lonely venture into a battlefield in the wake of a large scale killing. No traffic. No lights. Either off in the scrub or on the hardscrabble.

"Balls to the wall," Joe said. He had sat up and was rubbing the sleep from his eyes. Which, when I came to think about it, was almost supernatural. A moment later, out of that desolate trek, had slowly appeared a string of low watt lights across the hard surface and the shadows of men shifting between some outbuildings. As you can imagine, both of us were getting very alert at this juncture. America had just spent the previous few weeks trying to incinerate this ancient land of the Tigris and Euphrates and once again, here we were, the emissaries of that same destructive force, daring to drive up to this border crossing into Iraq and put our pale faces in front of these Iraqi guards.

I don't know. Perhaps they didn't care – either way. I still tend to be taken aback that, seemingly regardless of circumstances, for some, it's often business as usual. I mean the paunches, the dead eyes, the glass of tea, and the pack of smokes. The slow laborious inspection of the pages. The calling of the supervisor to also thumb through the pages. Just Joe and I sitting there under the moon in the cold Hamada, with me doing my damnedest to effect a respectful nonchalance and Joe just coming by it naturally. Sort of twiddling our thumbs on the edge of the unknown.

If we chose to be rational, sitting there and shooting the breeze in the cold night air, odds were that we were not worth hurting and probably worth listening to. But when thousands of dog-faced Iraqi soldiers have just been mowed down by Yankee gunships, like wheat at harvest, then, when you think on it, it may happen that some grieved brother or sister might just walk up to us there on our bench, normal as could be, and once in front of us, as we look up at her, just raise a revolver and blow our brains out.

Certainly, it was not like walking through the dead in the aftermath of Gettysburg. Not in Baghdad, that is. It was rather those cement slabs and re-rod. Collapsed like mushrooms, as Joe used to say. That and the stillness of a city without life, without circulation and movement. And into which Joe and I drove, up and down dead streets, occasionally coming upon people picking through the rubble or scavenging for wood. Here and there was a light bulb working off a generator or a pan of coals heating some tea or kebab. These were the first days. A traumatization. Before "degraded life" in this nation became normal and decapitalization, as the euphemism went, began on a massive scale.

It had been most unusual – our meeting with Minister Sahha. It was a modern steel and glass construction, undamaged, but without electricity. So here we found ourselves, "Joe and me," sitting in the lobby of the building with some guards milling about and twilight upon us. By nightfall, these two lackeys with flashlights had appeared out of a side door, sort of like the headlights of a car, into the lobby and signaled for us to follow. And then the four of us had begun the ascent up this barren stairwell with these monstrous shadows being cast by the flashlights. Moving up toward the minister, nine flights away, with Joe and me looking at each other quite circumspect as we followed the lights up the well. It was an easy place to imagine the worst, what with the shadows dancing around us and our two escorts grim and uncommunicative. Quite relieved, as it turned out, when we reached the eighth floor and saw a side door onto the stairwell opening and light being emitted, followed by another functionary also going up, nodding to our escorts and then looking down on us without comment.

This counsellor had done foreign relations for a country with a half million men under arms and enough fossil fuel under ancient land to keep it prosperous for eternity. And now we, two persons of little significance, were being ushered into his cabinet with no one waiting before us, nor none after. I remember distinctly it was a black cable that had carried light to our discussion...a short talk, I recall, accompanied by the hum of the diesel generator, apparently stuck in the room next door. His nerves were frayed. I had seen this before and knew to recognize it. This man who had practiced diplomacy in foreign capitals was now so strung out it was an embarrassment for us to watch him try to get a light to his cigarette or the demitasse to his mouth. All the while, his eyes avoiding ours. Very quick and furtive as if an important call were coming. Momentarily.

The terms were familiar. "Just a different application," I had told Joe. We would truck in from Aqaba – food and medicines – on condition we could target and monitor their delivery to all victims, to include Kurd and Shia alike.

All told, we had argued, it would be a pipeline outside of Saddam's secret manipulation or none at all. "Please understand," I had said, "we represent millions in the United States, and we are preparing a humane response to those in need. We are hoping, from an office in Baghdad, to draw America's attention and resources toward repair and healing." But he was not paying attention. We were very small fry. And he had damned well been around enough to know we would be lucky enough to deliver a fraction of what we were claiming.

In the end, I suppose we got time with him...either because he thought we might be bearing an official message or because he had nothing else to do. Or, perhaps even as Joe had offered, "Because we were the only ones who would walk up nine flights of stairs." Anyway, finally, he had agreed to sign an accord along the lines we presented although I suspected that he was too frazzled to be counted on. Not, I guessed, because of this national catastrophe, but more probably because Saddam was at that very moment circling the wagons and this diplomat, I supposed, was not sure whether he was inside the circle or out.

Thus, it appeared we would take the money that had come in for the long suffering Kurds in the North, but use our own license to spread it around both geographically and regardless of faith to anyone who could no longer put food on the table, to include the families of Saddam's dead soldiers. Of course, the effort achieved far less than it might have since our public affairs people muted the universality of our distributions and only dared whisper about our command and logistics structure in Baghdad, knowing full well that Americans would not be so merciful toward Iraqis in general...not so soon on the heels of kicking the bejesus out of them. No, for the silent majority, it was, at that moment, the Kurdish minority in the North, specifically and exclusively, who were deserving.

Then in a moment of courage and individual license, those private citizen monies we received were matched with US government monies. A political appointee to State, Andrew Natsios by name, bucked the specter of Jesse Helms, the notorious conservative in the Senate, and did the right thing. So there you were, at the end of the day, with both taxpayer and citizen "will" having been bent to serve a better purpose.

"I don't understand," I was asking Joe afterward, as we drove back past the wreckage to our hotel. "How could our Catholic Conference 'pile on' for a just war while the Bishop here has been going public for weeks in support of Saddam? Where the hell is the Catholic universality in all this?"

Joe just pursed his lips into that tight smile of his and put his arm on my shoulder. "You know the answer to that, don't you?"

I was now looking askance.

"You know," he said in a parody of our associates from State, "our Conference doesn't have friends...only interests."

There you had it. Our conservative Bishops beating on the table to destroy Saddam while Bishop Bidawid would sit later in the day talking to us about the tragedy visited on his country with a bigger than life portrait of Saddam behind his head and a little pocket size replica of his Holiness on a far wall.

It was a program that was to last nearly two years, until the time came when Saddam saw that no political advantage in the US could be squeezed out of it and when the liberties we took to assure accurate monitoring were just too shocking to this particular regime to be sustained.

I was lying on some grassy knoll east of Sulaymaniyah, during a subsequent visit, among more of those dog-faced Iraqi Infantry, who were at that time facing off in the distance against a similar brigade of Kurdish Peshmerga. At that moment, the essential emptiness of these efforts began to stir in me. I had a bit of straw in my teeth and was lying back on my elbows and was staring at a profusion of wildflowers in the valley. I was thinking that I, we, Natsios, Joe could turn donor intent in Ethiopia, in Angola, in Iraq – you name it. We could be better than our constituencies and then take care to only whisper about our duplicity. I mean, granted it sure as hell did provide heartfelt surprise and wonder when Yanks like us appeared and put out our hand in friendship to some poor soul whose God had put in such a benighted land...and our supplies did get to places otherwise neglected. But all in all, we were doing precious little about changing the dynamic of Americans and Arabs – the relationship between this dog-faced infantry troop and his opposite number in the Kurdish opposition across the valley and their relationships to the man who sat next to me, back in the States, in the pew on Sunday, or at the bar on Saturday night. Nothing that happened between these distant people got altered. On the contrary, the relationship was most often blackened by the intermediary of the White House or the media, the first for propaganda and the second for publicity, and we, overseas charities, were...well...almost wistful in the light of that dynamic.

CHAPTER 2

Right Relations

Michiko Ota, a disciple of Martin Luther King, was expelled from the US for subversive activities in the 1960s. She then spent ten years in the Sahara as a contemplative nun and turned later on to biblical exegesis. I had met her for the first time just after the first refugees had begun leaving Iraq in the fall of 1990. At that time, she was the head of a Japanese NGO called Hands of Peace, which had collected funds to fly Vietnamese back home.

We were sitting around Amman one evening, and I was going on about how nothing makes much sense in the Middle East unless one starts with the Sun and the Shade and Water and man's relation to them. She had taken that comment as an introduction to what she had called "The Water Above and The Water Below." Next, she recounted how she had been taking her students from Osaka to the Holy Land for work-study programs and how they had found the concept of justice foreign and references within the Abrahamic faiths to it confusing.

She had led them to Genesis...to the passage of life "between the waters above and waters below."

The waters below, she explained, referred to the civilizations that grew up alongside the great rivers of the region – the Nile, Tigris, Euphrates – and how these rivers lent themselves to man's manipulation and supplied networks of waters for the sustenance of tribes. Man exerted control over the water. Hierarchy ensued. The man/god prevailed.

The Hebrews by contrast, she elucidated, had wandered the plains of the Levant with small ruminants. Water fell from a mysterious source on everyman, equally. Sustenance was unpredictable and heaven sent.

These then, Michiko argued, were "The Water Above and The Water Below." In the second instance, the divine was knowable and was the provider of sustenance according to his manipulation.

In the former, the divine was unknowable as was the provision of His sustenance.

The "water below" produced manmade hierarchies that ruled with certainty.

The "water above" produced ultimate belief in the mysteries that affected everyman, equally.

Jesus was a creation of the "water above" experience. His God was unknowable. Sustenance was for every man equally.

These conceptions, she concluded, had formed the basis for Right Relations or justice, as the Greeks called it. These Right Relations are founded in the unknowable nature of the mysteries and in the mutual dependence of mankind.

Of course, as Michiko would explain, that early myth of Jesus as the harbinger of Right Relations soon raced through the world and drew to it all who had suffered from the presumptions of the "water below."

Soon on, Christianity, succumbed itself to hierarchy and even, on occasion, to a knowable God.

CHAPTER 3

Shock and Awe, Amman, Jordan, March 2003

Twelve years later, after almost a decade of following the war in the Balkans east from Zagreb to Belgrade, culminating afterward with a rather sentimental assignment in Hanoi for a couple of years, I was back on "GO" again. Yessiree...new King...same place...different charity.

It was really just a fluke. I mean, my being booked into a place called Best Western. In the fifth circle of Amman.

The journey took some courage on my part. The weather was miserable outside. Snow slush and cold wind and all I had was a thin raincoat and some old dress shoes. One of which had a hole in the leather sole, which, of course, got my sock soaked as soon as I stepped out on my several forays.

I kept a smile on, but I could tell that while the citizens might be pleasant enough to me they didn't like what I represented. It seemed this time the King was for it – with equivocation, of course, given the Palestinian population around him and the uncertainty of how the venture would play out in his kingdom. And the taxi drivers would chat with me, but the few folk left in the hotel had grown silent when I had come down for breakfast. And I remember getting stalled in traffic outside a mosque on Friday and thinking I better shrink down in the cab as the faithful were leaving in large numbers, agitated it appeared.

I had some donor funds with me – not much – just enough to provide Iraqi's with something symbolic. And a couple of Christian contacts I had made helped me out around town.

Snow, ice in the streets, all the foreigners gone. And yes, in Florida, one could imagine CENTCOM and its preparations for war. Its panels of terminals, the forest of dishes and antennas. The huge heave up of the massive logistics involved. Yes, in that March of 2003, we all heard the trembling "of an army charging upon the land." The greatest amalgam of technology and commo ever known – smarter yet than that assembled for Desert Storm twelve years earlier.

And then, we could also imagine a somewhat less capable group in Washington, in the White House, at the Department of Defense or State driving the larger stratagems for transformation in the Middle East – setting forth from America with unprecedented idealism. And prevarication.

And so, my friend, a shopkeeper with scant revenue these days, picked me up in his rattletrap, and slowly we filled a couple of rented trucks with relief supplies, had their tarps painted with our charity identity, negotiated with some possible drivers, and watched their price go higher each day with the increasing imminence of war.

Afterward I went back to my room, watched CNN and BBC, and reported on progress to my HQ on my T-Mobile.

That first week in March, there was still hope. Talks were attempted, some vigils for peace had sprung up back home, but no trigger had yet been pulled. But if one took time to think on it, one knew that George Bush was surely intent and that Saddam was surely willing to sacrifice his people.

And so, equally, these were days of uncertainty for relief organizations. Nearly all of them expected large refugee flows to the surrounding countries, similar to 1991, but this time composed mostly of Iraqis. Several outfits were doing their assessments. Tents, water and hygiene, food, non-food, health, "vulnerables." A few of them were looking to make a statement or to be a witness or to do a reconnaissance. They wanted to get into Baghdad as well – to be there with their small supplies or to transmit the symbols of solidarity home or to huddle with those in the way of that army upon the land and the terrible uncertainties of how someone as mad as Saddam would handle his defeat.

I lay on my bed. The heat had gone on the blink, and then one day the toilet started leaking – so now it was dismal inside as well. I kept my coat on under the covers, read text messages from HQ, and watched the news. The trucks were ready for the next day. No refugees had appeared. Bush and Chirac were trading insults; England was steadfast on principle; and some other lesser countries were lining up. Turkey was reluctant, and Russia upset. Germany said no.

Gloomy, cold, alone.

My HQ, like most HQs, would decide the "whether" on a host of institutional variables; the "when and how" on the basis of the info you chose to give them. Getting the presence, the position – whether the trigger got pulled or not – had implications for overseas charities. To be relevant and to get noticed often meant survival. Advocacy, new programs are built on "first presence."

I knew the road ahead. The very late departure from Amman when nothing is stirring and then the headlights appear in the dark. You drain the last of your beloved coffee and light the equally beloved smoke. And then you pull yourself up into the cab with a man you just met that afternoon – a man from whom you will get no second chances if he deceives you or fails you. I mean, you like his smile. His hands are strong and so you're off, feeling absolutely vulnerable at any time should a BMW race out from behind a berm and kidnap you or an F-I6 swoop down and take you out.

No, it's just you and he in the cab, and he, by culture and religion, is much more prepared to go than you.

I knew that stretch – very lonely, as I said, until you hit the Euphrates.

And so I lay there in the Best Western waiting for a text message and really figuring that the only justification I could give myself was not "platform for program" or a great resonant advocacy – I probably needed to be brave so as to be able to live the way I had wanted, but had often failed.

This time, however, the text came back, "The Board says no," and I felt simultaneously off the hook but also deprived for the reasons mentioned. A few days later, Tommy Franks's army crossed in from Kuwait and Saudi Arabia, heading for Baghdad. Operation Iraqi Freedom had begun. In the north of Iraq, US Special Forces joined the Kurdish Peshmerga and headed south toward Kirkuk and Khanaqin.

So now, I would wait out the war and watch the show as I had in 1991 – that unforgettable moment in history when Peter Arnett had broadcast from the roof of Al Rasheed amidst the pyrotechnical bursts over Baghdad.

This time it was billed as "Shock and Awe" – and that it did – with different interpretations depending on your perspective.

A long way from Leatherstocking, I was thinking. From war paint and buckskins. Now everyone was wired or wireless. Uploading and downloading to and from satellites. All connected in a vast electronic net. This was the mother of all arcades. And now, instead of Arnett on the roof, we had live feeds from embeds.

I think everyone could have guessed the results. For most Americans, there was a satisfaction – a settling into their easy chair with a drink and some snacks.

For those from Secretary of Defense Rumsfeld's "old Europe," there was an empty sense of irrelevance – a bitter reaction from those not listened to.

For Arabs, it would be transformative, leaving them eventually as pariahs before the world for a generation to come.

The war's full significance was not yet fathomed by America. For now, it was only the Pentagon, the arrows on the charts, the overhead displays of the unrelenting Army of Tommy Franks heading up the Tigris and Euphrates while special ops units came down from the North with the Kurdish fighters. Inexorable, the advances. Three weeks till the Americans were sitting in Baghdad, dismantling the statue of Saddam in Firdos Square. The Republican Guard in disarray. The leadership fleeing and a comic mouthpiece left chatting senselessly to CNN.

Soon after the advance had begun, I called up a Jordanian businessman recommended by my headquarters and was invited to visit him at his office. It was one of those spacious affairs reflecting the vanities of the position with leather couches and chairs at one end, a large brass coffee table, and a console with several TVs, all on and all tuned to different channels: Al Jazeera, Al Arabiya, CNN, BBC.

There were other Arab businessmen there when I arrived, some in exile from Iraq. All fiddling with the remotes for more or less volume between sips of tea. I sensed I was there to provide the "American commentary" of sorts – though all of those men had either studied or had done business in the States or the UK.

By any standard, they were rich and cosmopolitan. Yet, as we gathered there over the next couple of weeks, I saw all too clearly that as much as they had hated Saddam, they hated this public humiliation at America's hand much worse. They said foolish things about how the first week was just a plan to draw the invaders into some sort of cul de sac. And on another occasion, how surely Saddam would defeat them at the Gates of Baghdad in some sort of rough approximation of the siege of Leningrad.

As each of these fantasies dissolved, they spoke less to me, averted their eyes, discussed other issues in Arabic, and at the end, it was almost as if the war were inconsequential. Finally, I remember, when the statue got pulled down, they had stood up, one by one, and left. My host felt awkward with just the two of us sitting there. He turned off all the channels except CNN and went over to his fancy desk and made some calls, came back, and apologized. He had to go. As I stood up, he looked at me and shrugged – as if to say "such is life."

There they were: the London School of Economics, Michigan State, victims of Saddam, exiles. Yet in the foolish gestures and in their resignation at the end lay the whole issue before us. A civilization once; the center of the world once; and now, since oil, spiraling down to insignificance on the world stage. Worse – exposed to the world as laughing stocks at the hands of a terribly swift force from a future century.

It was that, the Iraqi humiliation, more than anything, that the American government had miscalculated. That degradation would trump the great gift of liberation the US had handed to the Shia and Kurds as well as the presumed and actual jump start for the introduction of an "open and pluralistic" society in the Arab world.

At the heart of it was Arab pride – all the more so because they had nothing these days to be proud of.

With time, the war allowed for Zarqawi; it produced the Sunni insurgency; and it spawned the ascent of Moqtada Al-Sadr. Could it serve as cold water to the face of Arab complacency? Perhaps. An incentive for them for renaissance? Maybe. But only if the visible aspects of the historic humiliation vanished quickly and even then the West would pay for some time to come in terms of terrorist attacks and more grievously from the deterioration of its own civil liberties.

CHAPTER 4

Back to Baghdad, April 2003

I decided that since Baghdad was now so open, it no longer made sense to rush in the two symbolic trucks. Their entry into the mess would seem more pathetic than meaningful.

They would come in later, eventually, when I had found someone who would make good use of their contents.

Nonetheless, the events still had me standing on that Amman street in the middle of the night, with a Styrofoam cup and a smoke, watching for the headlights on the car that would take me to Baghdad, but now at a much decreased fare than when I had first planned to go.

This time it was a GMC with two Mennonites as fellow passengers and a driver who – in that age old dynamic of "who owns the trip" – he who pays or he who drives – made it clear that he was captain. His command included what other contraband we would transport, where we would take breaks, what music we would listen to, how much air we would get, and an occasional commentary on how we should perceive the war just ended as a war, he alleged, much less disgraceful to the Sunnites than we might have supposed.

We four rolled easily into Anbar at dawn. Really nothing to impede us after the last Jordanian checkpoint. Some special ops forces checked our passports once. Very California, I thought. Bronzed, camouflaged, T-shirt, sunglasses, tousled golden hair, standing on the crest of a sand berm with a sort of lackadaisical grip on his M-16. More Hollywood than Leatherstocking, for sure.

And then, yes again, the mangy, scavenging dogs and after a few more kilometers eastward, the endless hardscrabble flats.

At that moment, in the chaos that emerged after conquest – the looting and score settling – the principal fear was no longer getting hurt by F16s or by the Republican Guard, but rather by what was to become the infamous white BMW that would periodically shoot out of Fallujah or Ramadi, move alongside your GMC, point the automatic at your face, and direct you to pull over where you got taken behind the berm, pushed down on your knees, and then relieved of everything you owned, save the vehicle.

We had parked about twenty kilometers down from the border until a few more GMCs had joined us and made a sort of convoy, knowing full well it could not protect us, but only suspecting that it might make us "not worth the effort," considering other lone targets of opportunity on the road.

Then there it was – the insidious BMW, the fear of being on your knees with the muzzle to your head, and the vast barren landscape where anything could happen. A place inhospitable to life itself. And so, God willing, it would be ten more hours of this fear with two taciturn Mennonites and a conversation that was mostly restricted to passing the water and passing the bread. We also endured ten more hours with the abusive driver who gave no deference to his passengers – the Mennonites stoic in the face of this situation – and no deference by the driver either for the increasing numbers of burned out tanks and APCs and trucks off to the side of the road that had been offed in a few seconds of thunder by a Western air force.

Then, as the sun began to set, we met the first mud brick villages, the date palms, donkeys and sheep, then tractors, threshers, canals, and berms...transitioning to towns, utility poles with the wires all tangled, small shops with some colorful plastic goods outside on display, kebab stands, and black shrouded women in abayas coming home in a flock or alone, stepping predictably behind their husbands.

Finally, we passed over the Euphrates and then the Tigris, and once again for me, I reminded myself to remember how much the water had meant to the once great civilization of the land between two rivers.

By now, we were clogged up in the outskirts of Baghdad, into the cacophony of a sprawling dysfunctional metropolis, which, despite the "Shock and Awe" or perhaps because of it, was not manifestly broken. Not its buildings or "infrastructure" in any case...an aspect that was changing, I should add, as the thousands of looters from the Shia slums in the northeast began to gut everything of value once held by the dreaded Baathists, while the victorious Yanks stayed resolutely perched on their tanks, ever vigilant to the possibility of an attack on themselves. A very remote possibility in April 2003.

So we maneuvered the best we could around neighborhood roadblocks set up against the bands of looters and around the coalition checkpoints toward the center of the city – Firdos Square. We passed the empty pedestal and drove toward a broken down hotel for NGO types called Al Fanar where we were told there was one too few rooms for the three of us. We had been brothers on the trip, but I and they too, I suspected, now wanted to part ways. We had come from different places, the Mennonites and then I as the cultural Congregationalist. And we would go forward differently; they into advocacy for a reversal of US policy and me as an implementer of that policy, albeit often according to my own interpretation. And so I had given one of my travelling companions my key and had gone out into the cacophony to find other lodging.

Just down the street it was. The Palestine. But in that short distance, I had left the chitter chatter of the ardent humanitarian workers, all keen to know which Iraqi association was available for partnership, and all in an atmosphere of disdain for the larger enterprises of George Bush.

And into the hotel of preference for the world's media, most of whom had traveled up the two rivers as embeds and now were free to poke around. And so I ate what was left to serve, which amounted to some pieces of chicken and some rice. I then went outside and bought a beer to drink slowly by candlelight in my room, along with my last smoke of the day, meant to signify reflection just prior to sleep. I was there, I thought, with little food, no electricity, but certainly at the center of the world's attention.

The next morning left no doubt about being at the center.

I had already gone through the line at the restaurant and received the two pieces of bread and the one egg we were all allowed and then made haste to get a good seat in the lobby so as to make the most of it – the commotion at the center, the media stars circulating, their fixers arriving and departing, off to emerging stories around town to which the world would soon be glued.

I stayed on for a while, not star struck, but to try to capture what I knew would be more real than the events the media covered. A global force it was, right up there with Tommy Franks's army or the Federal Reserve.

Outside the hotel, in the parking lot, you could further marvel at its might. There were monster generators and masses of cables and dishes, and transmitters to satellites that brought the media stars to every nook and cranny on the globe.

Back then, in those early days, it was safe as you please just to skip out of the lot and onto the street and jump into any available cab with only some greenbacks and a scrap of paper with some addresses in Arabic. Back then, in late April, there were no blast barriers, no perimeter, no razor wire. Just the almighty American armor stationed at strategic points and an eruption of freedom; an incredible ground burst of it to include poor folk helping themselves to public property, leaflets and posters galore, and almost continuous demonstrations around Firdos Square as the people passed, as in parade, before the media stands. Manifestations for Islamic law, fliers for Assyrian rights, and sundry other advocates were coming out of the shadows, speaking freely for the first time in decades. So, I strolled out to the concrete apron around where Saddam's statue had been and watched the ground burst, tried to feel its energy, and see its currents. I chatted with bystanders; I mingled in the parades. I said things to myself such as "Birth of a Nation," and I believed it. Around me were the ubiquitous money changers with the stacks of dinars, rapidly depreciating, and a few entrepreneurs selling minutes on their Thuraya's to folks desperate to tell family back in the diaspora that they were okay.

A few hours later, I needed to jump out of this swirl and do what I do, which is known in the trade as "mucking about." Basically, I walked in concentric circles from the lobby of the Palestine – aimless – taking tea in a kebab joint, walking into a Chaldean church and chatting with a priest, finding a bilingual student to jump in my cab with me and spend the day. We drove out to Section 38 in the Shia slums where a few inquiries in the street soon had me sitting on a carpet with a Shia Sheik under a portrait of Khomeini staring at us. Men of esteem from the neighborhood slowly filled the room and answered my questions about the conditions – that vast swamp of black water around the buildings and the smoke from the garbage dump blown down the alleys.

My day goes on like this awhile: chatting with an old tailor, dinner with a Greek Orthodox priest in Baghdad. Then bright and early the next day, I drove up north to Mosul on the highway, littered with the burned out carcasses of Iraqi armor and the shot-up likenesses of Saddam, behind which stretch green fields of wheat to the west as far as the eye could see. Pizza with some shabab on the corniche in Mosul. Interviewing Kurdish displaced, now squatting in a bombed out army base.

Eyeing the beautiful black eyes of one of their girls. Buckets, foam mattresses, a brazier – a pot of tea. On to mass at Saint Toma in the old town...ducking under the Aramaic script above the portal, the very place, I am told, the Saint set out for India.

One mucks about as long as one can, hopefully uninterrupted by reading or seeing anything the stars are transmitting, just absorbing the scene before the long ride back to Amman from whence one's findings will get transformed into a proposal for humanitarian aid.

CHAPTER 5

From Kuwait to Kut, September 2003

Emergencies and the charities that respond to them attract diverse and often unwieldy groups of respondents. They are drawn to the flame for money, excitement, fame, and sometimes self-definition. Some are first-timers; others do it for a living. In any case, they are quickly living together as strangers...sleeping, eating, and working together. Feeding each other's strengths and weaknesses and, of course, each other's cultural biases. And you, the designated new leader must pull all this together into some sort of functioning team, often in a chaotic and fearful environment. So when I walked into that "Iraq-support office" in Kuwait that first night and opened the door on them – the motley crew – they were all sizing me up since they knew I was to become some sort of factor in their lives.

Complicating the dynamic was that within relief charities there is often little de facto command structure. Will and decisions have to be imposed by force of personality. When you walk in, no one stands up. Eventually, someone finds a chair for you. God only knew, they were wondering, why the ever inscrutable HQ had dropped me in particular amidst this mix of Europeans, Asians, Africans, and Americans, all quickly assembled off a rolodex of the willing. I can assure you that I, as "newly anointed," tossed and turned in bed that first night, already thinking about who among them might serve as friend or foe.

It was now September 2003, six months after the invasion. And during the same time, I had been moving in and out of the Amman, Baghdad, Mosul axis. An allied contingent of the NGO invasion had come up from Kuwait in April with other donor funds to settle among the Shia in South Central Iraq.

That night of my arrival, our expats from Iraq were huddling back in the Kuwait office for what had been their third temporary evacuation...having just yesterday decided that the I.E.D. (Improvised Explosive Device) recently thrown against the side of one of the residences, called Picasso by the expats (the owner apparently painted), no longer constituted enough of a threat to keep this gang away any longer.

So we drove north to the border the next morning in these huge land cruisers, "fully loaded" as we used to say and with all the apparatus necessary for both High Frequency and Very High Frequency communications, both between each vehicle and with the Yankee base in Kut. I was given the honorific handle Yankee Mike 1 and a seat in the back while the security and logistics guys up front were demonstrating their facility with radio protocols and 4x4s.

In the beginning, as I had mused earlier, this consecrated land was, first and foremost, sun and shade, water and sand, and how that played out on tribe and Allah.

Now, it was still that, but with oil very much seeping into it over the last century. Seeping into it, infecting it, and changing it. I had seen the changes driving in from the Kuwaiti airport the night before – the Western accoutrements like TGIF, the malls and boutiques selling everything from Philadelphia Cream Cheese to Jaguars, the bankers emerging from their establishments in the spotless white dishdashas. The city had had almost a complete facelift since Desert Storm had pushed Saddam's army out twelve years earlier and, when seen from the air, was sparkling in its dimensions.

Before long, I was sitting at the border waiting for my passport to get processed, watching some fat uniformed Kuwaiti leaning back in his swivel with his glass of tea pinched between his thumb and forefinger yelling out the open door, an arm's length away from him. Twice he had yelled, until a skinny Sri-Lankan man stood in the door. He was promptly told he was there to shut the door. Yes, oil had definitely seeped into the monarchy and was surely an influence in the country I was now entering. Such had been the case since the days British Petroleum first arrived on the scene, which coincided, I believe, with Churchill's decision to fuel his navy with oil and with the advent of Ford's mass production of the automobile.

I knew that inside those mud hooches we were passing there were breezes whisping through, colorful carpets and pillows, family portraits on whitewashed walls and often steamy dishes of lamb and rice laid out on the middle of the floor. But the view from our 4x4s was different. They were rather mud brick settlements that with time and the elements would melt back down into the terrain. Ubiquitous rubbish was baking outside in the stillness of the noon-day sun. Along the route, the mosaics of Saddam had been defaced by small arms fire. The once extensive network of irrigation canals was now clogged with bulrushes and silt. You felt the absence of humanity outside those shelters, on whose roofs now for the first time ever satellite dishes were tentatively emerging. Here grew the incongruous technology that would be both insidious and transformative to both tribe and Allah.

We were still in the aftermath – about five months since the Marines had pulled down Saddam's likeness in Firdos Square. The residue of Saddam's military, so mercilessly scorched by the Cobra gunships and the Abrams tanks, had not yet been pulled away for scrap. The convulsion of the springtime had not yet been digested by those in the recesses of these settlements where I could imagine almost perpetual debate went on as to how this liberation of the Shias would take form. Baathists, Sunnites, decimated; Shia religion and tribe ascendant. Imam Ali, Imam Hussein, democracy, freedom were on everyone's lips in the Shia south as was, I was sure, where the profit lay in all this turmoil. American dollars and cents profit, I mean.

It was mid-afternoon before we arrived in Kut, and I was being led up some metal stairs outside the backside of what the expats had named the Four Seasons Hotel, a dilapidated old regime joint, very much reflecting the general dilapidation of the town itself. Behind me, by a hundred meters, was the Tigris, a broad languid flow, carrying within it, I sensed, the poisons of a thousand miles. We had rented and rehabbed the second floor, the most recent location after a progression of earlier offices starting with the floor of the Red Crescent in April where the avant-garde had first worked and slept.

At first impression, I was having my doubts on the location, but was told by Chris, the security adviser, that it held several advantages. Among those were its back to the river, a perimeter wall around it, proximity to an Iraqi police post, and, he winked, "kebabs downstairs and it even has a backroom where beer can be had."

Once in the door off the landing, I had stepped into a great commotion of dozens of nationals running around the hallway and latching on to the appropriate expat boss now back from evacuation. Eventually, someone attended to me and pointed at a desk and a computer – just aside a window with a view of the river, the bulrushes, a few fishing boats and the Arabian sun which was beginning to set behind them.

At first, the nationals didn't know what to do with me, nor I with them. They had all been hired at $100 a month on the basis of knowing some English. They each had a boss, but few had titles yet. They were exultant at our return. And "did you know," one informed me, "the I.E.D. [basically, in this instance, a paper mache firecracker that had sent the expats and cars careening south] was not aimed at us."

"Oh no," she said, "It was for the owner of Picasso House, a real snake in the grass."

Then Paul, my deputy, came into the room and took the other desk while Zeena, an English teacher during the ancien regime and now our gatekeeper, let the "decisions needing to be made" enter, one after the other after another.

My head on that first day was soon spinning with the details involved. A rural Sheik and his delegation wanted a water treatment unit for the bad water from the Tigris, or a leveling and gravelling on the dirt track leading out to the main asphalt road, or a zinc roof on the thatched mud school. A contractor replaced him, upset that he didn't win a certain contract, and now alleging corruption in our office. Then the finance guy and the procurement guy could not reconcile "contracted" and "spent" and were making mutual accusations and then someone important had a son to be employed. Then it was the grand Ayatollah Sistani's representative in Kut, Sheikh Jawad the Venerable, who wanted to see me, on whose heels appeared the owner of Picasso who wanted recompense. And then at precisely 1700 hours, the women had fled to waiting cars, followed thereafter by the rest, except for a precious few who presumed themselves responsible or who had glimpsed the Western mind, Paul's mind and mine.

Ah, Paul. Years earlier, he had kicked about with me briefly in the Balkans in a minor role. An anomalous character in Kut amidst the others. A white stripe through his thick Mexican hair, duck walking across the tiles with the constant pen gripped in his left hand, always immersed in his milieu. A scholar. Ravenous in this instant for the word, root and suffix...the great etymologies back to Muhammad. Uncomfortable though, I knew, with the violence, with the swashbuckle and the attendant swirl. An odd partner when seen beside me, the facsimile of the aging American manager.

Paul drove me home to Park Palace, our residence – so called because inside it was ornate to the point of ridicule with its cherubs and chandeliers everywhere, its prints of Victorian ladies of leisure reposing by an English stream, and a park across the street with nary a trace of green.

I had asked Chris, who also lived there, why our guards were inside the wall. "I mean, how can they see anything?"

"They refuse to be out there at night without weapons," he answered.

"So we have night watchmen who can't watch anything but the stars?"

"Pretty much," he answered. "We put them on the roof once, but the neighbors went berserk claiming they could see too much."

That first night in Kut, I definitely needed what I called "surcease." And surcease I got. Paul plugged *The Matrix*

Reloaded into the DVD player while he settled down, simultaneously scanning some recondite treatment on "the siege of Kut" a hundred years earlier while Chris chucked me an MRE (Meals Ready to Eat – gifts from the departing US Marines stationed nearby). Yes, the US military had come a long way since the "C rations" when I had been in Vietnam. Against my expectations, this food was gourmet ready to eat – international cuisine – with a Tootsie roll as a last minute surprise. Chris, Austrian by origin, and open by nature, marveled at my delight for what he called grub. "Doesn't your wife feed you?" he asked. "Oh yes," I responded. "Delicious Italian dishes, in fact. But you, as a security man, should know well it's all about context and sitting here at Park Palace in downtown Kut, this is more than I could conceive." To which, this "long drink of water," as my mother would have called him, had snapped his fingers and passed me a Heineken. "Here's to context," he toasted.

About halfway through the film, I needed to be alone. I knew from previous such assignments that I had to keep some distance. I also knew that starting tomorrow I couldn't hide behind Paul and Chris and that all those decisions needing to be made would, at a minimum, require my opinion. I needed to lay back on my inch and a half of mattress, have a last smoke, and lift myself up for the next day. I took two aspirins for the dreamless sleep, turned on an overhead fan for the drone of the whir, then finally checked that my handset was working and on the nightstand next to my head. Hands on my chest in repose, I listened to Chris tell Hassan RTO (Radio Telephone Operator) that all was good at Park Palace, followed by "roger that" at Dolly House, and finally at River House.

Over the next few months, our relief organization made some progress. "Staff, Systems, Structure, Strategies," as I used to say at the weekly briefings. The 4 S's I would repeat daily. And later on as concerned the program investments, I added the 4 C's: Community mobilization, Construction, Creative Activity, Community Service. That became the way. Step by step, inexorable. Keep the message simple and repeat it constantly. Fewer moving parts, the better. Don't try anything too ambitious. We desperately needed successes. The staff had never heard of an NGO, much less of the sustainable changes we were contracted to make. Participative decision making, competitive tendering, transformative investments would never be fully appreciated by the majority of the staff. There was that first time, I remember well, when I had returned some project content to some national staff to be improved, and it had come back to me a couple of days later, unchanged, but now in a folder with some delightful sketches of imagined gardens on the cover. We lived with that.

We marched forward with the first S. "Nothing," I told the staff at the weekly meeting, "happens until we have a team who know their positions and who are all defining win in a similar way." And thus HR. began: scopes of work, position descriptions, performance plans, salary grids. What a nightmare.

CHAPTER 6

South Central Iraq, January 2004

January in Kut was dismal. Black water. It covers the town during the winter rains and the hardscrabble surface doesn't allow for any percolation downward. And, of course, Saddam had allowed no functioning infrastructure for draining it.

The concrete in our projects didn't dry and our "burn rate" or "money spent" was significantly behind donor expectations. We had a contradictory grant from the State Department – one that insisted on participatory decision making and local ownership at the community level, normally a painstaking process involving, in the parlance of our profession, knowledge transfer and behavioral change.

And while we were attempting to do these things with folks that hadn't seen hide nor hair of any aspect of civil society for decades, we were also supposed to achieve "quick impact," meaning we were to demonstrate visible evidence of American largesse so as to give hope to the Shia for a better tomorrow. And so we were plugging away to get communities to "own" their investment decisions but also to get through the process fast enough so that a new school or clinic saw the light of day. Of course, the donors – the State Department and the Department of Defense, now within their fortified enclave in Baghdad (AKA the Green Zone) – were, in turn, under extraordinary pressure to show the White House and Congress measurable results such as beneficiaries, jobs, and most importantly "burn rate," all the while emphasizing the transformative impact on local governance.

Frankly, we weren't doing very well with most of the numbers. In fact, the Green Zone had threatened to lop off a third of our AOR (Area of Responsibility) and give it to another NGO. "Are you sure you are counting correctly?" They would ask. "Maybe you should go back and recalculate." They said. "Your numbers seem awfully low."

And then there were the questions beyond the numbers. Were we really changing behavior?

When we sat down with the Mukhtars, Sheiks, and the other folks in the communities to go through the mobilization process, were we really growing an appreciation for democracy, or were we rather being indulged by a culture much older than ours that played along so as to get an infusion of cash for a few Iraqi contractors? It was hard to tell.

By January, the general population of South Central Iraq was all over the liberation like half-starved dogs on fresh meat. Dishes had mushroomed on many roofs, no matter how rudimentary, and with them, "forbidden sites." MBC/Channel 2 had the whole city transfixed at 2100 hours with their menu of Hollywood movies. Even in squalid little apartments with bare brick walls and oilskin tacked up to protect the woman and her gas cooker from the visitor's eye, there was a dish on the roof and Hollywood on the screen while we tried to get through some desiccated chicken wings. Newspapers had popped up overnight with any news they wished, whether it was fit to print or not, and citizens everywhere were trying to define the relations between freedom and democracy, mostly in spectacularly unsuccessful ways.

Rules were the problem. The heavy hand of Saddam had been there so long and was now lifted so quickly, that the first response was anarchy. Every night as we leaned over our MRE's at Park Palace, our windows rattled intermittently with the repercussion of another antebellum Baathist home being bombed. The policeman at the intersect across the Tigris was no more than an observer, and the cordon sanitaire that we had established around our "tendering process" was probed daily by Iraqi contractors who assumed an entitlement to win.

"These folk are damaged," I told my housemates. When they come at us, they look normal enough, but then when you get to manage them, you see what Saddam did. They fly off the handle at the first rumor. A few shots in this or that neighborhood can become a massacre by the time it reaches your ears. A woman seen near an expat becomes a whore, ruined. A man denied a benefit spends the indefinite future trying to malign the character of anyone who is rumored to be enjoying such a benefit.

Also into that vacuum came the mysteries and faith. They had returned from Iran or from underground and were now making Najaf and Karbala once again preeminent in the Shia world. Millions now would soon make the pilgrimage on foot to the Holy Cities, progressing onward with their bandanas and staffs. We heard the drumbeat and sway of what I called "flagellation music" as they flailed themselves in great rhythmic processions.

And so it swirled – this dynamic of the fixation with Brad Pitt at night along with the lawlessness and the resurgent zeal for Allah.

Other than the occasional frayed nerves from the bombing of the Baathist houses and the reprimands from the donor on the numbers, in retrospect our life was almost pleasant compared to what would come. Portraits of George W. were scattered around the souk. We went around town freely, got our teeth fixed by Dr. Ali, our hair cut nearby. Once a week during Ramadan, we played league football as an NGO team, and lo and behold made it to the final eight with me in attendance as honorary manager.

At the end of January, we packed up and left the Four Seasons to ensconce ourselves into the Al Houra neighborhood. This move was what Chris called "acceptance strategy" in contradistinction to deterrence strategy when one adopts a quasi-medieval approach of fortified residences, armed forays out of the perimeter, and body armor. By now, that withdrawal had become the obligatory method for the US government as well as the principal Western contractors and charities in Iraq.

For us, Al Houra was the neighborhood that agreed to bring us in – to let us live on their street, attend their marriages and funerals, and shoot hoops with their kids. We, in turn, watched our DVDs and drank our beer in seclusion from them. We built the neighborhood sidewalks, taught the computer keyboard to their teenagers, and ran electricity to their homes from our colossal generator. We promised not to watch their black draped women when they walked to market in the afternoon.

We even established a neighborhood watch – as much for them as for us – to stop either zealot or criminal from hurting us or them for harboring us. There were no visible arms (notwithstanding the Kalashnikovs stashed near every citizen's bed) and no blast barriers.

Instead we relied on "hue and cry," a neighborhood crowd massing, and the fear of any intruder for the consequences from Tribal Law, should the neighbors or their guests be violated. In the Arab world, once invited past the threshold, the devil himself is protected.

Could our acceptance be penetrated? Probably not, as long as our neighborhood was already cohesive. Perhaps with an RPG (Rocket Propelled Grenade) from a distant rooftop, or a burst of fire by a car speeding by, but these would be meant to scare as much as to kill.

However, within our "acceptance strategy," one insidious threat did remain – the Judas.

We foreign humanitarian workers were worth a fortune. Zarqawi and his Al Qaeda affiliates would pay plenty for those of us from a coalition country. Such a captive allowed them almost unlimited airtime before they severed his/her head.

So, yes, there was the threat of Judas...the old gardener who trims the lawn, the woman who cleans the house. When they went home at night to their poor circumstances, a word could creep out about the American in the neighborhood. If it creeps out again, and again, it may reach the ear of an assassin.

Other threats came from the local contractor whose bid was not sufficient for the school you built or the employee who was just released for threatening to I.E.D. his supervisor on a matter of "dignity." They too may let it slip, accidently on purpose, before criminal or zealot, about the American in the neighborhood.

Still, notwithstanding the Judas, the power of the neighborhood or the village was strong and, most nights, we slept well.

The more difficult issues for us were, first, we had to venture out from our neighborhood. We were employed to promote salve and transformation across wide swathes of Iraq. For that, we had to have a larger, albeit thinner, acceptance...as we sat on a dozen floors in a dozen homes, discussing projects with communities. For us foreigners, we first had to have guidance from the notables, as we called them. In the Shia heartland, this process had mostly come to mean the Clerics, those affiliated with Ayatollahs (past and present) Sistani, Hakim, Sadr (the father). Each week, we gave them the opportunity to suggest investments in salve and transformation. What they said at Friday prayers about us could have the population seeing us as either "Zionist Crusaders" or friends of the community. We traveled at their pleasure.

Even so, the reach and impact of the notables did not run into all places and into all minds in a place as large as South Central, Iraq.

For that, there was only stealth. The vehicle that was indistinguishable from most of what was on the road. The spontaneous and unpredictable visit. The bare essential of a meeting and the expeditious farewell. The shirt an Iraqi would wear, the stubble an Iraqi would allow, sometimes a keffiyeh, the dark glasses to hide the blue eyes, and, of course, my talisman, my Cal cap, invisible under my seat along with the sat phone. And finally, the one car ahead for reconnaissance to sense whether the police at the checkpoint would whisper my identity to the criminal or the zealot.

And then, second, ironically, there was the evident material assistance we gave – a school, a health clinic, plastic sheeting for the displaced and migrants. Definitely, a two-edged sword as pertained to protecting our skin. Indeed, as our community acceptance spread among the beneficiaries, so too, in some dark places, it was noticed as a dangerous accommodation with the

West. For us, there was not much way around this dilemma. Every chance we got, we put an Iraqi face on our work, but, at the end of the day, folks knew who had the money.

The third issue for us humanitarian workers was the principal donor. In our case, that was the United States government, which granted us taxpayer monies. Of course, they employed a "deterrence strategy" and thus lived and worked in the various fortresses, the principal one being the Green Zone in Baghdad. The workers rarely left them. But, when they did, they came to visit us in armored cars with an armed detachment, often South Africans. And, of course, any blending we had sought to do with the locals then became suspect. Was our intent really as "unencumbered" with the "political" as we swore every chance we got? Yes, the distinctions between Non-Governmental Organizations and US government donor did indeed confuse and endanger.

CHAPTER 7

The Avant Garde

"So quickly in Kut," I had mused, "you, free man from America, are constrained." Like clockwork, I retired to that thin mattress before ten to light my smoke and scan the horizon for what little I could collect...just trying, I was, to lift up over the daily rat a tat tat with another bedtime speech to myself. On this night, I had drifted backward toward Suffield Academy, those dense textbooks that had tried to take us chapter by chapter from Olduvai gorge to the wooden tablet chair in Western Civilization class...increasingly anxious as the minute hand persisted around the circle...and then the Prof. who had been strolling back and forth before the blackboard, droning on, would pivot..."put your books away." The snap quiz, sometimes as many as three a week, which together represented 30% of our grade, which along with our marks on essays and the finals made 100%. The final...just walking in circles outside the cavernous gym reciting over and over again salient facts...soon to take our place among a hundred others at plywood tables and apply our undivided attention to questions until the closing minutes as we scribbled wildly with an ever more careless orthography of hurried looping circles and strident straight slashes...in a mad dash...till the inevitable. "Put your pencils down," pronounced the austere proctor and all fell still...all ending some days later in an apprehensive huddle of school boys around the posted marks on the central bulletin board...for all to see...how much we had learned compared to the others.

That fortuitous concentration of storable protein – grains and mammals – which had been domesticated about 12,000 years ago in the fertile crescent and later along the shores of the Yellow River – allowing, through a quasi-Darwinian evolution, for a dominance over less advanced neighbors. Dominance, defined as a procreative and creative explosion that pushed further afield, eventually reaching the West and steamrolling everything in its wake. By the time that dominance had traveled from the Fertile Crescent to Europe and then across the Atlantic – or southward from the Yellow River along its other track – its prominence was assured. These civilizations killed, displaced, or assimilated everything in their way.

A textbook, that had been committed to my memory at the time, and played back ever since on cue for various appreciations.

Prostrate, I peered into the cloud of smoke above me, occasionally hearing bits and pieces from the watchmen now under the lamp on the street outside...in all likelihood mocking the whistles and horns they had been issued in place of AK 47s.

"Violence begets violence," I had told a disbelieving audience. "Make a racket and the neighborhood will run 'em off."

And within that civilizational flow, I reflected, those great fluctuations – of vitality and knowledge, together and apart, which like a river meanders though never loses its course, notwithstanding its diversion. A course since Byzantium and Muhammad to the southern shores of the Mediterranean where it swept all before it till its Arabian steeds were prancing on the shores of the Atlantic and with time were capturing and incubating all learning in Caliphates along that course while European tribes remained stranded and uncouth, the popular image being tearing flesh off the bone at the entrance to a cave until...and here my memory failed. Who knows, I thought, but, in any case, here we were taught to reference among so much else and so many others...Christendom ascending, Renaissance in Florence, Prince Henry the navigator, Luther, the bloodshed at the Gates of Vienna in 1683 and then Newton, Kant, Les Philosophes...seemingly unlocking what had been dammed up for hundreds of years and leaving the fabulous Islamic Caliphates to stew in some sort of polluted back water while those now enlightened uncouth set forth to conquer or assimilate the rest of the world "and still do," I asserted in my refuge within Al Houra...as this night's ponderings on such things had gone about as far as my thin education could allow me.

"And still do," I mused, "albeit in a more insinuating way than Hiroshima and Dresden. I mean we don't fight to the death as we did then." It still made my palms sweat to reconsider the prowling of those monitors checking, as they did, for the wandering eye or the hidden script with significant dates on the inside cuff. All those facts and figures crammed behind the forehead, bent over the final paper and submitted by a sharp point of graphite.

I reached down to the floor and took another cigarette from the pack, lit it, and took a big drag on it. "Eh voila," I said out loud, as I exhaled, "we, the insinuation." Hobbled in my case by the chronic ailment in my bones. Engendered at first by the pounding of them on the tarmac in front of my boy and later by the pounding of them behind him. I massaged the swollen knee to feel if it was receding. Like a soccer ball with a slow leak. Over days, it would reduce back to knee bone and would be normal for a while. Now moving my hand slowly up my body to other more recent afflictions of the corporeal...the red stress dots on my face, on which I obsessed, checking them in anything which gave off a reflection...the metal cap on my lighter now in my hand. I suspected people thought I had AIDS. Photos made the dots even redder, revealing a face maligned with red pox.

"Backed up, of course," I continued, "by the 5th Fleet anchored not far off in the Persian Gulf with enough firepower to assure that all this would stay in the back water till Kingdom come."

"Imagine that," I said to the walls, "that vast grey armada dozing and maneuvering and flexing while we like good-hearted microbes penetrate the backwater trying to neutralize the poisons."

"Get these Arabs on message, damn it," I laughed, "with all that Luther and Newton wrought."

"Ah," I stretched on my one and half inch thick mattress…"My Avant Garde."

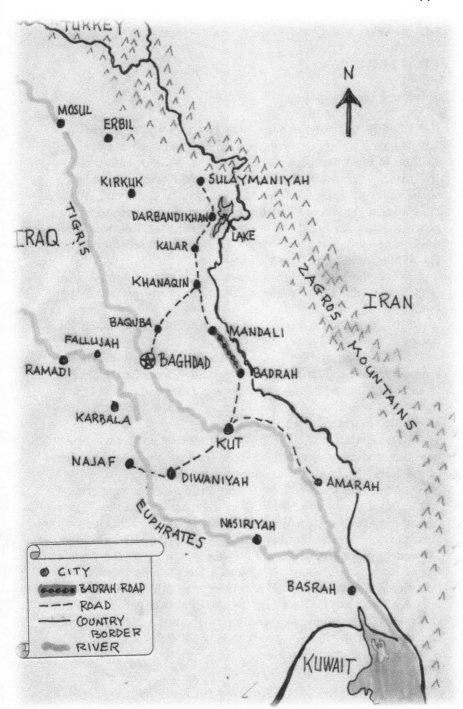

CHAPTER 8

Salve and Transformation

Even before this war, about a year before we had moved into Kut, a small contingent from our agency had been far north of Kut, up in what had been since 1991, the Western enforced "no fly" zone, the land of the Kurds. They had been engaged in a small relief program in Sulaymaniyah (Sullei for short). When the Kurdish Peshmerga and the Coalition Forces moved south, down the Iranian border to Khanaqin, they had followed their trail, eventually in April of 2003, sleeping under some old eucalyptus trees at the Central Water Plant.

Since then we had continued to run a small WATSAN (water and sanitation) program there, basically trying to get potable water into folk's homes. In Sullei, we had left behind a small back office to do some procurement and balance the books.

Sullei, free since 1991, now had a twelve-story hotel. It had a grocery store and amazingly a checkout that applied a scanner to barcodes. It even had Corn Flakes and Peter Pan peanut butter. In short, it was a sort of secular Mecca and was now where we all decided to travel for a summit.

It was, we hoped, a place less restrained than Kut where we could let our hair down and do some free thinking. A place free of the daily I.E.D.s and black draped women.

And so, we made a convoy and left our safe neighborhood and traveled northeast until we were right up against the Zagros Mountains, very sharp and snow swept in the winter. Our way was mostly a dirt/macadam piste, called the Badrah road, flooded in places, which ran along the old front of the Iranian war fifteen years earlier. It curled beside the berms and minefields that had been used to protect Iraqi artillery and armor.

And so it was that our cars eventually moved into Khanaqin and then kept moving past our outpost there through Kalar and Darbandikhan and into the gaudy lights of Sullei.

"Meetings," I had read, "should never be tabula rasa; rather they should serve to test and support prior assumptions." I operated on that principle as I tried to take hold of the proceedings the next day on the mezzanine of the Palace Hotel. Most of our discussion centered on commonly held "stipulations of fact."

We all knew that the donor presumption of making Shia folk more democratic by letting them choose their projects was fanciful and impossible to prove in any case, given all the other incoming aspects of liberation.

And we all knew how unsettled their psyches were from the frightful years under the ex-regime – damage that would not disappear within the lifetime of this generation.

And we knew that Iraq, since oil, created nothing. Not one creative aspect to it. And that a person, town, nation that creates nothing dies and was dying before our very eyes.

The air in the meeting room was alive with ambition and presumptions and with time came to swirl more and more around the thoughts of our Albanian woman, a real firecracker, who had come of age under Hoxha. She told us we would marry up the teenage hopes and dreams with opportunities for creation and that we could do this transformation on a massive scale. By nightfall, this argument and its attendant details had clearly won the day. Applause even, as we trailed out to reach the grocery store before it closed.

And so now, in addition to our 4 S's, we now got deeper into those 4 C's: Community Participation, Construction of Platforms for Learning, Creative Activities, and Community Service.

"Hot damn," one of the Americans had said. "Transformation in South Central – neither Channel 2 nor the masses flagellating." For the first time in decades, the area would have original art, theater, poetry, science fairs, inventions, a better mousetrap, an Internet connection to the outside world, the free exchange of ideas. Unbridled. This change would be a renaissance "on terms owned by generation next."

Afterward, I sent the following email to my boss at HQ for presentation at the annual meeting of our Board of Directors, laying out the logic for our plans over the years to come:

Subject Line: An NGO at Work in the Shia Heartland

"We benefit from millions of dollars from the US taxpayer and receive oversight from the United States Agency for International Development [USAID, an appendage of the State Department]. These funds are invested in an area of Iraq called South Central by our donor, but is more accurately known as the Shia Heartland, which describes a great swath of hardscrabble land from the holy cities of Najaf and Karbala in the West to the Iranian border in the East.

The development process we are instructed to follow involves approaching a neighborhood or village and asking that a representative group choose an investment from which the residents of the area will benefit. As we do this, we push to "flatten the hierarchy," meaning to have the Sheik or Mukhtar involved, but not dominant. And we insist that women be represented. Of course, both of these insistences run counter to tradition. Still, they certainly speak to some profound yearnings among some of the population.

While the project is being debated by the community, we also insist on one final component: that the investment be owned by the community, meaning that they are the primary stakeholders in both design and maintenance from the beginning. We demand quantifiable evidence of this "ownership." Either cash or labor as a reflection of "sweat equity." For 100k dollars spent on a school, the sine qua non for the community contribution is 15k.

Sound good? Well...not really. In the first instance, a few Western civ types are not likely to overturn thousands of years of traditional decision making, even as history may be on the newcomers' side. In the conservative rural areas of the heartland, there is often token observance of our insistence and little doubt left in my mind that after we drive off no Western infection of the old thought process has really occurred. By contrast, in the urban areas, those self-same places where the SAT dishes, cell phones, and Internet connections are proliferating the fastest, more authentic "flattening" does take place.

Women. A very delicate subject in South Central. Other than the epithet of "Jew-Crusader" hurled at you by a zealot, only the accusation of interfering with their women can get you killed faster. Interference can mean as little as an infidel being caught in a public "pat on the back" with a Shia woman.

So, for investments touching on women, there must be a respected Shia intermediary to take the investment in hand. For an Internet center for women, a religious Sheik should propose and manage it. Keep in mind, a woman has no choices in the Shia Heartland. There is no "kissing off mom and dad and taking a bus to the big city where one waits on tables and struggles through night school." No, in South Central, women who don't comply are destined for either suicide or prostitution, no matter where they flee inside Iraq. They may be more vocal in the urban areas of the South, but, in the end, there is no actionable dissent.

"Ownership" is also a goal that often means we must settle for less. Much of Iraq is a country of entitlements. Or dreams of entitlements. A tribal leader provided, the religious leaders provided. The government still allows a monthly food basket for all Iraqis. Energy is almost free...as is health care and education.

Then, there are the 50C summers that certainly discourage toil.

Scratch the surface of most Shia Iraqis, and they will tell you they expect, before long, if all goes well, for a Sudanese or Egyptian guest worker to plant their garden and serve them tea as they did before 1991.

It is indeed a passive population. There is nothing in the thousands of little stores across this Shia swath that is created there. Neither by necessity nor by happenstance. In the end, if neither tribe nor cleric nor civil servant will provide, oil will. Not to mention, they look forward to the imminence of paradise just one short step away and where all earthly needs are met.

The net result for local participation and ownership in our projects is disappointing. There is usually some desultory response to roll up the sleeves and pitch in for the 15%. But the school wall only gets one thin coat of paint. The trees around it are indeed planted, but usually not watered. When the storage tank on top of the toilets needs filling, the responsible party is nowhere to be found.

Ever wary of our obligation to both donor and presumed beneficiary, we have fiddled with the original formula. We, soon on, concluded that the ubiquitous and profound passivity was indeed one of the foundations for despots and represented the greatest challenge to an open and free Iraq.

We, human centered investors, came to believe that without authentic participatory decision making or local ownership, we were ultimately only left with the construction, be it a sewer or health center or a park. Against the risks we were taking, we could not be satisfied doing "bricks and mortar" when, in fact, any good Iraqi contractor could do as well."

We were there in the promotion of Right Relations. That had to be the value against the risk.

And so we amended the approach by offering a more select menu to the community, meaning that if creativity and connectivity were key antidotes for despotism, then we would focus almost exclusively on investments in schools, libraries, museums, Internet centers, science fairs, recreation halls, theaters, and community centers. We would offer a community such a "platform" if they would "own" the effort – not by slapping some whitewash on the walls or planting some grass, but rather by joining with their children in using these physical platforms for community sourced, activity based, supplemental investments in art, narrative, music, invention, and connectivity. In sum, we redefined the notion of "sweat equity" so as to align it with unmet demand by those most ambitious and idealistic among an emerging generation of youth. Managing a poetry recital or science fair in the community center replaced slapping whitewash on the wall. For the parents of the teenagers in those places of learning, we would bank, perhaps unrealistically, on their appreciation that for Iraq and for the next generation to prosper, there would have to be these opportunities for creativity. (After all, an Iraq that creates nothing of value for the global society is a country that has become little more than oil and consumption.) We hope to leverage the parent's love for their children and their future and, in return, get our heretofore elusive "ownership."

Further, these teenagers – boys and girls – could now be connected through our ICT (Information and Communication Technologies) investments to other voices and other ideas. Their centers would have Internet connections and the transformative projects in creativity would create the beginnings of a new interconnected culture that would allow them to participate in the surrounding global society. Absent the renaissance that these platforms for learning and transformative projects could produce, most other investments in Iraq had marginal value. The alternative to renaissance was passive accommodation to the extraction industries, non-participation in the global society, and a prolongation of autocracy.

Or so I believed, in that winter of 2004.

CHAPTER 9

WDC Comes Knocking

And then – ecce miraculum – during that selfsame winter we had distinguished official visitors, the first ever to arrive without a squad of "shooters." And, as events turned out, the last.

We had driven north that morning from Kut in our "blended cars," indistinguishable from the mess of Iraqi traffic alongside us, and had waited for them to exit an Iraqi shuttle bus at a staging area a kilometer outside of Baghdad International Airport (BIAP).

Congressmen Wolf and Shays were pioneers. Pro Consul Bremer and company had told them earlier that they must stay "in the security bubble" from the moment they had stepped off the C-130 from Jordan. That would have meant a chopper into the Green Zone, a series of official briefings, including some from notable Iraqi's imported for the occasion. They had declined and, in what must have been an interesting conversation, were then told, "You can get out on your own steam if you go through with this."

In retrospect, that winter and the several months to follow were to be that historic window when hopeful possibilities failed to take root and worst case scenarios emerged. It was the time when the chaos following the toppling of Saddam's statue in Firdos Square gave way to ever increased death tolls. The chaos had begun nine months earlier with the massive looting in Baghdad alongside the "hunting of Baathists" in the Shia heartland. No less than 1300 years of Sunni rule had been erased in an instant by General Franks and the onset of a great national void while official Americans, uniformed and not, sat on their turrets at strategic intersections or in their cubicles at Saddam's palace and lived a complete policy vacuum within that void.

American notions and plans for good governance were "refreshed" before they had barely begun. America had been reduced to the impotent observer as 25 million Iraqis scrambled to make some sense of their own transformation, slowly at first, and then moving in 2004 from heated rhetoric or clandestine plots to the first manifestation of savage warfare.

So, as Wolf and Shays moved south that day, they felt the incipient chaos. They saw the stacks of smuggled goods crowding the sidewalks, peered out at a damaged city with no functioning infrastructure, neither electrical grids nor water mains, and got stuck soon enough in the mother of all traffic jams with not one uniform, American or Iraqi, in sight. With only, on occasion, some daring citizen jumping into the middle of the mess to try to clear a way. On this day, it was my manager, Amar, who eventually made an opening for us to sidle through. With me, all the while, trying to keep the conversation as mundane as possible with the two congressmen who were definitely wide-eyed at what was on the other side of that one-eighth inch of windowpane.

Two hours of this, in our blended cars, winding our way through the cacophony where, still, in that month, everything was possible and nothing was possible – where rebirth and death lived one within the other.

By mid-afternoon, we had finally popped out onto a straight-away south flanked by bulrushes and mud hooches in the distance but now, oddly, with dishes sprouting from some of their roofs in further evidence that Saddam's world had been penetrated with yet to be determined consequence.

Yes, they were afraid. They had never met us before. The whole weight of the American government had told them "not to go." And here is the point: Mr. Wolf and Mr. Shays, without fanfare, without any certain positive returns from their constituents, needed, seemingly, for their own worth to get, as they kept saying, "the policy right."

We had pulled into Kut just as that sun was setting in beautiful salmon colors over the Tigris. The guards noted no arms at the gate to our house and confirmed the message with the sign in the hallway: "no arms allowed." At about the same time that the sun disappeared, we heard blasts, and our windows rattled as self-styled vigilantes were gutting more Baathist homes with grenades.

Notwithstanding, the congressmen were settled enough by dinner. I mean it must have been clear we, the hosts, were no fringe element. There was a young engineer from Walla Walla ("The place so nice, they named it twice," he told them); a young Moroccan-American woman from Portland, Oregon, who did monitoring and evaluation for us; a former platoon leader in Vietnam from New England. And others like us. We acted like Middle America – like the folks in their districts back home. So, there it was – the windows rattling, the quick looks at us from Mr. Wolf and Mr. Shays, and then Mr. Shays said grace, and we said Amen, and then we dug into some tough mutton and stale rice and got the most nonstop, intense interview of our respective lives.

"How can you live without arms?"

"The neighborhood protects us," we replied.

"And the religious sheiks?"

We told them about the famous Fatwa from Ayatollah Sistani that had been read all over at Friday prayers. That we were okay – not part of the occupation.

"Can you go to the souk without guards?"

"See this haircut," I responded. "Yesterday in the souk." And so on deep into the evening.

But, and here was and is the essence: "Our life," we told them, "is not sustainable." As instigators, insurgents, and zealots roam the void, the official Americans react predictably. An American troop is shot, and the response is, well, asymmetrical with the attendant "collateral damage," meaning civilian dead. And then the US military and their civilian staff raise their perimeter walls even higher, only to sortie out in armed convoys. With time, and "we already feel it," we told them, we are caught alone in a shrinking and confused space and position. American foreigners but "citizen Americans" very much outside any perimeter.

The next couple of days they lived like us. A trickle of tepid for the morning ablution, greasy eggs, sitting cross-legged on hard floors before every religious and tribal sheik we could muster up. And then, without warning a quick detour into the slums – down by some burning fields of rubbish – quick in with Mr. Wolf and Mr. Shays to ask more questions of the squatters who were totally bewildered as they rushed to make tea – quite incomprehensible to them that an American Congressman was sitting before them, with nary a weapon in his vicinity.

So, that last night in Kut was quite emotional. After the prayer by Wolf, I said something corny about how much their visit had meant to us, especially as we faced a darker future. But, corny or not, it was true.

Over the years to come and as Iraq came tumbling down into the abyss, I was brought back to Washington, D.C. a couple of times a year by my employer to make testimony. I would always stop by to see Mr. Wolf and Mr. Shays. Times would indeed change. My team would have to move north to Khanaqin where we were safer and neither Wolf nor Shays could again go south and live outside the perimeter.

But what they had gleaned had made a deep and lasting impression. Their experience gestated in their minds, eventually surfaced, and went public in 2006 within the covers of the Hamilton-Baker Report. Finally, belatedly, some more careful thinking survived the horrible aftermath of 2004. A very fledgling national introspection emerged. The report was, of course, both late and insufficient, but it salvaged some sanity and some bipartisanship, which finally got American citizens thinking hard about what we had wrought when General Franks crossed the Kuwait/Iraq border in March of 2003.

CHAPTER 10

Relocation, April 2004

There are only a couple of months when the weather was pleasant in South Central – when my brain was not starting to boil from the heat or when I was not forced to bury into a pile of Iranian blankets at night and cocoon within them against the desert cold.

April is one of them. What green there is shows itself then. You can sleep straight through the night under one blanket, yet not have to recline with the roar of the air cooler.

The black water begins to subside, and lovely Zeena the gatekeeper sits on the swing at lunchtime in her pastel hijab reading her Jane Austen. Or wide-eyed Salam, the communist, bounces through the gate in his "I have a dream" T-shirt – his newest promotion.

Yes, signs of renaissance. But sadly against the backdrop of other, more ominous developments. It had been a year now, and still we were the only independent development workers in South Central. Across the river, unemployed men grumbled for want of income. The parade of infrastructure contractors paid out of the $21 billion congressional supplemental had yet to materialize – all tied up north in the Sunni Triangle, it seemed. There were fewer expats in the Baghdad restaurants. We felt more vulnerable there and now seldom left South Central. The price on our heads had risen, I had heard, to 50K for an American. That was the street value. Captured, he or she was worth a million as an advertisement for Al Qaeda.

Both ran parallel – the blossoming of those curious young minds and the advance of the sullen men across the river who were confused and threatened by the "new Iraq," a nation too disturbing for their current dispositions.

Since the salve and transformation summit, we had shed
expats, now down to a dozen. The security man, Chris, left,
handing over his paramount duties to me. He had lived with Paul
and me for six months, this evangelist for "acceptance strategy."
This ardent ex-cop from Austria with his shaved head and those
eyelashes as long as a camel's. He had dared to build our safety
upon a local Iraqi embrace and a cadre of local believers who
now, he assured me, would step up. It had been a great mix – us
living together. Chris who had all the technical knowledge and
the protocols, Paul the Arabist, and me the veteran. But now, we
expats were single-minded as we were passing over our duties as
fast as possible. On one hand, we were telling the nationals,
"This is your country, you need to own this work." And, on the
other, preparing ourselves for both a new Iraq and for one that
would sink into the abyss. Either way, this message translated
into, "If an Iraqi can do it, the pale face should get the hell out."

God only knew where the country was going. Those spring
days, my colleagues and I swung from hope to despair and back
again several times a week, sometimes several times a day. And,
all the while, like a Greek chorus, the international press corps
kept wailing at the top of the hour from the Palestine hotel in
Baghdad – a sort of drumbeat on the daily violence.

We somehow chose to keep hopeful. I told townsfolk about
the imminence of the supplemental legislation in the US and
about the part that had been assigned to Kut – over 200 million
US dollars for major infrastructure. During the spring, we ran a
cleanup campaign across the city, called "Kut – City of the
Future." We hired more Iraqi women, and we fired contractors
who looked for personal gain. By the end of March, we had
established over fifty "Platforms for Learning."

As development workers, we had prided ourselves about
knowing what was going on. "Finger in the wind" is how we
phrased it. After all, we attended local funerals, joined in Hajj
lunches, raced the boys down the streets on their bikes. We were
Mr. David, Mr. Paul, and Mr. Chris to our neighbors. There were
only a handful of expats who lived like that in Iraq. So in
retrospect, we should have seen it coming. The giant T barriers
were being raised by the Coalition Forces around the old Baath

party building – the concertina wire strung around it, the imported security forces, and then the installation of the Coalition Provisional Authority (CPA – a US created interim government). The 4x4s were scooting around the area with the first official emissaries of Jeffersonian democracy going from neighborhood to neighborhood with their coterie of shooters, preaching to wary folk about participatory democracy. They were especially wary since, as the days got warmer, evidence of my promise of the imminent largesse offered up by the US congress had yet to appear on our horizon.

"And these are our friends," I had complained earlier to those visiting congressmen from Virginia and Connecticut. The Shia, I had meant, "who comprise 65% of the population." Then, more recently, my friend, Sheik Sattar of the quiescent tradition, had warned me about the American conception of an Interim Constitution. "We will never accept the Kurdish veto," he had said. "We will not be cheated by Baghdad and the North. We want a popular vote now. The Governing Council has nothing to do with us."

Change came down on us faster than any of us had imagined. The Coalition Forces (CF) decided to go after the populist Cleric, Muqtada al Sadr. He took refuge in the holy site of Najaf. He, a wayward firebrand with an incomparable Shia lineage through his martyred and revered father (Grand Ayatollah Mohammad Sadeq al Sadr). He, who these days spoke to and for the sullen, the outlaws, and the marginalized. And who publicly disrespected the hierarchy of the quiescent Shia Clerics. By April 5th, his street militia, Jaysh al Mahdi had replaced the local police forces on the roads out of Kut. So now, the Shia street, so recently liberated from Saddam's clutches was transitioning into the hands of the rabble, provisioned by Iran. While they were far less violent toward folks like us than Zarqawi and the Sunni extremists, certainly they represented an ominous turn for the worse.

On the following day, I got a call, desperately, it seemed, insisting I travel to our branch office in Diwaniyah, about two hours west, which meant slowly struggling by car through the streams of pilgrims as they traipsed on foot during Arbayeen for their annual mourning at the holy city of Karbala. Among them, I noted, were the militias of Muqtada al Sadr.

I found the staff there very fearful, huddled in the reception area. The ex-pat in charge was upstairs packing out. Jaysh al Mahdi had taken over the town; the new police, trained by the Coalition Forces, had melted away. We all knew that those tainted by their association with the West should beware. I remember asking them to stay calm for a while and to let me take us through the logic of the situation. Then there was an outburst at the door and a couple of Jaysh broke in, very wild eyed, and wove across the room gyrating their AKs at me, stopping, fitful, about an arm's length away and invecting "Jew." My instincts, as far back as Vietnam, told me that any second I would feel some very high velocity rounds tearing up my body just before my lights went out. I stared at the tiles, since their eyes held nothing for me, and lit a cigarette...and then another...sucked those babies down to the butt in great inhalations. I waited, on that fearful edge, interminably, it seemed, as the national staff fawned shamelessly and begged the assailants for mercy for what was, despite the obvious, a friend of their people.

Meanwhile, as fate would have it, Ahmed, one of Chris's security deputies, unseen in a back room, had jumped the back wall and found some of the more traditional Sadr Sheiks to intervene. With time, they distracted the Jaysh long enough into the yard outside for me to sneak out into the back, over the wall, and run down an alley, along with the other expat in tow, soon after to slip into Ahmed's car who eventually got us to Kut.

That night, my national staff took us into their houses to sleep.

At work the next day, I remember Zeena being whisked home by her brothers and Salam looking glum. Then we found a knife of mysterious origin stuck in Paul's bedroom door, with a bullet and keffiyeh laid beneath it. A note told him to get out or die.

On April 8th at about 0130 hrs, I heard the automatic fire begin around the CPA complex about a kilometer away from the home where I had been hidden. I moved my mattress closer to the wall. Strange, it was almost cozy, like having shelter in a hard rain. The fire lasted about an hour and then stopped. The next morning, I was told that the CPA building was in the hands of Jaysh al Mahdi.

The nationals gathered around me and told us that it was time to leave, that the Jaysh was out of the control of their leaders and would hurt us. So, over the next few hours, we sent the expats north in stages to Khanaqin along the Badrah Road. In the end, about noon on the 8th, only a Jordanian and I were left. I remember thinking that I should leave then when the streets were empty and the folks at lunch.

But the neighborhood elders would not yet allow it. "You must eat with us before you travel," they told me – and many courses at that – while I, doing absolutely no justice to the food, nervously watched the sun recline outside their window.

Finally, they invited some Sadr friends to escort me out to the Badrah Road where, quite anxious, our drivers, the Jordanian, and I worked our way over the dirt piste along the Iranian border toward Khanaqin where the other expats had already congregated, seeing me turn into the office at last after dark. "All the cows in the barn," was transmitted by the manager there to the HQ in the States.

CHAPTER 11

Khanaqin, Remote Management

Two weeks later, we were still in what was called "remote." We had no idea of how long this would last. We drove down and met with the national staff about midway between the Shia heartland and the recent Kurdish appropriation. They were still running the program down south and, by all testimony, running it well. We expats were suffering from impatience. Being in "remote" was hard on the nerves. Our national staff told us that the American soldiers who came back to retake Kut were not the same anymore. "One year ago, we brought them flowers. Now the kids throw stones at them. They have their lists," Tall Muhammad, our Kut security guy, told me. "They make their raids at night, and they terrify everyone in the neighborhood. But they don't get the bad ones anyway." The next day, I got two emails from the satellite connections we left behind. This first, below, was from Zeena, who was also one of four women on the local provincial council, created by the Americans as a prototype for local governance:

> "Besides, I would like to tell you that the council is active again. We have been given very broad authorities signed by Bremer. We are selecting a new governor for Wassit in the coming week. I have been chosen to work with four committees: Educational, Cultural, Public Relations, and Females committees. It is great David; it is no longer a decoration. Duties are assigned to us weekly and I do what I can on Sat to finish my Tues work. I feel active and I am trying what I could to serve my country, though not liked at all, but time will come when people will realize that I work for them and not for the Americans. I know some are angry but they will have to change their views in the NEAR FUTURE. Believe me it is Wassit's future that we are building now."

Then the second email came from Tall Muhammad, again informing me that another "list," not a CPA list, had appeared – this one tacked to shops in the Medina. The list stated that the following would be "hurt" if anything bad happened to the Muqtada al Sadr. Zeena's name was on it.

The events of April had changed the landscape within the Shia heartland, significantly. The American designed CPA apparatus, as well as those American organizations contracted to support its objectives, were no longer seen as legitimate by many of the Shia population. We had witnessed its structures attacked and in some cases destroyed. Its principal US contractor for the promotion of a democratic Iraq, the Research Triangle Institute (RTI), had come under a dedicated and almost universal assault by the recently ascendant Muqtada al Sadr movement and had been evacuated. The various other government structures sponsored by CPA – such as the police, the local governing councils, and the CPA-appointed provincial governors – were now no longer seen as legitimate Iraqi institutions either, but rather as extensions of the Coalition Forces. To some extent, this situation had already been the case, but now, after the Muqtada al Sadr uprising, public opinion had shifted further toward their illegitimacy.

The unequivocal "lesson learnt" we got from the April uprising was that the American objective of planting and growing a replica of Western liberalism within Iraq would have to reflect the more traditional Iraqi respect for tribal and religious influences. Within the Shia heartland, pluralism and secularism were now tainted by the American brand. That was not to say that many folk in the Shia heartland did not yearn for the type of opportunities provided by a more open society. They clearly did. After decades of being denied the possibilities of participating in a more modern world, they were hoping for integration.

Then why, we asked, did the Western-trained police disappear as soon as the Jaysh al Mahdi took over the streets? Why did the moderate majority retire to their living rooms and let the glassy-eyed Jaysh take over the streets? The answers were various and complicated but also connected directly to the possibility of independent charities such as us resuming activities in the South.

Of course, there were no traditions of equitable governance in Iraq. No real reference points so that the assumption of democratic principles, as defined in the West, could have an indigenous starting point, no habits, no practice with the necessary social contracts. There was only the "hear-tell" of how other societies in the West live and the hunger to have those opportunities for their children. This yearning had grown exponentially throughout 2004 as satellite dishes proliferated across the land, as well as mobile phones and Internet access. From almost no connections with Western culture, there had been an explosion of links. In the living rooms of expats who had worked for us in the Shia heartland, there had been frequent references to the contest between Najaf (the center of the Shia Religion) and Channel 2, a commercial, Western-oriented station from Dubai that played a succession of Hollywood movies. Left uncomplicated by other forces, clearly Channel 2 had been winning an increasing share of hearts and minds. For many women, Oprah had become a role model.

In conjunction, we had begun to follow through on our summit and to use the platforms for "transformative" programming to link Shia teenagers to other sources of knowledge through the establishment of Internet centers in their communities and through encouragements to be creative through a pursuit of the arts and science. Young women were equally represented.

However, this fledging renaissance had no defined Iraqi organization, nor did it have any leading spokespersons. The new secular political parties, created after the war, were not seen as independent of the Coalition Forces and, as such, not legitimate. The older Baath organization had, of course, totally dominated the previous governing structures and had stamped out any emerging leaders not faithful to them. At the time when all things Baath were excised by the Coalition Forces, there were few other recognized voices for the aspirations of those who would modernize the country.

Further, there were, at the same time, other forces that were obstructing modernism. Among the most potent of them was the extended presence of foreign soldiers on their streets. No population accepts this for long, even as they were attempting to provide – often carelessly – the necessary security for the population to begin benefiting from its release from the horrors of the Saddam regime.

Meanwhile, the power of the Clerics in Najaf had grown – not because they spoke for a historically religious people but because they had a growing organization; they were indigenous, and they had their hand on a growing sense of Iraqi/Shia nationalism, which had grown even faster as CF soldiers stayed in those cities where the promised American largesse was piddling against expectations and where the attempts to plant a Western model of governance became often ludicrously inadequate. And so, with its organization growing, the Najaf Clerics had grown their reach, and as the pilgrims had streamed to Karbala for holy celebrations in the spring of 2004, their influence became pervasive.

Then along about the same time came the interim constitution and its principles, engineered by the Americans, which had seemed to allow certain undue protections for the secular and western Kurds, while constraining the power of the Clerics in Najaf. The expressed intent of the CPA to wait longer for direct elections was seen in Najaf as a further constraint on their ascent to power in Iraq. They believed they had been cheated continuously by Western powers over the past century, and they were dedicated to now getting what their numbers (65% of the Iraqi population) led them to believe they were owed. The longer the "one person-one vote" elections were postponed, the more they feared that deals would be struck in ways that would limit the role of the Shia – especially the power of the Najaf Clerics. The confrontation between the revered and quiescent Ayatollah Sistani and the CPA over the interim constitution and the timetable for voting had led to heightened tension throughout the Shia South. The earlier praise for President Bush among the people of the South now turned hostile. They spoke of an abandonment, such as they had received from Bush's father.

It was into this cauldron the Muqtada al-Sadr had jumped – the young renegade Cleric from Najaf who now took the voice and the stage away from the quiescent Clerics like Sistani in Najaf and actively began railing against not only the current political process, but against the existence of any Western influence within Iraq. He was not respected by educated Iraqis, nor by the quiescent Clerics, nor by the tribal leaders, but he now had the resonance on the street fueled by President Bush's declarations to capture him – even as he was sitting in Najaf surrounded by his followers, and ready to become a martyr like his famously martyred father. By mid-April, the Coalition Forces had recaptured most of the areas taken by the Muqtada al Sadr army of faithful and were soon at all strategic points inside the cities of the South. However, the Jaysh were still there...melted away...but there.

The Americans now needed to negotiate with the Najaf Clerics, particularly with the quiescent ones, and through them to limit the disruption from Muqtada al Sadr. But because of their public declarations, neither Muqtada al Sadr nor President Bush had allowed much space to effect such a retreat. The CPA maintained that this group was an extremist fringe. That was true. But Muqtada al Sadr now had the banner and the battle cry for Iraqi nationalism as well as for Shia eminence. Whether his capture and destruction, along with all the collateral damage that would cause, would allow for a modified resumption of that renaissance referred to earlier or whether it would spawn a hundred daily acts of sabotage to get rid of all foreigners remained to be seen. Could the prospects of a better life (meaning pluralism, democratic participation, economic opportunities, and the rule of law) do successful battle with zealotry and nationalism among a people with only fear and distrust as a legacy from the Saddam years? That was truly the question. And if the "yearnings for renaissance" in any way prevailed (surely modified), would they not prevail more often because of Channel 2 and "transformative" programming by NGOs like us than because GI's patrolled the streets, and US contractors forced a Western model of governance upon them?

And so it was, into the summer, we had stayed on, about two hours north of the Shia heartland in Khanaqin, in Kurd controlled territory. Our national staff continued to visit us from the south, and we tried our best to manage the programs by remote. The national staff were strong enough to continue this for some time. I still believed that we would return, as security would permit.

But I also knew that absent any indigenous force for law and order, with only a shadow of governance, these residues of the Saddam regime (the criminals and the assassins) along with the new born Shia zealots (Jaysh) would intimidate the general citizenry either to hide away from the growing divide between CPA and Najaf or to get in step with the new zealots.

We, even as we had been independent of CPA, and even as we had responded to the "yearnings for renaissance" of many Shia, without politics or prejudice, would eventually fall as a victim to the divide. With time, our staff would become afraid to come to work, our expats to travel south.

Absent the triumph of the moderates, the quiescent Clerics, the traditional tribal leaders, and the average Shia family, our larger hopes and dreams for the birth of that viable Iraq, which I had dared to hope for back in those early days when I was to be found wandering around Firdos Square, would slowly give way to those prophesies of "abyss" as wailed daily by the Western press. The marriage of convenience between Muqtada al Sadr and the "outsiders" (Zarqawi) and the Sunni "dead-enders" would die the minute there was no common enemy. What would follow would be a terrible sorting out within Iraq by a resurgent Sunni opposition and a disorganized and divided Shia movement with little capacity for governing its zeal and a Kurdish population that would wish a curse on all their heads, take Kirkuk, and resume their independent course. And should the nightmare not be stopped by overwhelming force, we knew that neighboring countries would intervene and look for advantage.

And so, throughout the summer, we, the expat managers, hunkered down in Khanaqin.

We put up our antennas and connected to our national managers on the other end of the Badrah Road, or alternatively we were seen roaming around the compound with the SAT phones to our ears. Very antiseptic compared to what we had had. Bed, breakfast, laptop, lunch, laptop, dinner, bed punctuated by the great embrace when once a week our Shia staff would appear on our doorstep for consultations – and by constant trepidations as well that the pressures we expats fled would soon scatter to the winds what good we had begun.

Then in late August, the Marjariah (the supreme council of Shia clerics in Iraq) rose, followed by the liberation of the Imam Ali Mosque in Najaf from the desecrations of the Jaysh Al Mahdi.

Yes, the venerable, dark eyed, quiescent Ayatollah Al Sistani had landed in the Lower South – returning from medical care in England – and now his convoy moved on Najaf –

coalition gunships on his flanks – the power of his preeminence growing with each kilometer north. The confrontation ended on the 25th of August with the rabble dispersed, the keys to the Shrine handed over to Ayatollah al Sistani, and the Muqtada silenced for the moment.

A few days later, I felt I must lead. We managers had to show our faces down there even if we had ceded the management responsibilities for a role now more proximate to that of investor and coach.

I remember there was no farewell that morning, Paul was up – to track me by Thuraya. Ahmed Qadir – the ex-trucker, ex-smuggler – would drive me to the point where the Kurdish influence stopped and the Shia began.

I had gotten up much earlier, in the dark, to get ready in my head. I went through every detail. My forced abduction and the manhandling till I was on my knees. The round into the back of my head. For someone like my Kurdish friend Qadir, he didn't need to go through this process. Already, he had seen two of his four brothers shot dead. He just made his appearance known to me – that he was ready when I was – and then left me to my coffee and thoughts. Maybe I would squeal like a pig if I were captured, tortured, killed, but by sunrise, I had reached a point where I didn't think so. I believed I could die okay.

We checked our commo with Paul, took a left turn out the gate of Khanaqin, and drove across the desert south – a very dead, hard desert with its reddish ridges and mounds melting down to the flats and gullies. South of Mandali, Ahmed passed me off to Tall Muhammad and Safa, who wrapped their arms around me and quickly pulled me into their sedan.

And so I arrived in Kut – to my eye very familiar with that stern gaze of Ayatollah Sistani or the benevolent countenance of the deceased Ayatollah Sadr plastered in all the public places, the baking of an August day, the trash dumped everywhere, the black plastic bags caught up in the ubiquitous razor wire, the disrepair – a right and quick left and right into the compound with me still hunkered down in the back with my keffiyeh. Then I was ushered through the front door and past the inner door, finally flung open, and pulled into the meeting room, from which a great gasp ensued. It was packed with all our staff. Unknowing. I was led to the front. Men shook hands ardently and the women, all now compelled to sit on the side, smiled with both affection and discretion. I had fifty-nine minutes, Tall Muhammad told me. I gushed for most of it – about solidarity and brotherhood and forces that divide and courage for staying with us over the last four months. Then they pointed at my watch, and, in a blink, I was in the car and leaving Al Houra, past my house, my street, my neighbors.

As it turned out, that set the pattern over the months to come – from one hour to one overnight to several overnights. Them up, us south – hopefully in random, unpredictable ways. Somehow, the trips managed to keep us as one despite all that would pull us apart.

CHAPTER 12

Khanaqin

"Welcome back," the doctor had said to me, the day after my return from Kut, straddling me as I lay beneath him, curled up in agony on the tiles, feeling some sort of corrosive eating through my gut.

"Walnuts," he deduced. Shelled, which our ersatz cook had thought to place on the kitchen table and which I had quickly put in my mouth, given my long intimacy with their "black cousins," so lovingly cultivated by me and my family on our patch of land in New England many years before the notion of living in Iraq had entered my mind.

"Rat poison," he pronounced…from some Iranian walnuts in a dilapidated warehouse stored there since before Tommy Franks. Then the doctor had dropped some pills in my mouth followed by a swig of Pepsi that soon shut me down well into the following day.

Khanaqin, since April, had become my new home. It was the terminus for that frayed thread of road from the south, and, since

2003, it had been a Kurdish intrusion into the Shia heartland. The area was flanked by Iran to the east and a miserable flotsam of Arab refugees who had been pushed west toward Muqdadiyah as the Kurdish Peshmerga had advanced. Seventeen months had passed since our agency had made an initial outpost there, slept under an empty water tower, and received some American largesse to control a variety of pathogens in the town's water. The outpost had also served as a secure way station for expats leaving the southland, intent eventually on arriving at a dirt airstrip far north in Erbil with a shipping container nearby where one signed in for a seat on the Beechcraft to Amman.

So picture it. 50C at noon, arsenic in the well water, Nicholas Berg's severed head still roaming about our collective minds, remote from our team in Kut, despondent. The hurrahs and hooplas that our first team rode in on, in April 2003, now were long gone. More often, we were weeding out those who had become disgruntled; in fact, we were often forced to weed those replacements just after they had arrived from Erbil.

We remnant expats had been occupying an old Baathist residence and had made it habitable, adding some guest rooms for our national staff travelers from the south and erecting a small square of cinder blocks on the roof for me and my mattress, affording me easy access to the sky as well as to any midnight stirrings on the street below.

Bedtime…there I was most nights in my cinder block hooch on the roof. Often with "click click click" in my mind – like those old 3D View-Masters from the 1950s and their revolving images. I imagined now my remaining emissaries of the West touching down in the summer of 2004, like incoming parachutes, now living in an ambience of death. "Ashes, ashes, we all fall down," I sang to myself. "Such a terrible landscape we inhabit. An ambience of death," I repeated. "How can we refute the zealot's cry of 'no joy on Earth' when here there is most often 'no hope on Earth.' Never a right angle, all pipes leaking, circuit boards shooting sparks, a thousand date palms planted to no avail because no one cared enough to water them?"

"Can you conceive the landscape in Kut and Khanaqin?" I imagined I was lecturing to a concerned audience back in the

US. "Consider its poor Shia and Kurdish souls sent by Saddam two decades ago to perish by the thousands against the human waves sent by Ayatollah Khomeini. And only a few years later, in the aftermath of the first Gulf War, their kin slaughtered when George Herbert Walker Bush abandoned them to a resurgent Saddam."

At this point in my imaginary lecture, I crossed my arms on my chest. Then the paralysis came fast. First, a thick fog settled in, impairing my thinking and my speech. Then my brain froze into a cube and cracked like lake ice. I could feel the cracking...and then lights out, as we would say when I was a kid, until or unless I was awakened by the horns and whistles of the night watch.

But the encouragement I received in bed from the applause for my imagined stump speeches rarely endured past the morning coffee. Soon enough, I would get aggravated that too few of my expat employees could explain to themselves or to me why the hell they were working in Iraq – other than for oil and Israel.

Regardless, unpremeditated as they were, the terms *rationality*, *secular*, and *modern* were supposed to be their purported attraction. They were to be the initial preparations for eventual Arab assimilation into a Western-inspired global order. But as seen by many of the more suspicious residents of South Central, this Avant Garde was only the latest manifestation of a devil, a long-term intruder from the West. His "war on political Islam" was their war on "Jew Crusader," which for now, for this gang of foreigners, only meant asymmetrical warfare whereby the zealous opposition to them played to Western media so as to provoke a West with no appetite for body bags or, for that matter, for severed heads – an image since Berg that also kept a lot of the gang from bounding out of their beds in the morning. Poor souls who took the calls on the sat phones from loved ones back home in Peoria, who pleaded with them to come home, sending them off to their quiet retreats at night in secluded corners of the compound so that they could be alone on chat, murmuring intimacies in the corners of bedrooms.

Through the eyes of those around me and for most of those who had shipped out for this mess in Iraq, there was never a sense for a grander cause – no compelling idea to justify a sacrifice – just a lot of free radicals tossed about among the latest sociologies on the ground as the Arabs tried to find a way out of the backwater.

Meanwhile, the neocons back home were all lit up about stilling the Iraqi zealotry with their own sense of manifest destiny while the political left joined in an unholy alliance with media and the Iraqi insurgents to get the film of both the bomb and the victims in the can by 6pm (ET) so as to hit the prime time news in the US. While most Iraqis in Kut and Khanaqin just waited in their homes for this invasion to pass, sensing that it was a lesser tragedy than 300,000 dead from Saddam's no account war with Iran and soon after with Kuwait. They smirked when I asked about the outrage of Abu Ghraib. "Dirty pictures," they scoffed, "nothing compared to what Saddam did behind prison doors."

So, who the hell came? Who was carrying the latest load of Western civ? Who was coming so soon after Berg had had his head severed by Zarqawi and placed on his corpse still dressed in the orange jumpsuit before the picture had sped around the world on the Internet? Who the hell came? Was it just a hodgepodge of actors who came for a payday? Or for a better personal narrative back home as heroes where there were none? Or for a couple, I supposed, with images of T.E. Lawrence dancing in their heads? Whoever came, I would try to meet them in Erbil at the airstrip as the Beechcraft came in from Amman and watch as they had walked through the reception container. By the time they had made it to Sullei, about five hours south where we broke the trip, I had an idea of whether another mistake had landed. Some would immediately cocoon up as they realized that the price on their head was real and that "no" they were not going to have some South African commando sit outside their door at night. Or sometimes to the contrary, there arrived those few who would bolt the curfews when no one was looking, feeling they had a personal immunity, not because they read the streets better, but rather because that was the personal story they were selling back home.

In they came, the new arrivals, never ceasing to amaze me at the comfort many hoped to derive from a uniform, any uniform, notwithstanding the nincompoop inside it and their dismay to find none at our location. In its absence, they latched onto anything for well-being: tinted windows, sat phones, thick skinned vehicles, concertina wire. Then often, finding the above insufficient, they found someone to sleep with to get through the night.

In they came and out they went, since there were few in HQ who had a clue about what was needed. I handed them the UNDP 2002 report, a landmark anthology by Arab scholars describing the extent of the backwater, and a list of what was allowed or not, along with my explanation for the rules and finally the number for my phone "which is never off."

And if there were incoming expats who could not accept that as enough ("I didn't sign up for this shit"), then soon enough they would be going back up the road to the container to sign in for the trip out.

There they were – what the enlightenment had produced 300 years later as the "soft power" allied with the grey hulks of the armada in the Gulf – all in the framework of the neocon occupation as relayed in the morning calls from Rumsfeld and Wolfowitz to those acolytes who radiated the evangelism out to those bewildered "willing" who would push the cash out and then report the magnificent results back. Those acolytes had brushed most American scholarship on the issue into the nearest available trash bin and trotted on – jut jawed, prow into the weather. Most notable of the acolytes was Bremer, but he was only the first of a long line of apparatchiks who preached the evangelism of the American narrative. Another was former deputy national security advisor Jeffrey. I remember him well, his spittle and dribble, as he fumed at me that it was "damn well not an occupation." He then summoned some young intern to regale me with the story of an Iraqi women's group, which, thanks to American largesse, had recently produced some embroidery. The occasional US government inspectors also came through, contracted to speed through South Central in squad-sized formations with their M60s on swivels at the back of Chevy Suburbans, sweeping the barrel over the local citizens.

Windshield analysis they called it – no stops – just to verify the project existed. Or once upon a time, our own precious USAID liaison with the Green Zone who had the balls to descend into a mud and wattle hooch, insisting on tight jeans, sitting on the carpet, her legs spread in a V before the venerable and wizened religious sheiks to lecture them on women's participation.

"Jobs, jobs, jobs," the staff from the Green Zone would keep hollering at me as if they would appear magically with no market. That or to build ever more monuments in praise of the trickle of largesse, frankly anything. "Just make sure they own it, make some damn contribution," they yelled. "How about some light bulbs for the tunnel at Derbanderkan?" I asked my employees. Yep, for a fee, the locals would supply the light bulbs for the British made tunnel. Presumably, making the tunnel theirs henceforth and, in the process, jacking up our beneficiary count each time a car passed through it.

And the Iraqis, still eating their couscous inside as twilight came to Kut and sighing at the incompetence. It was their oil money after all which was paying for this, they would all concur, referring to Bush's pitch to his Congress in 2003. I, forever the Yankee, never understood how America could afford such waste or what the return was. What was left behind – corruption as America dumped the money off in paper bags, literally. Or America as a massive floundering malevolence.

So, there you go. That was our gang's infrastructure – our US government's enabling environment. Jeffrey's tantrum and our USAID representative spread eagled in the hooch – and an M-60 on a swivel as their hard-skinned vehicle raced through town.

"Never mind," Paul and I laughed, "let freedom ring." Somewhere, we fantasized, at 30K feet up this disgrace must be making sense.

And thus the winnowing of my Avant Garde went apace. Often, in any case, useless as purveyors. There was Angela, the poor woman from Westphalia who was brought in to repair the books in Khanaqin so ruined by her predecessor – a tubby old colonialist from Namibia who upon arrival had wasted no time securing a clandestine source of moonshine. He consumed enough so as to be dumb to the consequences, and in my absence he fell permanently prostrate on his bed from whence he had insisted on a continuous mentorship of his twenty-three-year-old bookkeeper from the Sunni heartland, periodically to shift from counseling her on accruals to explain the very nature of the newly arrived freedom she was receiving...to include making some original interpretations of the original Koran as concerned a man's right to her rosebud.

As my car was pulling in, the bookkeeper went fleeing across the street in a flood of tears bewailing her fate to the gathering bystanders. She would soon have her brothers in Baghdad, I feared, saddling up to kill the colonialist and maybe anyone else who got in the way. So my ham-fisted driver and I gave him twenty minutes to pack. We stuffed him in the car, restrained and mumbling rubbish until halfway to the airport when he went into deprivation shock. We had to hunt around for another pint of moonshine, which he emptied in one extended gulp and then slumped into a coma – only to be reawakened long enough just outside the container when we fed him another pint before lifting him into the plane.

And so now poor Angela was parachuted in as relief and was not understanding her predecessor's numbers. She, soon on, had been criticized for her incomprehension by her senior at HQ who had sent the "insufficient" numbers back to her. She stayed glued to them all day and night in a quasi-hysteria to get them right despite my several warnings that numbers weren't worth it – especially not when we saw what our Department of Defense was doing with numbers – or rather with paper bags full of numbers thrown off the back of Humvees to collateral casualties.

Still Angela shook and cried – becoming a wreck over the inherited mess – and I then reached softly to her elbow to beg her to relax at which she snatched her arm back, baring her teeth, and cowered. Others reached out to her, and she seemed similarly terrified of the pat on the back and would become tongue tied with her insistences of being able to do the numbers. Then in the corners of her mouth, she would froth, and given the heat, it would bake there. Thus I had to concoct a lie about a finance workshop in Amman which, smelling something, she said she could not attend. As a consequence, I had to make a real meeting in Amman and even then watch her halt and resist the whole way north to the Beechcraft and get very agitated each time and then froth and then, of course, even if one's hand only went out in a gesture of peace – never touching, mind you – she would cower. And so in the waiting space of the little airport, I was all the time on tenterhooks that she would break down or disappear out the door and what could anyone do since she would not be touched.

The next morning, a kind heart from our staff in Amman had managed to persuade her to sign the release papers, making us no longer liable. Then soon after, I was flying back to my gang. Not much later, I heard from that saint in Amman that Angela had indeed confided to having suffered from pre-existing conditions – since childhood – and would I be a reference for her for the next job?

Eventually, the books got solved with the arrival of a close approximation of a model Avant Garde, an Oxbridge man named Andrew, an actual representative of the enlightenment. With his degrees in the Classics, he had come to numbers late as a way, a trade, to earn a living while he peregrinated. He took us home in Iraq as regards the numbers. He had a steady hand, an encouraging smile, patience with the nationals, and only the sharp bite for nonsense.

Ah, my Avant Garde. Yes, this motley team would plumb the depths of this landscape to assess "demand for what the West had to offer." Where, as it turned out years later, only literacy (English and Arabic) and the Internet would survive. Authored by that one woman amidst the many who had landed in South Central and with the national name, Albana, no less. This daughter of the Hoxha regime was a child of aberrant Western belief, but eminently Western nonetheless, and, sadly, one of only a few to find and seize the demand and eventually to draw thousands to those doors, so as to read those mysterious subtitles for the Western shows. Or those labels on the jars at the corner shop. Or in some cases to create that email to Katie in Kansas. Amidst the millions of dollars eventually transferred to us – these tens of thousands – only these sowed a disruption that survived our absence.

But even as we insinuated transformation, truth be told we still needed bricks. Millions of bricks or we would be told to leave. No bricks meant no burn rate, which meant no cash transfers from the Feds, which meant our NGO collapsed like a house of cards. And so even as women streamed to the Internet and literacy programs, that dynamic unfolded alongside the preposterous, such as the municipal pool in Kut that was reluctantly approved by the wide-eyed engineer from Walla Walla. The pool was the welcome response to local hopes for aggrandizement despite my timeworn advice to reduce "moving parts" to the absolute minimum. "If they move, they will break, and when they break, it will die," I said.

"It'll sure burn money," he argued. Always a boon, we both knew, for our financials and for the satisfaction of Washington.

"And what will we do with a pool?" I asked, begging for more information from this All American from the great Northwest.

"Well, each year kids drown in the Tigris. We would have swimming lessons. For women too," he added quickly.

"And you know the first time the purification system crashes, it will never be fixed?" I asked.

He demurred on that point.

"So how much?" I asked.

"300K USD," he said.

Well, I would not have bet a penny on it, but the town – what with some preliminary inquiries afoot about the site – was inflated with pride. A pool would be something to distinguish Kut from similar cities in the South.

And so they built it. These engineers. On the banks of the Tigris so as to afford easy access to a constant supply of water. Then, of course, the cement basin began sinking before it had hardened, so more rigging ensued by building a hill on the location and then pouring a new basin. But that action elicited complaints from the town's people. A tall wall needed to be built because the town could see the women on women's day from outside the perimeter. So now a great wall was constructed, which cost almost as much as the basin, with the price tag now exceeding 600K USD. Then some people argued for a roof to protect the bathers from the sun. Then some wanted hot water, so they could swim in the winter. In the end, I put my arm around my friend from Walla Walla, and we just closed our eyes to all of it. The pool was now a Town Cause, a cause célèbre. I didn't even want to discuss it with the eager engineer from Walla Walla. It would be, inevitably, five years from now, just another skeleton on the landscape.

Ahh...my Avant Garde

And then who else...since there were many stories to choose from. My Greek, my zealot for sincerity. He pried incessantly into everyone's motives for doing good. Eventually, he became a solitary figure, estranged from our current representation of Avant Garde.

It had been strange to get a Greek. I had never seen one in this line of work, notwithstanding their preeminence in the Western civ we were all selling. This one had come from a castle in the Peloponnesus, subdivided so often by siblings over the years, that, according to him, his piece was now barely two rooms. That and a reference to his aunt was all he had offered. Short, stocky, and swarthy, the black hair atop his forehead stood up by pomade like a picket fence, which given the culture in our commune for jabbing at peculiarities, invited a grin.

So like that he had introduced himself, "I am Drakoulis" and then extended his hand and showed a magnificent set of teeth, which, as we were all to learn, were kept that way by his constant habit of strolling through the compound and its yard, vigorously brushing. Sudsing up his mouth, elbow gyrating, face twisted.

Drakoulis, quickly reduced by the gang to "Drak," took a room and dropped his pack. And then came English. He had enough words if you were to count them. But it was quickly apparent that he didn't have the hang of it. So, meaning to be understood, he needed (sometimes desperately) to circle, often, exerting himself to finally zero in on what he was trying to say. Unfortunately, at meals, where we were all elbow to elbow in a high-volume chatter, Drak often fell aside, to silence and eventually left – just stopping by the table afterward to eat some residue. With time he became progressively introverted. Sneaking off, under cover of night, he walked without purpose in the surrounding neighborhoods. For which, while I could not extract a promise to refrain (he said he could not allow himself such a promise), I did extract his understanding that I would fire him if he continued. There were also the uplifting substances that I suspected supported his walks about town, not to mention his midnight séances on the roof.

I think they were mutually supporting: his inability to congregate along with his disdain for the overall enterprise for which we were employed. All of these misgivings and insecurities emerged against the backdrop of his sense of family with his nationals in Amarah (a branch office east of Kut under his supervision) whom he visited from the remote compound in Khanaqin whenever the Jaysh were in remission. Even physically separated from "his" Iraqis, he was with them on chat at all times of day and night, explaining the prospects of renaissance as understood by a Greek. He nagged me constantly for permission to visit them more often, to stay there longer, even as the place was rife with violence and zealotry.

Still we had a special relationship. As if he had been spying on me by moonlight from his window, he would see me alone on the rusted swing in the front yard and come down to smoke with me. He sat beside me to absorb my late evening verbal meanderings, from Homo Erectus to "Shock and Awe." We designed interventions with no regard for the donor's Logical Frameworks or for GAAP (Generally Accepted Accounting Principles). Together, we tried to get it right. In Amarah, he dug up the remnants of an artist's guild that dated back to Saddam's secular years – Baathist years – and argued for an atelier. This plan was unfolding at the exact moment that the Jaysh al Mahdi was swarming on Amarah, pronouncing abject piety and dumping free spirits in ditches at night. This mayhem forced our atelier to be built under another guise into which a few brave creative souls were secreted to apply paint from a palette or mold some clay with such discretion that the religious thugs would not know what was underfoot – leaving them to remark on the magnificent renditions of Imam Ali and Imam

Hussein at the entrance – and selling cheap prints of the same in the market.

But then there were his other relationships back at remote. Particularly with the women who proved most awkward when he had them alone. They for their part took him less and less as funny and more and more as a pain while Drak in some rough equivalency drilled in on their alleged fraud: what did they bring to Iraqis, except English practice and Generally Accepted Accounting Principles? Finally, after some months, Drak had become too much, and the women had pleaded to be free of him. I was too far removed to know the details. Maybe there had been untoward suggestions as well. Sex implied by the swarthy Greek, and implications refused by the pale white American and Polish women.

As a consequence, I deported him to the back office in Sullei, five hours more distant from Khanaqin and even farther from his family of nationals in Amarah, with only a couple of taciturn Arab men as companions. Unrequited, he remained persistent, ever pushing me to expand the limits of his travels in the badlands.

"It was nothing, David."

"Nothing?" I almost shouted in his Greek face, "You a Westerner...a Christian..."

"An atheist," he corrected me.

"Don't play fucking games with me. A Western Christian type...slept on the same floor with a 24-year-old Shia princess in Amarah with the fucking Jaysh outside your window?"

"David...I swear it was nothing...we were in different rooms...I told her to go back to Kut, but she said it was okay."

"Fuck," I shouted, "between you and Zeena...you'll get us all killed." I was infuriated. I wanted him away. And Zeena, my precious gatekeeper in the Shia heartland, longing to let her hair fly free. Well, yes. But not, if I could help it, on my watch. Far, far too much collateral damage for the rest of the gang.

But I needed to sleep on my dismay. In my mind that night, he was gone, back up to the airport as yet another reject. But as the hours passed, I wavered. My Greek friend, did get it, better than most – why we were supposed to be here – and he certainly had enough distinction to see the fraud and to ply the badlands.

Then it hit. The decision was made for me. Evidently, he had not quit the expat women as I had assumed. He had shifted his focus toward a newcomer, running her down on chat with his constant queries, till she had thrown up her hands. After all, it seemed he was inalterably fixed on being the self-appointed "sincerity cop," and would not stop. Till finally the "fresh eyes" – fresh from "culturally appropriate" in progressive circles of the US – had copied all his righteous, belittling chat, pasted it to an email and sent it to HQ as a prima facie case of "inappropriate behavior" for which he was urged to leave us.

CHAPTER 13

Vietnam, 2004 Op-Ed

Later on, that September, there were a growing number of Op-Eds and other such analysis that compared Iraq to Vietnam, which, as a veteran of the later, interested me and prompted me to send off my own thoughts, which were never accepted for publication. To wit:

"On first reflection, aspects of the American situation in Iraq seem similar to those in Vietnam. In both wars, we were crippled from the start by our incapacity to read the weather; never once to be accused of having our finger in the wind. In the vernacular, we backed the wrong horses...Thieu and Chalabi and company...and the wrong battles, underestimating, catastrophically, the indigenous forces, respectively of Vietnamese nationalism and Arab pride.

Then with that over-arching and abiding disability, as American policy was applied on the ground, our liberal democracy clove to its perimeter – both cultural and military – most of the time. The forays out into the country where folk may not want you are increasingly limited and circumscribed. The asymmetry of the firepower, the disingenuous vocabulary of 'hearts and minds,' rubble/blast-barriers/razor-wire, the undercurrents of nationalism outside the perimeters, the sense of us being so foreign to the place, the public confusion back home, the liberal/media drumbeat for bringing 'our boys' back – all that still exists in Iraq as it had in Vietnam. Fear exists too – along with the exquisite intensity of occasional feelings and the abiding longing for the best of the world you left behind.

And finally, there was the 'lie' – the unwillingness of either Johnson or Bush to level with the TV audience. Both the Gulf of Tonkin and WMD (Weapons of Mass Destruction) were essential parts behind a President's will to subordinate 'facts on the ground' for a more existential cause that, in and of itself, would encourage citizens to agree to sacrifice blood and treasure.

But back then, in April of 1969, my presence existed as a uniformed and armed troop on the periphery of Russian expansionism, engaged in a proxy war that did, in the end, further bankrupt the Kremlin and send me home, wounded. Vietnam lost three million precious souls. America withdrew to the safety of its economy. The Soviets, fifteen years later, went 'belly up.'

Now, in September of 2004, almost thirty-five years later, I am un-uniformed, un-armed, but, truth be told, still an Avant Garde for the liberal democracies. I work for one of the few private humanitarian organizations still left in Iraq, funded in its entirety by the US government.

But. And there is a 'but' – some critical differences exist. For now, in any case, cell phones, satellite dishes, and Internet connections proliferate here as if there were no tomorrow. The sign of the times is the mud brick hooch in Southern Iraq with the SAT dish sprouting on its roof.

Hundreds of newspapers of all persuasions, political debate on every street corner, the makings of civil society. Yes, indeed, Iraq is roiling with unchecked freedom, open access to ideas, and public argument.

In contrast, even 30 years later in Hanoi, even with its booming economy, there are few such accoutrements of liberal democracy. The dead hand of the communist party still prevails.

Further, and this is the heart of the matter: This is not a proxy war involving two hostile global powers. Rather, it concerns whether a tolerant Christendom and a tolerant Islamic world accommodate each other? Do 400 million Arabs participate actively in the global community, or do they revert to despots, other forms of absolutism and/or fantastic dreams of bygone Caliphates? And as for us, do we embrace our historic neighbors from the fertile crescent? Embrace them in such a way that it cannot be interpreted as subjugation. And do this all the while protecting the sea lane through the Strait of Hormuz and the inviolability of Israel? Unlike Johnson's larger effort to contain and defeat the USSR, the investments we managed prior to 2001 argued for the incorporation of the Arab world and, to some extent, the Islamic world into a global society...a society currently inspired and managed by the West, principally America. In short, it was a vision of absorption that would save the Arabs and enrich the amalgam.

But then 9/11 happened – dropped into George W's lap – and that earlier sense of amalgamation that had been twisted since the inauguration became infected with mutual distrust and often hostility. Tragically, for many Americans, Arabs are becoming the enemy. Barely ten years after the Commies were dismissed. At times, I thought, it was almost as if we could not endure 'peace.'

No doubt, George W. has stuck our arm in a beehive. There is no 'on boats' such as when George McGovern was asked how to leave Vietnam. No Paris Peace talks as a fig leaf for expeditious retreat.

In Vietnam, America had wanted to stay, but, with time, got persuaded out. In Iraq, America, God knows, wants to leave (all too quickly), but cannot – not without a regional score-settling involving Turkey, Saudi Arabia, Egypt, Iran and Israel and the immediate onset of a global energy crisis.

Should Americans have let the Arabian Peninsula stew in its own despotic juices? Or, should America have precipitated an 'accommodation' that has an historic inevitability to it – though more difficult (read bloodier) with each decade of delay?

Should we few American humanitarian agencies ply the dangerous roads of Iraq in the promotion of transformation and salve? Should we play to this part of US foreign policy, which is fundamentally based on the propagation of liberal democracy among Islam and the Arab peoples? Or should we also have kept far distant from the authentic 'yearnings' of the majority of Iraqi's for the accommodation – on their terms?

Very high value – as I tell my team. At the very heart of Right Relations. What comes down over the next decade will not only be transformative for the Arabs, but for us as well. Certainly, Vietnam was instructive as pertains to the end of Western 'boots on the ground,' and the circumstances surrounding American occupations…but for Iraq and the Middle East the future is harder to divine."

CHAPTER 14

R&R, San Sebastian, Spain, December 2004

The road back, I suspected, would be tough. I had told my wife that I only had about one more of these assignments in me, maybe two.

I had wrenched myself out of bed and managed to get up and running in winter rain and wind along the corniche in San Sebastian, Spain. It was not really the road back since it was just a few days for Christmas R&R, but I was hoping that running would help me sleep – since the night before I had just lain next to my wife and had had these troubling dreams in rapid succession about the warehouse in Kirkuk and the dilemma we had gotten ourselves into.

There had been enough there on the run – sneakers soaked, the rain beading up on my glasses, the waves rolling in, the cove beside me – to bring back the memories of best runs. Runs so wonderful, few have had them.

So unlike, I had thought, how I meet the day in Iraq. At 0445, the muezzin from a minaret, right across the street from

my cinder block room on the roof, clears his throat – coming
across incredibly loud. Then he puts the microphone to his
mouth and the scratch of the beard on his mic makes a great rasp,
and by then I am more awake than not.

I crawl over to the rowing machine next to my bed, but now
twenty months into Iraq, I now no longer aim for 3.6 kilometers
in twenty minutes, but have instead lapsed into keeping my eyes
closed and just rowing in the dark at whatever pace.

After, it's down the cement steps to a shower where I hope
to get warm water because nowadays, in December, tucked in as
we are right next to the Iranian border and the Zagros Mountains,
there are those nights when I don't lie straight out, but rather curl
up tight as a baby in a womb under an Iranian blanket. Then, you
can imagine the disappointment when there is no hot water...a
factor of seemingly endless, inadequate, unsynchronized circuit
boxes, cables, wires, and erratic switches, which on a good day
may get our generator working in harmony with city electricity
for four hours a day.

And so hot water is appreciated as a perfect way to wake up
from what began with the muezzin who also gets electricity off
our generator. Then, she leaves it there, so I will take some of
Kaya's, the Polish woman's, shampoo and wash my hair, which
has rapidly thinned on top since I came to Iraq.

By day, I am often on adrenaline because of the proximity
of the killing, just across a stretch of desert, twenty-five
kilometers to the west. Nevertheless, I rarely forsake my bowl of
Egyptian corn flakes on which I pour some bottled water from
Turkey. This is my pleasurable moment when no one else in the
compound is up yet.

Sometimes, my Tunisian colleague, Abdel Hamid, will
come in and make himself some bread, jam, and coffee with
sweetener pills and then chat with me about a program or a
context for a program. I will, in any case, take my second cup of
coffee outside by this decrepit fountain, really a corroded pipe
sticking up in a cruddy tile pool – a construction that probably
broke down soon after someone took the time to build it. And
now I say it is the mother of all ashtrays since that is where I and
others flick our butts, hundreds of them, as the sun burns off the
frost – the sun coming up behind the dog pen warming my face –

and I enjoy those ten minutes as well.

Then I move to a bullpen where there are desks and computers with satellite connections, from which arrive dozens of emails nightly from around the world that I seek to answer and delete as fast as I can. So I do that in my corner of the bullpen while Kaya and Abdel Hamid and Sarah and Andy, and others who live in our compound come to work at 0800, as I tell them they must, so as to keep the discipline, no matter what, since so much around us is only a small push from chaos.

We eat lunch together, which brings me to sit among these hungry persons – my teammates, most of whom are quite young, quickly learning that all those textbooks from graduate school are mere straw.

I go back to my satellite connection until 2000 hrs when I go to the kitchen and take two cans of Turkish beer and a chunk of goat cheese and go to the fountain, knees shaking, and suck down the beer fast to get lifted up and smoke a few cigarettes and flip them into the "fountain-as-ashtray" while watching Kaya's seven feral pups – their mother poisoned by the town – huddle into their makeshift dog house for warmth. Then I go and check my emails, now arriving in a stream from the East Coast until I have done enough. I climb the steps to my room on the roof, get under the Iranian blanket, take my last smoke, make a speech to myself, and then, as I said, I just sort of short circuit and drop off.

And now, thirty-six hours into my R&R, I am with my wife and daughter in our nineteenth century apartment in San Sebastian. I had just done a thirty minutes run in the wind and rain, hoping that could let me sleep.

I had slept well enough the first night home when I had been so drained from the drive to Sulaymaniyah into our back office on the hill, now bristling with Peshmerga and then on to Erbil and the Beechcraft into Amman at night where I had my cheeseburger with Andrew, the classics scholar coming back into Iraq who, characteristically, chose something more elegant. Back up at 0400 to hopscotch around Europe to Biarritz where Annie had met me and where we had sat outside at the station in the mist with our white wines, waiting for the train to take us across the border, with me reflecting how weird it was to be there and not in Khanaqin, and finally up the wrought iron staircase where the schnauzer went berserk when he saw me, squealing and beside himself while my daughter offered me a somewhat less spectacular hug. After putting some Shepherd's pie in me, by prior agreement, by email with Annie, we had gone to a bar where I drank one tequila after another and took tokes off some compadres and bantered in Spanish such as it was and in general got to know all the patrons and bought them drinks and was in an arm wrestling match with a powerful looking Basque while his pal hopped around to a tune – his pal, with some of his front teeth punched out – while my wife looked askance, saying she had to live there and I didn't.

And so afterward, after the lovely surcease, I had slept deeply enough, but, of course, with a terrible sick feeling the next day while I went shopping for earrings and fountain pens and camera lenses so that I would have something to put under the Christmas tree the next morning. But which had been followed by that sleepless night and the constant fleeting worries about Kirkuk – worries just under the surface of sleep and extremely detailed, one after another, leaving me feeling that I was failing all over the place with no room for hope of finding a good way out. I desperately needed consolation – a new house on fifty acres where I could plant another orchard, now that the old one in my last house was likely getting abused. Those beautiful black walnuts, I remember, whose bark I used to stroke whenever I was home – and Hank whom I used to carry in my arms at sunset as I waded in the waves in La Marsa – and my boy who climbed the Col de Mosses at age ten with me in the middle of winter.

And so that night, each recollection, just under the surface of sleep had played out – down to the emails flashing on the monitor about the new branch office in Kirkuk, and the trembling as I straddled that sectarian divide, and those trips into the badlands with Qadir, intermingled with how the money I do get for being in Iraq gets sucked away by bills and volatile stock markets. Just all amalgamated into one turbulent stream of the farm slipping from sight, the cold of the muzzle on the back of my neck, the glittering multifaceted grains of sand between my knees, and the DOW ticker running in sharp detail through it all.

But strangely, half-awake now, lying on the bed, I knew those trips out there where the terrorists hunt would sustain me for the next bout of remote management from the Khanaqin compound where, regardless of my presence or absence, all those emails would forever fly in. Cozy, I would be for that brief while after Qadir and I returned, pulling that heater closer to my legs, curling my toes in the woolen socks while the bytes dropped down.

R&R...such an odd invention. An enigma in my case. Plucked out of war and dropped ever so briefly into my kin for Christmas day. Lifted away from my cinder block abode by man's flying machine and into this cove on the Basque coast.

I was sixty. I loved the run such as I had, but over the previous months, I had helped fill a whole cruddy pool with my butts and had kept stoked on two tablespoons of Nescafe to the cup, almost sludge.

And even though I could not really resurrect for a long time, that week showed me how hard it would be. A harbinger. The lungs burned. It was very hard to fill them up. The small of my back ached, and I had run less than three miles, and, as I laid down to write about my situation, I felt the blood percolating in a couple of broken down veins on my legs.

CHAPTER 15

The Election

By January of 2005, the whole world was watching the great George W. stumbling through the process. At times like a drunken sailor through the blood and mayhem, the Iraqi nation had moved toward national elections, the first in a series of three for the coming year.

Outside the Sunni Triangle, there was election fever with the party lists slapped on every flat surface available. It was a moment most Shias and Kurds had waited for, for centuries. For Bush – an unequivocal assertion; for the Shia and Kurds –

ascension to power; for the Sunnites – a precipitous fall from dominance.

In the two-week run up, the violence spiked. The Sunni insurgents made common cause with Al Qaeda to bring the country to its knees. Increasing numbers of martyrs were strapping explosives around their chests and walking into markets and mosques and igniting themselves – spraying bits of flesh and bones far and wide. The Shias wailed and the Kurds dug in. Still the movement to vote went inexorably forward.

In Khanaqin, we tightened the security protocols further – hardly showing our face – huddled around our dog-pen at night, wondering whether we were high enough on their list to be a primary target.

And then two days before the elections, a delegation of our national staff told us to retreat northward to Sullei. Almost prescient they were because the next day a dead-ender walked up to the entrance of a nearby school, to be used for polling, and "ignited." That certainly caused a few hearts to pause.

Election day finally came and, believe me, the Western democracies don't thrill to the event anymore – not like this where many citizens braved physical threats so as to be able to leave the poll with their index finger raised high, the tip colored "indigo."

Some in the Sunni Triangle would have their fingers removed for such treachery; others, the majority outside the triangle, would not wash the indigo off for a month.

The following week, there was a lull as insurgents and terrorists tried to figure out what came next after such an outpouring of voters. Whether this election was an auspicious advent of a transforming nation...or rather a provocation for more war. Think about it. Thirteen hundred years of Sunni dominance in a brief shutter of time now stood on its head. A Shia arc now postulated from Tehran to South Beirut...running right through Baghdad. Instigated, no less, by an oil man from Texas.

CHAPTER 16

The Evaluation

Coincidentally, there was a meeting of the minds (mine and the donors) that this was a safe and historic time for me to go to the Green Zone in Baghdad both to put some substance to the emails and to have them evaluate the program, such as I would present it.

The drive with Ninos, my Baghdad representative and all around fixer, would take me south but more west, right across the Arab/Kurd fault line, through the now renowned Baqubah. A rough place in its own right, but made so much more so when all those "new" Arabs that Saddam had engineered into the land around Khanaqin fled there overnight as the Peshmerga had pushed southward in April of 2003.

Now these tens of thousands of displaced, as they were called, were squatting around Muqdadiyah and Baqubah in bombed out Baathist camps. They had become our most recent beneficiaries, as we sought to expand our modest program in Khanaqin west into the Sunni heartlands. They were mostly mothers and old men surrounded by a half dozen kids with runny noses and dirty hands to whom we provided blankets and plastic sheeting and cookers, basically trying to keep them warm and dry in the cold rain of winter.

Strangely, I felt safe the closer we got to Baghdad, lost in the back seat of an old beat up car amidst the commotion and cacophony of traffic and commerce. Only at the checkpoints did my heart beat faster and that trickle of sweat roll down my ribs. There would be those among them, especially as we moved west, who would use their cell phone to alert the assassins farther ahead that "there seemed to be a foreigner in the backseat of the car coming toward them." Always a possibility despite my doing everything to fool them into thinking I was a tired old Iraqi man. Getting "snatched" in early 2005 was a daily occurrence – for money or zeal. Finding out they had an American was something heaven-sent for the terrorists and their suppliers.

Once past the last checkpoint outside Baghdad, I breathed

easier. We were now just one more undistinguished car amidst the commotion of a city mad with activity...most of it everyday commerce, small retailers, and traders managing the billions flowing through...much of the money, I supposed, representing the flow downward from American taxpayers.

In that circumstance, one does not feel threatened. There is the off chance of "wrong place and wrong time," but if one does the math, that is statistically improbable in a city of this size. There is also the threat associated with patterns, most especially sleeping in the same bed twice or visiting the same place of work in any regular way, adamantly proscribed by our own protocols.

So, yes, as long as I flowed within the commotion or jumped out in an unpredictable way and didn't stay too long, I could indeed move in Baghdad. All the folks I knew who had been snatched or hurt had been those who somehow felt they were too righteous about the war to be hurt – too righteous to jump from bed to bed or, most dangerously, those still encased in the coalition identity.

There was, however, one unavoidable hitch to my approach on these occasions. Eventually, I had to get Ninos to drive past the Al Rasheed gate – maybe fifty meters past the opening in the blast barrier – where I could jump out and sprint for it while Ninos could do some quick evasive driving and get lost in the traffic.

Once down the chute of razor wire, there were a series of redundant checks and questions by some bad mannered American reservists who were fresh from the mall – so to speak – quite distinct I should say from the regular infantry guys I had met, now saddled with trying to defend the Western occupation in a land completely upended in its pursuit of its own identity.

Then I popped out of the chute, and, it seemed, I had just been teleported to a Little America replete with green grass along with several Iraqis pushing brooms and pulling rakes to keep it the way Americans like...as well as joggers, double bacon cheeseburgers, and, of course, body scanners at every place you entered. Eventually, I ended up at either Saddam's former palace for the VIP meetings or at a newly constructed collection of tidy, minimalist offices that housed USAID – sort of like a low income retirement community – for meetings with the

Cognizant Technical Officers (CTOs) as they were called.

Over the twenty-two plus months since I had arrived by road from Amman, this trip was perhaps my eighth inside. Often, they had been for codels (congressional delegations), half asleep from the flight, and on two occasions to brief Bremer and Negroponte. Once, even, to explain to Hillary how it was out there in the "Red Zone."

It was hard to get in their heads. I usually had less than an hour, and there were usually four of us, and then I had to figure the questions took half the time. So, in the end, I had maybe ten minutes to steer the "drunken sailor" straight. In my case, I wanted to explain that there were great risks in taking the Shia for granted and that despite all the so-called "committed funds" there was precious little being "spent" down there...where, I added, one could do good without having to tie up half the money in security costs.

Well, they listened. Politely, I should add, but then, often abruptly, they had to put an end to the meeting. Armitage or Wolfowitz were on the phone, I guessed. I doubt there was much policy going on in Iraq that did not emanate from Washington.

On this particular trip, as I said earlier, I had been summoned to be evaluated. Of course, normally these program evaluations should be done in the field where the investments can be seen and the beneficiaries touched, but by 2005 the donor oversight had largely disappeared "for security reasons," so donor impressions were gleaned from our visits to the Green Zone or electronically. They called that process a "remote evaluation."

Beside the CTO from USAID, there were the two contractors who were there to help evaluate my organization – basically on how well we had used taxpayer monies to achieve the goals we had agreed to, back in the spring of 2003.

Under the heading of "if you don't laugh, you'll cry," I did indeed get my evaluation. I was asked a few dozen perfunctory questions for their checkboxes in a pre-fab conference room. But about halfway through them we got the "duck and cover" from a Gurkha on the end of an intercom, and we descended under the conference table while some incoming exploded quite far from us. "More incoming today," I was told, "than usual," and thus the suggestion "that we continue the evaluation whilst sitting under the table." And so we did. Cross-legged, neck bent beneath the table top, the questions and the tick boxes laid out around us on the floor. Mission accomplished, it seemed, as finally we were told, we were "good to go," employing the vernacular of the place.

As it turned out, I barely made it out the Rasheed Gate on time for my connections. Basically, the same sprint in reverse till we were back in the commotion, circling around till it was quite dark and then abruptly into an anonymous driveway where gates shut behind us, and I was scooted into a foyer – curtains pulled, a phonograph playing. Then my Orthodox friend had smiled and asked, "A glass of wine, Mr. David?"

CHAPTER 17

Our Baghdad Representative

I believe that Ninos had his hands in the cookie jar most of his young life. That and his unique religious confession, which in 2005 was almost nonexistent elsewhere, had enabled him just the paths he sought to grow his treasures and not get hurt. Rather, they were interstices, less paths, that ran through the great and dangerous religious and political forces at play since Saddam had emerged supreme in 1968. As one of the last remaining faithful of Father Yunan's Greek congregation, he and his folk were no threat to anyone and sometimes quite useful for that same reason. Even at age 30, which I supposed him to be when I had hired him in 2003, his red hair remained tousled, his face freckled, and he had a willingness to serve that was endearing. When I asked for something quite beyond the reach or imagination of my regular staff, he paused for a moment of rumination, ask a question or two, and then clap his pudgy hands as if the solution had now just become apparent. Then he asked for my concurrence on delivery and cost. Most of it was contraband…fuel when there wasn't any, whiskey for Christmas, various seals and stamps for permissions when none could be had.

And Lord knows what else he did since by prior arrangement he did not have what one would call "regular office hours." A fair guess was that he made most of his income trading cars. Buying cheap, making repairs, and selling dear. Yes, back then, Ninos more often than not had grease under his nails, unthinkable for my Arab managers. "So when are you going to Detroit?" I would ask him. He demurred. I imagined that he was making too much in those fast fading interstices to attempt to dislodge his Mom from the family home and drop her so late in life into the new world.

It was Ninos who often drove me through Baghdad even in the worst times when it meant certain and cruel death if we had been spotted by any of those on the hunt for apostates. He had kept the car frame battered and discolored, but had put a V8 and all the enhancers under the hood. He rode low as well, his right hand attached to a marbled knob and there I would spot him up the street, cruising toward me, modulating the power, the body reverberating, waiting for me to leap out of the dreaded gate of the Green Zone and dash – as much as a sixty-year-old could dash – into the back seat and throw a keffiyeh over my head.

Usually seen with his traveling companion, Abdul Satar, alongside in the passenger seat. A Shia boy from Bag as well, the son of a doctor who was, perforce, practicing in Amman. Now he was minding the family house and running a money exchange for his own sake on the nearby corner. No grease under his fingers. Wan, untouched by the weather, mournful eyes – quite undirected, for the moment – amidst all the polemics swirling about him.

And so, this time, after Satar had slipped off near his shop, we had circled in the dusk on Baghdad streets until dark had fallen, until finally Ninos would connect on his cell and a few minutes later would swing into an open gate that was immediately shut behind us.

There was his mother in the amber. Loving to have someone like me secreted home by Ninos. Indeed, a glass of wine was put before Mr. David among a colorful array of glass dishes filled with sweets. She just sat there, with her hands clasped in her dress, asking Ninos to ask me what more I wanted while I sank into the upholstery and felt quite removed from the filth and violence outside…within this ambiance of plaster embellishments and faded wallpaper and fringed lampshades. She was plainly nervous before me, her first American, this rather old and shabby representative of all that "Shock and Awe" that she had been privy to, huddled in her church at the time where the good and gaunt Father Yunan presided. I had asked her about America and the cousins in Long Beach and without needing Ninos for the translation she said, "Heavens no." A resigned smile had followed. "I'm too old to leave," she sighed. They were remnants…Ninos and his Mom. She had her church and this bit of her civilization inside her gates, some family in the new world, and Ninos to keep them afloat, without her knowing the half of it.

After she had retired to bed, I asked Ninos to take me up to the roof and show me his clandestine piece of original work. Back when it had meant prison, he had taken an old tin shell of a water reservoir and tailored it with some metal shears, so he could put a dish within it, unseen except to the sky. And through this dish, into his sanctuary, he had allowed the best and the worst of America to stream. A crime his mother shuddered to allow, save for her trust in her son's sense of appropriate technology and his promise that "no one could ever know." If not a daily devotion to their church or to Baathist regulations, they had this together, up on the second floor, till one or the other had departed for bed.

By 2005, those earlier interstices in which he had knocked about Baghdad as a young man had transformed. Ever shifting weather was what Tommy Franks had wrought, which had brought Ninos to a new game, extending his finger each morning – so to speak – and raising it into the air above the hood before he ignited that V8 under that battered frame, gripped that marbled knob, setting off on his race across hardscrabble and ruin, from Basra to Kirkuk to parlay larger deals, increasingly those pertinent to the disintegration of the Iraqi state.

In my mind, he was now the pudgy Orthodox boy on my Thunder Road, well into the night, with his barely muffled motor turning into the gate. Mopping his brow with his handkerchief as he trod up to the second floor, much as he had from before

Tommy Franks, to join his Mom before that aperture to the West. She still ensconced in the amber of her Victorian harbor, notwithstanding her growing interest in Hollywood, in particular the daytime game shows.

Later that year, he had departed the Kurdish enclave, close on to the Iranian border, late. Too late. I had warned him. But he wouldn't listen, so he had taken the most direct route right across Diyala, Satar by his side. But this time, the trip had gone horribly wrong...right outside of Miqdadiyah where they had been stopped by an impromptu force and taken off the road and behind the berm, soon to be on their knees in the black of night. Seemingly, his life had finally expired.

Well, Ninos had come this far in life on the strength of his wits, and it would have been something to watch him on the griddle that night with these zealots who had sworn off not only all joy on earth but also all dickering with apostates. Harrowing, I was told...how they were shoved toward an abandoned building, Satar now weeping without shame, knowing full well that he, as Shia, was the principal target and with Ninos still hunting desperately for the word that could turn the event – even as they were now being strung up from a rafter by their ankles with a continuous poking of the AK's at various body parts, most often the temple...until Ninos...God bless him...managed a bargain. Managed a bargain, can you imagine, strung upside down before men who had killed at random before and would again. Soon, he was calling Satar's father in Amman who screamed on the other end...that "yes anything." Anything to free his son, which at Ninos' manipulation became 200K USD. Tonight in cash before dawn. That offer...on the surface...seemed to appease.

Money for hostages. Zealots being zealots would have preferred different outcomes, but even they had their orders, certainly not divine in origin.

Ninos called Father Yunan who with undaunted faith in the Lord's will gathered the community that night to front a "bridge" loan for Satar and, of course, alongside him, for "one of their own." The understanding from their phone call to Amman at that late hour was that Satar's father would assure them reimbursement. "Anything," Satar's father had repeated to the parishioners. God knows who else was called to underwrite the loan – maybe even Long Beach. So the cash got readied and "seen" in Baghdad near the church even as Satar and Ninos were pushed back toward his car. Later, not until Ninos had confirmed they had been left alone at the border of Kurdish-controlled land, did the perimeter of the faithful let the cash leave their control.

I had been curled up in my bed on the roof of the compound in Khanaqin when I had first heard of the ransom during an early morning call from Satar's dad. His wealth, he said, had been vastly exaggerated by his son. "Couldn't you, shouldn't you, help with the ransom? After all, he worked for you." "Sometimes," I thought, "and only when I could reach him, which had been far less than required lately. So, you can guess the squeeze. Dr. Satar could not pay but a part of the 200K USD. A couple of days later, the Greek clan had gathered very stern around Ninos with Abdul Satar's dad on the phone – his son now next to him in Amman.

And so I bent the will of the agency to far better purpose than it was often bent and authorized transfers for renovations of our Baghdad warehouse within Father Yunan's church compound, of which not all could have been spent usefully – with the surplus going to help make other parties harmless.

Now, with some very ill will being directed at Ninos, he pulled the trigger. Thunder Road it was for thirteen straight hours from Bag to Amman...back and forth to the US consulate in Amman to connive one of those special visas for Iraqi collaborators (Christians a priority), back to Bag to decapitalize, to lay low, very low, hiding his imminent escape. To marry his young cousin in what I must surmise was part of another understanding. I rarely saw him after that. On the fly, he was. His mother's precious gems, God only knows what he was unloading, monetizing, and transferring to Long Beach...with his poor Mom, ever closer to her God after the Diyala event and now looking at California looming and a farewell with Yunan's congregation, soon to be reduced by three more. Not to mention my name being attached to yet another piece of consular documentation pertaining to Ninos's contribution to American values and interests, past and future.

Then one day, they had evaporated, escorted by the International Office of Migration onto an airplane to America. The next time I saw Ninos was a year later, on Facebook....in LAX. Yes. Beside a very muscular purebred Pontiac lowrider.

CHAPTER 18

An Increasingly Lonely Pursuit, March 2005

The next month, I left Iraq, briefly, to attend an NGO meeting in Amman, Jordan. There were about thirty organizations present that had or allegedly had operations in Iraq. Of that number, only a handful admitted they still had expatriate management inside Iraq. Others in attendance claimed that while they had evacuated the international staff from Iraq, their national staff was still, one way or another, able to deliver needed "goods and services."

Afterward, out in the hallway, a representative of a colleague agency had told me, "If you want to know what's happening with NGOs in Iraq, you really have to be in Amman." More cold water in my face. I knew that the fewer personnel inside Iraq, the more valuable we became as a soft target for what Prime Minister Allawi referred to as the "dark forces."

That is how they began to win. In August of 2003, they took out the UN staff at Canal Street, and the UN did not come back. A year later, they took away the two Simona's from their offices in Baghdad and nearly all the remaining NGOs took the Beechcraft to Amman.

The process continued as the Shias sought to form a government. The international media clustered in a few fortified hotels in Baghdad, the dark forces analyzing Western resolve back home, a Sergio blown up, Berg's head severed, the media dispatches suffused with expressions such as "Into the Abyss" and "Spiraling into Hell," thus leaving the larger part of Iraq, which was not "spiraling," without the support of those who might help.

The "Letter from Baghdad" in *The Atlantic* (William Langewiesche, Jan./Feb. 2005) was more of that self-fulfilling prophecy. His account at the time of his flight into Bag read more like an apocalypse than the enigma it still was for the rest of us. The problem was that so many reporters detested the swagger and evangelism of George Bush that they could not distinguish between that repugnance and an honest portrayal of what Iraq was struggling with. Normally, one would think that the international press would be focusing on the ascent of the great oppressed majority to political eminence instead of a daily drumbeat on the resistance of the Sunnis and the Baathists to the new political reality. The result was that instead of just the facts (with notable exceptions like Dan Murphy of the Christian Science Monitor) we got a continuous media exultation of terrorist incidents as if they represented the sentiment of the Iraqi people or the Iraqi nation...with such incidents growing markedly as the market for news of them grew in the West. Absent such incentives, this relatively small group of Iraqi insurgents who moved with impunity (thanks in part to Bremer's erasure of the existing Iraqi armed forces), would have been far less effective.

I was a soldier in Vietnam when the press pulled the cover off the lies of the Pentagon. Ironically, I am in Iraq as the press supports another lie, which holds that there are no redeeming virtues to the unseating of Saddam by the Americans, that life under Saddam was an acceptable alternative.

Upon my return, my team and I gathered where we lived for one of our periodic meetings. At the end of the discussion, we got to the principal issue.

Everything did, in fact, boil down to "threat versus mission," that rough calculation of the value we were providing the Iraqi people as measured against the threat to our lives.

The threat had increased since the January 2005 elections and would probably continue to do so as the new interim government tried to form and as Americans began, more and more, to consider the American midterm election. At the core of the contest would be whether the dark forces could garner enough broadcast media time to rattle the original presumptions behind the American interventions or, alternatively, whether there was enough constancy of resolve in Western capitals to stay the course for the benefit of those benighted folk who had moved bravely through one bloody election and who would need to move through two more in the intervening nine months.

We had agreed, my teammates and I, about the rough calculation of our value added. Whether through our platforms for learning, our sports and connectivity programs in South Central where we were transforming despair to hope for teenagers, our efforts to provide salve for the estimated 50,000 displaced in Diyala province – at a minimum, we were arriving as unarmed partners to the population.

The team had debated this problem. The growing threat against our somewhat modest investments in transformation and salve. This small gang struggled with the imponderables almost daily. Some committed through the current grants at the end of the summer; others of us hoped to be active through to the referendum in October and the final election at the close of the year.

The end of these large grants was usually messy. We wouldn't ever know how many HQ expenses had been charged to the grant, and the construction and rehabilitation of social infrastructure often involved change orders or extended delays if, God willing, more money finally did come to the Shia Heartland and, with it, the prospect of better profit margins for our Iraqi contractors materialized elsewhere. Then we would have to throw incentives at the construction bosses just to get our work done before the donor, the US government in this case, pulled the plug and forced us to walk away from half done "platforms for learning" as we called them.

Of course, with only a few months left on this monster grant and the sequel not yet designed, the staff was also checking out places where they could spread their wings. Iraq for them was now a bedroom, a laptop, a satellite connection, a rowing machine. There were only intermittent and jubilant visits from the national staff, our brothers and sisters in South Central, and once in a while we made a dash down to the Shia heartland – undercover, blended, and down the mountain road along the Iranian border.

Yes, my staff surfed at night on their wireless connections in bed and dreamed of benighted Africa and bare arms and shades. They also dreamed of 4x4s, and tea sipped carefree on the floor of a hooch. They shut off the part of the mind that deals with such things as seeing those killers in black garb rush in with such zeal to kill a Jew or infidel as we were called. They also blocked the thought that someone might snatch them and put them on a website with a blade sawing through their windpipes and their neck muscles and their vertebrae. They were tired of this life despite the love for our kin in the South who would give their lives for us infidels but who also gave no sign that they would mass, hit the bricks, and cleanse their towns of the butchers.

My son had emailed me that I had to get rational about where to live next, that I could not continue to be all over the place by which he had meant Hanoi, Baltimore, San Sebastian, Kut, Khanaqin, all in the last three years. I was now entertaining my most recent proposition about getting a hacienda in the mountains of Chihuahua (Paul's ancestral homeland).

I responded that we needed a last stand. Work in Africa, maybe, but what about our own land, I asked. The orchard, the gouging of the land, dragging the boulders from the stream. The aches and the elixir. But what also about governance in Mexico, I thought. About backlash and expropriation.

In the end, I knew, the children would look at me down through my fog on the linen while I passed away. They were already looking forward beyond their parent's dilemma.

CHAPTER 19

Cross Border, Summer 2005

"They are imbuing the soil with their blood," I said. "Sanctifying it and making it theirs. The field of Blackbirds for the Serbs," I added as I turned toward my Serb program director, "versus the footloose, the homeless, and the multinational who will not die for soil."

Attendance at the fountain was down...composed mostly of several new arrivals as the old timers were pushing off for more attractive emergencies elsewhere. We were more workaday these days. My didactics now were most often confined to my hooch at bedtime; my flourishes more an allowance from my staff than an encouragement. They remained respectful of me as a veteran, who led by example, but stayed reluctant to become interested students. I had eyes. I could see the attention waning – the eyelids heavy, the heads turned elsewhere. Toward the dogs. To the Satphone. "Sorry to be late, Mother, the boss was in the middle of one of his worldview speeches."

There we few circulated around the fountain, some bread and cheese, an Ifes or Pepsi in hand. We, the footloose on reclaimed Kurdish soil, so close to Arab soil, with the displaced, the remnants of the ethnic purges, on either sides of the line.

Empire, nation-state, treaty of Westphalia, the humanitarian imperative, global village, self-determination. Such important concepts we plumbed. School busing, ethnic cleansing, the wall in Palestine, the Schengen Accord, EU accession for Turkey.

All attempts, we figured, at defining Right Relations between peoples. To what extent do we conglomerate or separate? If conglomerated, then is it federated, allied, imperial, or national? If separated, then is it by race, ethnicity, language, religion, ideology, or geography?

And then, quite abruptly, I waved it all aside – the academic – and leaned in. "Imagine the fourteen-year-old Eritrean boy," I said, "in burlap, thin as a stick, peering at the images from *Baywatch* or *The Simpsons* at a store front in Asmara. Imagine the Shia housecleaner in Kut watching a re-run of *The Matrix* on the master's TV. Whatever they defined as Right Relations before is certainly getting redefined now in ways it never was before. For the receivers, they yearn for the abundance before their eyes, and, if denied, they insist on it – and if denied again, they eventually seek to destroy it."

So borders, we concurred, were now permeable.

But simultaneous and parallel with this transformation, we knew better than most there had also arisen fierce movements for physical borders where none existed.

On this particularly starry summer night I recounted to the remaining staff my personal witness as the heavy hands of the colonialist and then the nomenclature were lifted. "I was at work there," I related, "in the Balkans – peering down from Mt. Igman on the besieged city of Sarajevo – and in Georgia as heretofore inclusive borders dissolved across half of the land." More than twenty new entities, I had guessed, had thus far been formalized into new states. "But many more," I cautioned, "want independence from the former configurations and continue to insist on asserting their own language, religion, and culture. In fact, anywhere we look across the old Soviet periphery or in Africa there are incipient independence movements, armed insurgencies, crying for borders as a guarantee for Right Relations.

"So, there is the dynamic, my friends, our context: the global homogenization through the new technological revolution and the fierce insistence for borders around tribal entities.

"We are caught in it," I warned them. "We sit on all these ethnic fault lines – in Bosnia and Republika Srpska, in Kurdistan, in the Sunni triangle, in the Maronite stronghold, in Aceh, in Mindanao, in the Casamance, in Western Sahara. You guys know," I told the weary colleagues across from me. "Each side here in Diyala sits us down and pulls out their maps and agonizes over patrimony lost. They reiterate their version of Right Relations between them and their adversary. They keep us up late with the tales of the martyrs, often true, usually presented as proof of one side's historic preeminence rather than a reflection of a more insidious cause."

"And the counterpoint. All of it now," as I took the liberty to sweep my hands under their faces, "so dramatically unfolding in the Arabian Peninsula. The teenagers clawing down the heretofore isolation with no less passion than Berliners smashed down their wall. For all of it...Silicon Valley...Times Square...and Hollywood...for chatting with Suzie in Toledo or diving into Portland's digital library. And, yes, also, for some to visit the dark sites...the website of Al-Qaeda.

"Damn it, guys...can't you feel it?" – as I jumped up out of my chair, "that earth shaking beneath us?" I jumped again and they laughed. "Those popular yearnings for universal participation and sharing freed up for the first time in history and yet the horrific resistance by tribes and zealots to any accommodation with historic neighbors."

There was silence; no one else was choosing to fill the night air. Signs of a rumination preliminary to calling it a night. "Sounds like a wrap to me," said the man from Belgrade, with a twinkle in his eye. "Good night, all," I saluted, before I veered over to the pen to check on whether there was sufficient water for the dogs.

CHAPTER 20

Promotion

After the Samarra mosque bombing in February 2006, and the subsequent onslaught, opposition to the war in the US ballooned, and other coalition allies abandoned the cause. The number of foreign NGOs declined even more. Their respective boards made the calculation on cost/benefit – the benefit being the huge revenue streams and the cost being the close association with Bush's war – to include the possibility of seeing their staff decapitated on global media.

Those few NGOs that did stay moved to fortified perimeters, spending as much as 40% of their budget on deterrence and in the process becoming indistinguishable from the US military bases dotting the landscape.

During the ensuing months, we filled the vacuum and in time opened new offices in Kirkuk, Erbil, Nasiriya, Basra, and Baghdad. Never armed, we were always ensconced in a neighborhood that would protect us, one that we served much as we had done in the early days in Kut. Unsaid, but clearly understood by my HQ, was that I could take no casualties or the whole enterprise would be shuttered. Of course, as we expanded between 2006 and 2009 to a dozen offices across two-thirds of Iraq and the 50 million dollars processed through them annually, control and communication became precarious with only a handful of my most trusted lieutenants coursing the roads – as blended as possible – to connect the pieces into one strategic whole. Necessarily, more and more got delegated, increasing the odds of a casualty – the severed head on an orange jumpsuit –

and keeping me awake with that nightmare. But also leading me to brook no nonsense, no infractions. There was no longer any "flat" to my management. "Do as I say or take the plane out," became my constant refrain to the wayward whose disdain included saluting me as they departed. On the contrary, the nationals took to this hierarchy with ease. They could swim in those waters. With time, they came to revere me as was their tradition and habit. I was becoming venerable to them.

Meanwhile, the US government turned respectful. Any talk of insufficient "burn rates" or lopping off part of our territory was a distant memory. We gave them enough bricks and mortar, not to mention the colossal amount of salve thrown off the back of trucks to the massive numbers displaced after the Samarra bombing and received in return their muted concurrence to plant in parallel investments the seeds of modernity into millions of Iraqi women and youth, always fronted these days by religious or tribal sheikhs.

So, I strode, full of myself, described by some as "legendary." But also a man fully consumed by the petty, renowned for checking toilets and kitchens at each office, "where they ate and shat," as I would tell Paul, to assure the dictates of security were drilled in. Principal among them, in bold black marker on sheets of flipchart paper taped to the walls, were the inviolability of our contract with the notables in our various enclaves, the unpredictability in the way we must travel and the random mattresses on which we must rest our heads en route.

As we approached the summer of 2006, the execs back in Washington invited me to a dinner, not far from Rhein-Main airport in Germany to discuss "plans for the future." Very nice, I supposed, those little pink medallions of beef and a few precious vegetables on what seemed to be a vast china plate with traces of exquisite sauce meandering around them – for flair, I assumed. Far removed from the daily gruel we ate in Iraq. I could see them fidgeting, treading very carefully. My revenues now accounted for half of the agency's annual take, but left unchecked in all but the most formal sense, my program was inexorably seceding from the agency and then, somewhere circulating, were those inquiries about my health. "How are you feeling, David?" as they nipped off the asparagus tips. Those red dots across my face, tied as they were to my recurrent nightmares of my staff in orange jumpsuits, were indeed making me somewhat scary in normal company.

Finally, promotion was broached – to Regional Director in Beirut whereby I would now be responsible for more of the bloody conundrums the Middle East offered up – from Gaza to Syria to Lebanon and significantly also for Iraq as they said, "to stay close to Paul and continue to modulate strategies and tactics." I was to have an office/apartment in Hamra/Beirut back where Annie and I had begun this trajectory into Right Relations in 1981 and where my daughter Hank had seen the first light of day. Not exactly a vacation spot, but then again Sayyed Nasrallah (head of Hezbollah) was not Zarqawi by any stretch of the imagination.

Leaving Paul. The end of a marriage – the celebrated odd couple. The Yankee cradling his cup of instant on the stoop before he pushed off into the badlands before dawn and the Mexican-American Arabist from El Paso at whose knees David sat night after night absorbing the great Arab narrative. Paul. Ungainly Paul, for whose very good heart I feared. Delicate fingers reserved for the keyboard or alternatively to dart across the communal table and pinch a chunk of meat and pop it into his mouth like a mint – walking through the office his left fist gripping a pen.

There he would sit with me unchanged since those first evenings in our rooms…with a book at his left hand turning the pages, a DVD playing on the wall before us, tapping out responses to emails as they flew in. And I would interrupt asking him something about the battle for Karbala in 680 A.D., and he would not respond, rather looking blankly ahead of him for about a minute and then, almost as if his brain had just found the file, the penny dropped and he streamed chapter and verse without a pause. A great voluble emission before the man whose communications day to day mostly revolved around "no." "No's" that Paul was sometimes reluctant to say himself.

In any case, we would not be uncoupled completely; we needed each other too much. I arranged with Paul for him to manage what we had created together while I found an apartment in a sympathetic neighborhood in Baghdad. I had my eyes on Sadr city, the teeming Shia slum for which I had suffered unrequited love since I had first mucked about it in April of 2003 – section 38 to be precise – where the city's refuse was burned creating a great fog that infiltrated all of the slum in addition to spawning a vast metal market for that which would not burn. It was Wolfe's swarm. In spades. Tripping through the black water at dusk, one eye on the packs of feral dogs hunting for any stray flesh from the day's commotion.

And so it was: for the next three years, I became itinerant. Managing from wherever a cell tower allowed. Me and my iPhone. Like a pinball ricocheting from Beirut to Damascus to Amman to West Bank to Gaza to Amman to Baghdad. "Haraka Baraka," I would say. Movement is a blessing. With my three passports and an array of visas. Red dots receding. Just speeding past the million moving parts that would now consume Paul and the other country directors. I was not the same now. No more eating and sleeping with the troops. My old bedrooms were occupied; my roof top hooch now an exercise room. Only in Beirut did I have a place to store my few possessions. Only in Baghdad did I spend enough time to savor the context.

Other than the two short wars (the July war in Lebanon in 2006 and Cast Lead in Gaza in 2008) when I did have to take the tiller, the rest was guiding, persuading, and as before uttering the resounding "no" when staff went astray. The resounding "no" as well when an "unsavory" at HQ thought to interfere.

CHAPTER 21

Obama, November 2008

On the eve of the presidential election in the US, I found myself biding my time at Baghdad airport, occasionally rising to confirm and reconfirm gates and departure times and marveling at the thousands of US contracted personnel being corralled for charters bound for Kuwait. A nation of mongrels, I had thought.

No symmetry or grace to them. All sixes and sevens in a kaleidoscope of cheap colors. American exceptionalism, I mused. At which time, an Iraqi acquaintance, a vendor, noticed me and took a seat beside me. I put my paper down.

"What about the black man?" he had asked, pointing to Obama's photo on the front page.

"What about him?" I responded.

"He will never win, will he?"

I fully understood his question. Black men were Africans who served tea to Arabs. Not to be confused with captains of the hegemon.

I told him that if Obama won, it would be the greatest gift to America since Lincoln, which only increased his confusion. "Imagine," I told him, "a black man on TV every night. And as a Commander in Chief, no less." At which point, I could tell that he was suspecting I was joking, pulling his leg.

"What about them?" he asked, referring to all that lumpenmass being slowly herded toward the gate.

"We'll see," I replied. "He says he's closing down this war. Fact is," I added, "we don't know how to manage it. Never did and maybe never would. Look at them. They belong back in Arkansas, pumping gas, dreaming of the weekend pig roast." This comment made him visibly wince.

"And once they leave, the rest of you will leave as well?" he asked. He was looking genuinely pained. "Iraq is not ready for that," he declared. "Our neighbors will pick our carcass like a chicken at Eid."

That great swatch we now inhabited, from Kirkuk to Kut with a lot of unsettled stops in between. There it was, I recalled, as I grabbed my knapsack and pushed off toward my flight. A nation state with no foundations, like a house built on sand. A Shia government with no reference points for government. A country made desperately sick by the now deposed tyrant and a hegemon, which if it were not doing "Shock and Awe" or turning a handsome profit, was downright hapless about drawing Iraq into the Western orbit.

By early 2009, we did indeed have a black face nightly before American media audiences, and soon after, those long lines of contractors were being dwarfed by the largest logistical operation in my lifetime as an occupation Army retreated, leaving a billion dollar embassy in Baghdad as the principal residual sign of the US presence. Our rapidly shrinking program shed bricks and mortar – taking what funds we could still find to spread our gospel of transborder relations for "generation next." Seemingly, the only viable option in the cloud of dust we Americans kicked up on our way out was an idea yet to come of age, which was that with time, private capital, social media, and Skype, America's entrepreneurs and civil society could influence what the neocons could not.

So, Paul and I knocked our heads together figuring out how our work across Iraq for the past many years, absent the bricks and before long, absent the official Americans, could be an influence in Baghdad and Washington DC. Our worth would soon become our personal relations within the Ministries and within the Legislative Assembly, our investments in transformation, and our possible but improbable effect on American-Iraqi policy henceforth.

We both concluded that while "Shock and Awe" was long gone, oil and Israel would serve to keep America interested in the Land between Two Rivers. That and the hundreds of thousands of Americans who had passed by – some into the line of fire; most in a carpeted cube with beer and cheeseburgers down the hall.

So Jadriya it was – a stone's throw from the embassy and Ambassador Hill, a friend from Kosovo days, and, importantly, a neighborhood on the doorstep of the swarming Shia slums to the northeast which I, not Paul, was betting on as the primary weathervane for a modern Iraq.

CHAPTER 22

Al-Jadriya, 2008

Sam was waiting for me in the kitchen, hands clasped around a mug held above the Formica tabletop. She was young and ample and seemed to my sore eyes, midst the inferno Baghdad was becoming, undaunted by "the dark forces." In any case, no sleep in her eyes as I slumped over some dry cereal and water; no residual twitch from the mortars lobbed into our vicinity the night before. I teased her with some muted words from *Oklahoma* :

> "Oh what a beautiful morning,
> Oh what a beautiful day,
> I've got a wonderful feeling,
> Everything's going [our] way."

She had, by the end, put a little music in it, seemingly amused.

"So, what brings you to Baghdad, my dear?"
"Well, a plane," she had laughed.
"I mean, this is mostly a Yankee notion," I said.
"Well then...how about adventure stories over supper?"
"Such as," I asked.
"Well...such as...a hundred years ago, from the Rhine Valley, by steamer and trains, and then, twenty years later, most of my family was moving again. This time around the dust bowl in some old contraption. You know," she smiled, "we weren't always so well fed."
"And?"
"So, eventually I broke their hearts, family and fiancé, or so they swore. Was doing an awful lot of reflecting at the time. I figured I would have been just looking at crops and hogs by day and buried in self-inflicted fantasies by night till I had shuffled off that old mortal coil. Coincidence, it was, probably, that got me hankering, dreaming really, to put my feet on that heralded Arab Street. Hell, there it was, year after year, coming into our living room nightly. And so when Baghdad popped up on the job site, I jumped. Faxed HQ my degree from State and a somewhat modified CV, got processed, and then three days later, came down to breakfast with a ticket in my hand. It seemed there wasn't much of a line."
I had my head down slowly stirring my coffee, even as it never had milk or sugar in it.

"There is no street, really, where I live," she said.

I said nothing.

"I know I am not especially 'indicated.' Is that what you mean?"

"Believe me," I said, "the Americans here, well the majority of them, are nowhere near this street – heralded or not. Most are born and bred for a long life on Cherry Close or some such in the heart of suburbia. We don't get folks from Bed Sty or South Central LA or, for that matter, from the Great Plains."

She laughed.

"And believe me," I continued, "suburbanites generally aren't worth shit in this business. They're just available – not for long, mind you – just until they can scurry back from their fortified perimeter to Washington DC, proud as can be of whatever soil has clung to their shoes, which they will reference till they die. Look around. Look at who has stuck on our team: a Tunisian, an Albanian, a Pole, a Serb, an Azeri, a Russian, a Sudanese. And yes, exceptionally, Paul and I – from Texas and Vermont. Oh yeah, can't forget, and my wide-eyed friend from Walla Walla. Fact is that most of the folks spreading the American narrative these days are not even Americans."

There followed a silence – both of us puttering about with the last of our breakfast.

"You really think you can shed the farm for this chaos and violence?" I asked. She looked back at me, sorta square in the face, not smiling now, probably aware of my reputation for summarily sending "non-indicated" recruits back to where they came from. "I'll tell you, Sam," I added, "why your family's heart broke. It wasn't because you were leaving. Rather, it was because they must have thought you certifiable. To be lying in bed mornings on fresh sheets somewhere on the Great Plains and to be dreaming of this." I pointed out the window. I threw the last of my instant down and laid my hand on her shoulder. "Let's go," I said.

"Nice," she said. Her favorite word, as I came to discover.

I put my index finger to my mouth.

So, ten minutes later, she descended wearing an abaya, a black shroud over all that good health.

I gave the address to two of my faithful, recruited for the

occasion. Two cars. "Stay close," I told them. This was one of the essential risks – that one of them would get separated in traffic – the other being the makeshift checkpoints where for nearly five years I had been pushing my luck as a sick old man bundled up in the back seat. So the four of us gathered in our driveway repeating several times worst case scenarios and what we would do, which sometimes was precious little. We might be taken by the Jaysh. But they would present their prize to their commanders. And from there, we could, time and circumstances allowing, get an endorsement from the holy cities down south. The Shias, even at their worst, did not do orange jumpsuits.

We squeezed out into the inferno, now part of the swarm, soaking it in till we arrived at the designated shanty not far from the burning refuse in Section 38. A flyspecked oilcloth, some tea from God only knew where, and our tentative sips, hoping to limit the pathogens, while the district official upon whom we had just landed unexpectedly welcomed us like manna from heaven, keen as he was to provide for his people, despite the source. "Yes, in principle," we explained after a multitude of back and forths, "we could build a 'platform for learning' in his district as long as he had the religious sheikh's approval." And, I added, putting my forefinger to my eye, "any misuse of the money and we're gone."

Then a couple of women came in and coaxed Sam away, to the evident relief of the men around me. Tough Okie or not, I got nervous. One of my guys followed her.

Through the open door, I could see the "stares curious" of the boys growing by the minute into a semi-circle around our presence, retreating a few steps each time my host yelled at them. I was feeling the seconds ticking away.

I got a glimpse of Sam now, beyond the street boys, standing with the women beside a vacant lot strewn with rubbish. With only a few hundred words of Arabic at her disposal, I could see she was getting answers, nonetheless.

"We're going," I announced abruptly to the official.

"Touch it, hear it, smell it." I was telling Sam back in the car. "Size 'em up, friend. Look into your host's face, see if you can spot a duplicity, a nervousness, and more importantly, watch how the gang around him watches him. Life skills, right?" I asked her.

She, now reflecting: "Same as when a stranger back home at night offers you a lift."

I was wagering, never sure, that she took the ride. "And then split, lickety-split," I continued, "and take the untoward road back." There we were, Vermont and Oklahoma, in an abaya and a keffiyeh bumping along in a blended beat-up, through the billows of smoke and piles of refuse and the quintessential urban cacophony. Until, toward the end, I had interrupted it all: "Your show, now," I said. "You have his number. Tell him and the women who will run the center to meet us in Jadriya. After that we can decide on the Internet center."

"Thank you," she said.

"You'll do fine. Do as we are advised: slowly, slowly, quickly. Never let anyone know when you will pass by again. And, by the way, keep my guys here as close to you as sweetness on honey. No offense."

She laughed. The only American farm girl outside the perimeter, I was betting. God bless Oklahoma. This was our big toe into Sadr. Sam, I mean. For better or worse, distant indeed from the Great Plains, she now had her Arab street in the land between two rivers.

Jadriya would also be a bureau from which we would commute to the great government buildings of America and Iraq to peddle our alleged antidotes for despotism, incubated in Section 38, Kut, Khanaqin and many stops in between. From Albana to Sam, with love. Two possible and singular points of light amidst the deluge of official waste.

CHAPTER 23

Dinner Uptown

Occasionally, on my trips back to the US – as an agency advocate for their interests in Congress and at State – I would be invited by persons of privilege to take the train north on weekends for dinner parties in Manhattan apartments. It was an orchestration – someone of wealth, an artist perhaps, a few pretenders, as well as someone who had "just arrived from Baghdad/Damascus/Beirut," AKA the humanitarian. The wealthy and the artists – they could just sort of be. His wealth or her paintings were already known. But I was expected to inspire with good. Yes, amidst the silk and the filigree, I should have three good accounts of exceptional altruism. Something, in the main, to win the hearts of the women present since it long had been my experience that the men usually didn't buy it.

It is one thing, over there in the Middle East, to remind one of the subalterns not to forget to email the weekly human interest story into HQ so that yet another success could be presented on the web before those who had spent as little as a dollar to give some desperate child some gruel for a week all the way up to those who had so magnanimously coughed up a 100 dollars so as to buy his mom a goat. But it is quite another to present such crap face to face before a sitting for eight, who, before you had even begun, were prepared to pat you afterward, perhaps with a sigh, much as they would the family pet at a particularly endearing moment. So you can imagine the silence and the profound disappointment when I, unable to allow them their "pet" moment, said that if one has perspective or can gain perspective that there is no qualitative difference between what I had done, back in the day, on the roof of that cinderblock hooch in Khanaqin, for example, from what Sal, the pickle man in the corner Deli down their avenue, does. At this point, the host was seen frowning into her soup. "Correction," I said, "Sal, to his credit neither sells a pickle which is not a pickle nor does he wantonly cheat the scales (I was guessing here)." Around about here, the host asked Artist something-anything about her work. But this particular time, Wealth had spoiled her meanness and in that space when Artist was trying to fathom such an empty question, Wealth slammed the conversation back to me. "Interesting," he said, as the help was placing the main course before us. "Tell us more about Sal and what you were doing there on the Iranian border." And with that door now flung wide open, I strutted right through it, knowing at a minimum, that there would be no petting afterward.

"You see," and now I began in a way that every field hand recognizes – through their daily stories of sacrileges (and yes accompanied by loud field guffaws) – that is, when measured against the unsuspecting heart who had just typed in her credit card information for a cow for Ahmed, let us say. "It's the humanitarian business; it's the relief industry; no shareholders, no measurable impact," I continued. "The margins on bare-boned altruism are huge and the well-paid stalwarts of this business and industry have no more divinity in them than Sal or for that matter Flo who styles your hair." At that point, the table had caught me glancing at my distinguished host, knowing full well that her hair stylist would never be called Flo. I pressed on: "But my business, which unlike that of Sal and Flo who would quickly be undone should they sell underweight pickles or apply cheap highlights, can tell folks back home that we are fixing the Middle East, and despite all evidence over the ensuing decades to the contrary, feel no compulsion to change our business model, lower our salaries, or even rework our pitch. So, yes, I can tell you I currently do live a dangerous life and a very unhealthy life, and I attract a lot of money for the charities that employ me, and, maybe, on a good day, I may have even advanced the possibility of my country controlling the global narrative for another generation – which from where I stand is probably a good thing. But as for good, the way you expect it to be made manifest, I am afraid, my friends, you have been deceived and mostly you have been deceived because you want and need to be deceived on this issue. You need to believe that buying a cow for Ahmed through a well-heeled middleman makes a difference since it soothes your own troubled soul a bit and since you will never be caught in your self-deception unless you are willing to visit me in my milieu, which," and now I paused to survey the table, "I am sure none of you plans to do anytime soon." Here I swallowed an inch or two of Bordeaux and then hammered my point home – now in full out preach mode: "In thirty years of accepting your money to develop folks overseas, I can say categorically that almost no project there has survived our departure, principally because we were never anything but the exclusive owners of its illusive success. Secondly, after we left, there was no earthly way to sustain the

110

subsidies needed to keep the project alive. But" – index finger in the air high over les pommes dauphinoise – "not to worry friends, the purveyors of America's interests and values, meaning the overseas charities, managed to pocket at least thirty cents on the dollar for their overhead."

I dared now to retract my finger into a fist. I knew I would never be asked back, so I had nothing to lose. In fact, I knew they would even avoid taking the elevator down with me, except perhaps for Wealth. "Win-Win," I exclaimed. "Shut down their industries and their fraud, send their workers like me" – I moved my fist onto my heart, the same way the Shias in South Central do – "home to earn an honest living and get whatever residual good that exists in Sal, Flo, and the woman who sought to help Ahmed and let that jump at the speed of light across the intervening seas and borders to Ahmed's front door and if he is too poor to be connected, I assure you that soon enough, with a bit of a search, you can find an electronic address for his mosque or church or coop or business. If, in fact, since even before the time of Homo Sapiens" – and here I was wrapping up, bringing the linen to my mouth – "we are all wired for altruism…so then let it pass, please, uninterrupted without it being defined, captured, and abused by big charity and its fat margins."

I was relieved to be out on the pavement. Wolfe's raw and unsettled land – the groaning continent – braving the north Atlantic, Yankees, Southerners, and Africans working the land around towns where the tap of the telegraph and the wail of the locomotive gave them to wonder about the great hear-tell of the multicolored, polyglot, pulsating, pullulating swarms of swarthy immigrants, eight to a room, under the machinations of those Yankee carnivores who raised steel and poured concrete like no tomorrow in that great symbiotic amalgam of squalor and opulence, freedom and desperation. And I could feel the dynamic – in the mess and muddle of faces and languages as I walked downtown. Clacking through the street past the panhandlers, musicians, street vendors, working stiffs, dealers, and executives, I walked back to the Hotel Chelsea. Here, Burroughs, Dylan Thomas, Bob Dylan, Ginsberg, and so on incubated the music and prose to inspire the world. Clacking down those threadbare and dayglow halls to my metal frame bed for the night, with an original radiator spitting steam, I knew one damn thing for sure: that there on that walk were American interests and values, which had been usurped by the faceless charity fonctionnaires who now felt vested to make that interpretation before the world.

So this Uptown memory gets rolling around in my sun baked brain the next time I am visiting the Shia heartland. Imagine: back in 2003, Paul and I had to assure the locals that the streets would be cleared of our male staff each day by 2pm and kept cleared until 4pm, so the women of Kut could walk past our offices and not fear being seen, emerging out of their gated confines in a parade of black tents, perhaps to meet at the little grocery store at the end of the road and trade a rumor or two.

Then, barely two years later, quite by mistake, I remember that day when I had been given a peek by an adolescent girl flying out of a room in the home of a native son to which I had been invited. The women were huddled before a TV glued to Al Arabiya and simultaneously engaged on their cell phones, all the colors of a rainbow. In a relative heartbeat, they had moved from a small gossip at the corner store to calls from over the horizon.

Yes indeed, reminiscing now, in 2008, on that constant refrain, "new technologies turning old sociologies on their heads."

CHAPTER 24

Al-Basra, 2009

By the summer of 2009, Gaza (Cast Lead) had been long gone from the headlines, and I had transferred the mop, so to speak, to the designated director (none other than my pal from Walla Walla). I had arranged it with Paul for me to fly into Basra and to see what I could do about standing up a proper operation of literacy and connectivity in the ruins of what had once been a magnificent source of hydrocarbons and their derivatives before Saddam had starved it half to death in 1991.

112

It had been a year since the Jaysh had been defeated in Basra by the Iraqi army, its fighters dispersed into the surrounding mud and wattle slums licking their wounds, though still quite able and willing to drop occasional mortars down the tube toward the coalition airport base, hoping to hasten the departure of the remaining British soldiers and assorted contractors. Meanwhile, Iran would fiddle for advantage and the multinational oil companies would sniff around, both aware that capital would remain the coward until a modicum of law and order could allow Basra its place in the sun – with time eclipsing the other bejeweled pretenders like Qatar and Kuwait.

We were getting there late, replacing another American NGO, which had taken flight a year earlier, and assuming many of its local staff. Unlike our other offices, we had never had the chance to live together with these nationals and fully bring them into our definition of Right Relations. For security reasons, we had promised not to cohabit in their existing office; rather, we met in a clandestine way as we sought to take them from bricks and mortar to transformative investments. To replace the engineers with social activists. To reinvent the operations in Basra.

So about Java: Dr. Javanshir from Baku with a medical degree from Moscow, to be precise, sat at dusk with me on this bench of sorts, really no more than a plank from a nearby scaffold put atop some cinder blocks, with our backs leaning against a chain link fence. We were not too far from a concrete bunker where sometimes at the siren's call we would need to rush. We were nursing some alcohol in a brown paper bag and trading stories on the war in Nagorno Karabakh where he, in his youth, had served as a medic on the front. Until, one fortuitous day, he had been picked up in the flush of national independence by a western NGO, then circulating freely upon the former Soviet sphere, amply financed by the Peace Dividend from the recent rout of Russia in the Cold War. In fact, diving headfirst into that dividend, paying intellectuals like Java in big dollars to spread the gospel of Pluralism, Rule of Law, and above all Freedom – not an unimportant advertisement since Java seemed to my old eyes quite gay.

It was surely a buyers' market for these intellectuals with professors driving taxis and doctors bartering their skills for Marlboros. Thus a straight track soon emerged for Java to Afghanistan with the same western NGOs, but this time with the expat chevron on his sleeve. Not a full-fledged expat, mind you. He was more like an expat in waiting – toward that day, if ever, when he would have Western civ flowing unequivocally in his veins.

All of which had led him to be sitting there with me on the bench – just one short hop, skip, and a jump from Basra City, temporarily renting a container in the Brit perimeter around the airport so as to set up a back office until we could insinuate into the city along the Shatt al Arab. A time of transition, it seemed, as the Brits were packing out and thinning ranks, ceding the airport security to the Iraqis and the surrounding base to "contractors." And so Java and I waited to get badged and otherwise authenticated so that we could leave behind our beds and our computers in the containers and hitch our way to the airport from whence, sweet as you please, we could get to where the West was still being actively hunted.

Yes, thin as a pin with big bat ears, "un vrai sensitive." It took but a little imagination, or alcohol, to see him rise off the bench as iridescent, tiptoeing across the deck of the baths in Baku. His mother now stricken with cancer in Moscow.

Java, of course, did not sit at mess with the pneumatics, which is what we called all that pumped up contractor flesh. In fact, we abhorred it, made jokes about how it could deflate with just one quick cut of Java's scalpel. No, we weird un-pneumatics got there early and sat in a far corner. We, with frequent gestures, using words as a spring from which to tumble – and they, over there, who other than commands, disdained words or any derivative eloquence. Excepting, of course, a certain kind of eloquence surrounding root words like "cunt," "fuck," "under a truck," or "putting holes through Arabs." "Perforating them," they laughed. And yes, as for profit concerns, they did once make us an offer to escort us into town for an outrageous price.

The only other brush we had with them was after dark when the mortars came in as Java and I were sitting side by side in the concrete shelter, knee to knee with contractors, seeing their grim faces off the coals of our smokes. It was at close encounters like that, knee to knee, that one could know what one was made of and Java, who liked life enough, in spurts, but not so much as to dread its passing, had a very brave knee – until the very garbled announcement came from the megaphones that we could emerge. We returned to our bench or depending on the hour to our containers whose corrugated roof, I might add, could not stop a falling rock much less a descending shell made in Iran.

So, we waited to be processed, we fish in a barrel for the remnants of Jaysh al Mahdi, with our heartfelt yearning for our original mentor, TE, and the prospects of our future insinuation growing in our minds by the day.

Enter Hatem Al Bachary, a notable from Basra known earlier to me as a remote recipient for some small funds for the propagation of Internet Literacy. Now, with our container authorized and our status as the so-called soft power of the US occupation in the right databases, we left the chain link fence for the airport, and one late afternoon we watched Hatem swing up in his quite weathered car and beckon us in – wearing his trademark purple and orange barker's "get-up."

Picture him best under a marquis, boisterous, an assault to the eyes. Not anything suggestive, subtle, or sublime. He was now moving on from the Internet training to his most current brush with death, an amusement park. Yes sir, Donald Duck and Mickey Mouse in this marshland where the enforcers of "no joy" lurked in every recess and where the Persian Ayatollahs were no more than a stone's throw across the waterway. There stood Hatem, arms akimbo, who had visions of the great wealth at his doorstep should Basra be able to shed the war and give the Emirates a race for their money in pushing the liquid gold to the market.

Nothing dreary or backward about him. Amusement parks on the banks of the Shatt al Arab, a radio station with an arrangement for feeding the BBC, breaking ground on a modern hotel, biding his time until the oil infrastructure could be reconstructed. A barker beyond belief for the progressive dream. More than I could have imagined – with my comparatively modest attempts at transformation in South Central.

So he had secreted us into his driveway at dark and had bedding laid out for us and soft drinks and filter tips all arranged by invisible women, a bit unsure about the right way to receive such ragged representatives from the West, notwithstanding that he sensed we had loads of US government money somewhere up our sleeves.

Later that night, we all got filled up with steaming lamb and couscous heaped up before us in a dining room of blasphemous – if one was thinking of TE – Victorian kitsch, which like his suit was about 100 years behind the times and devoid of suggestive, subtle, or sublime.

We scooted out his back drive and meandered down some roads till we were confronted with the Jaysh's nightmare: a jangle of brightly colored pushcarts, pastel ice cream stands, little girls in sequined party dresses, and cars jockeying for space near a rainbow arch. So under Hatem's wing, and within the cover of his entourage, Java and I with keffiyehs pulled tight were ushered down a path through strings of gay festoons and all the mechanized amusements – the bumper cars and twirling swings and the carousels and extravagant slippy slides and delighted parents with their wide-eyed screaming children – toward a once removed table on the banks of the river...assuming our backs to it...with an almost electric astonishment, amidst the general cacophony, for the glorious platform now before us...and the "joint...oh my God...was jumping." It had all happened so fast from curb to the table, I hardly knew what hit me. I grabbed Hatem at the back of his barker's neck and shook him. The band struck up "In the Midnight Hour"...all that joy on earth...uninhibited...with all the Motown moves and the floor in front of us was hopping with boys...stomping those boards in a riot...and then behind them were...God bless them...the girls bopping frantically up and down from their chairs. They broke my heart with their yearning...hijabs flying every which way and dancing as much as a body could from the waist up, hands to the heavens in a swaying ode to joy: "We Shall Rock You."

I stared at Java and Hatem and feared this man was magic. Walpurgis Night in the heavy air of the marshland with Persia twinkling in the distance. I mean when seen against the jihadi so recently ready in this here city to meet their maker as martyrs for the destruction of joy, well Hatem was readying himself for his maker in unabashed praise of joy – to include the money to be gleaned off those girls going wild in the stands. I was breathless.

I mean: "You can't kill it. Can you, Java?" I asked.

"Not forever," he said.

Well, the rest was what I did – meaning if I had a business card, it would read, "Insinuating in strange places." So, "me and Java" got into a neighborhood – very discreet – into the house of Hatem's friend. Not to be seen on the street – just a cleaner, a car and driver, and a cook, courtesy of Hatem. So that was how we saw Basra – hunkered down in back, face to the window pane. And with time – random and far from our house – popping out to meet someone close to our cause, probable kin to Hatem – more Internet investments...amusement parks being far too far beyond the pale for any donor.

And then to the ensuing job. Now that the inaugural was done, Java and I started a little pipeline. Ensuring the same process for the subsequent recruits: some few days inside the razor wire with the pneumatics then sliding into the neighborhood as advised, "slowly slowly quickly," followed tentatively by up and down the street. And just like that, the new office in Basra slowly rose to the occasion – with the pneumatics back at base being an effective strainer of sorts as they fear-mongered what was lying in wait outside the chain link fences and, in so doing, separated out those few who would never be true to TE.

This, I concluded, was the best – with the likes of Hatem and Java, the Barker and the "Sensitive," insinuating...my God...amusement parks. No one in the green zone would have believed it or could have fathomed such a tribute to Western Civ.

CHAPTER 25

Bridging the Divide (BtD) Broached, August 2009

How apt, that at that particular time and place, this wooly haired Levantine – this erstwhile Secretary General of the Arab ICT

Association and occasional subcontractor for my ICT projects, this multicultural Sunni from Hamra, named Nizar – should drop on my doorstep in Beirut.

Coming at me in my fog of moral relativism. Head in hand at that particular moment as I considered the professed reason I had stayed so long – that being my obligations toward my family of national staff. And even though I had often exaggerated their devotion to our mission before outsiders, I suspected the reality was more equivocal. For many of them, this work might be no more than a precious job where few were to be had or perchance, despite the risk, at some undefined moment to have some of America's stardust fall on them. And hanging over my kinship – real or imagined – was that great canopy of realpolitik – of sole sourcing for the Bechtels of the world and fabricated metrics on performance engineered by the automatons in the Green Zone. All of which, by 2009, had already pushed me to the shadows where I siphoned what I could from existing grants to promote computer literacy on demand and to provide, under some purposely vague budget line, seed money for ICT start-ups and transborder relations with the "Other." It was an endless foot race, my heart accelerating in bed at night, between whether we could break borders faster than the zealots of various stripes could erect them...especially around those benighted women whose engagement was the sine qua non if Iraq were ever to compete successfully with its Sub-Saharan neighbors – the very same in years past who had swabbed their floors.

Rumsfeld had called them (the no joy on earth crowd) "dead-enders." I didn't know. I knew that they knew when death came quickly, it was painless. That the mortal coil was just so constituted. And the alternative? The West's extended dalliances and their earthly accoutrements which we hail and worship: sex, long life, and howling at the moon.

Once you see the struggle on the ground as immaterial to the essential physics of the matter, then Ahlan wa Sahlan (welcome into my family), Mr. Nizar. Allow me to be amused by your indifference to anything we presume to do besides raising the tide of your cash flow. Allow me to be amused by your amazing disdain for what we in the West call facts. Allow me to be fascinated about how you sidestepped the Koran to become "ethics free." That is to say that when I played with Nizar, I entered a wonderland where he dashed about Hamra in his silver Humvee, eyes like saucers and divining all sorts of fantastic possibilities. Date Palm plantations near Karbala, a Holy Water franchise outside of Najaf, the Segue franchise in Damascus. I mean who the hell in downtown Beirut hangs a portrait of the Governor of Texas above his desk? Who else closes down the whole damn phone system in the office so that the unpaid vendors won't disturb his dreams? Who else flees out the side door when his presence with me as Avant Garde might have shamed the deal that just walked through the entrance of the restaurant? Who also got me seated before all the presidents and prime ministers I could hope for – Saad Hariri, Michel Aoun, Fouad Siniora, Walid Jumblatt – and other assorted headliners he could pull like rabbits from his baseball cap. A trade, if you will, for the pale replicas of the deliverables he was supposed to provide my agency on the ground.

Enter Pierre. The eminence from Zahle (the Christian enclave in Eastern Lebanon) who under his father's hard hand hauled rocks as a teenager from the quarry of a nearby family mountain while his older brother Nicholas studied constitutional law at the Sorbonne. Now bald as a billiard, talcum enough to turn heads, brutal in the face of dissent, and awkward before any erudition. He was a cold heart in a land of such. A classic capo whose Christian domain was being threatened by unrestrained Shia procreation. (He once asked me if I could find out if the United States would fund a massive distribution of free condoms and other more permanent prophylactics so as to stanch the Moslem invasion of this God-blessed Christian enclave.) Buried two floors below his brother's party apparatus, he had his fastness, with a large oil painting of his deceased mother on the wall and an allied photo of a chapel built into his church to consecrate her in memoriam.

He also had his palsied left hand from a sniper's bullet, a vile and, at times, almost hysterical manner of crushing unallied opinions as well as a renown for laying out vast banquets along the river Berdouni for those occasional soft-skinned and well-bred visitors. And while he refused himself more than a taste, he almost personally put the mezza into their tentative mouths. Left uncurbed by Nicholas on such occasions, he would interrupt his rant on the Catholic plight with, for a clearer understanding, "Don't worry, we will fuck 'em," which definitely would have the juiceless diplomat beside him anxious about how that got communicated upward in the cable to State at day's end.

He had inherited several mountains after his father's death, and as the coast of Lebanon became caked in concrete, his fortunes trended up – spiked even, with the intermittent bombing by Israel and the subsequent financing by Gulf Arabs of even more formidable structures. This was his base – the quarries in several mountains and the confessional ilk that guarded them. They jumped at the tinkle of his bell to serve him more high octane sludge and guided his armored car to certain undisclosed rendezvous. The business in the mountains had soon extended its reach to illicit hijacking of the telecom traffic all along the border of Syria in cahoots with Assad and family, which also coincidentally served as a convenient brake to Hezbollah's advance on Pierre's historic fastness. Extended apace to equity in other comparable schemes. An exclusive telecom operation in Nagorno Karabakh. A significant share of the ICT market in South Sudan. Frontier markets they were called in business schools. Dangerous places with high margins if you lived to collect.

So, then, in a textbook illustration of how to master the chaos, which was and is Lebanon, Brother Nicholas managed the various alliances necessary within the government so as to arrange a half billion dollar award to the Fattouche family for damages incurred since the late 1990s when the Hoss government had been unwilling to permit them such a windfall from Lebanon's cherished mountains and thus had the quarries closed. Not an unusual series of events in Lebanon, but the pot of gold had arrived when the Internet was now publicizing these notorious affronts to the public good, some of which were becoming bothersome to Nicholas, if not yet to Pierre.

Enter Nizar – who like a bee had been buzzing around on the edges of some of Pierre's investments and who had recently been drawn in further when he had handled the communication strategy for Nicholas's re-election to the national legislature in 2009. For that, Nizar was rewarded with a mansion on Embassy

Row in Washington DC. And amidst these various events came the notion that it would be good for business for Pierre to cleanse his public image, particularly where it counted the most, in the world's only hegemon.

And so one day I got that visit on my doorstep in Beirut, inviting me to join Pierre and Nizar at the Hotel Phoenicia for an undisclosed proposition.

Of course, Pierre did not understand such things as cleansing his image or any possible benefit he might derive from doing so. Thus all such details were buried by his insistence to put some more mezza in my mouth and to refill my glass with champagne. Nizar, I was guessing, had probably filled his head with some vague propositions that David could bring to life. And when I persisted with my questions, Pierre waved them all away and told me to "ask Nizar." And when I asked Nizar, somewhat later in private, he simply said, "Make sure Pierre can meet some Senators and Diplomats whenever he visits Washington. Start a humanitarian organization and put Pierre on the board. Believe me, he will pay you well." Dig as I might, I could not get more. I got some Vermont lawyers to draw up all the preliminary papers necessary to protect me should things go wrong (money laundering came to mind). Those papers came in August to be spread before Pierre. He barely read the bold type at the top and then rifled through them applying his signature wherever I indicated. At the conclusion, he smiled at me as if to say, "Such nonsense, eh?" Then asked me if I thought America would bomb Iran.

CHAPTER 26

Leaving Iraq, September 2009

I had wanted to stay past the end of the occupation, even as we all knew that the Sunni insurgents and Al Qaeda would, regardless, continue to contest the future of Iraq on the streets.

But I had already signed the papers with Pierre and bizarre as the circumstances surrounding the deal were, I was enthralled with the idea of bringing my quest for Right Relations to America – quite unaware at that moment what form that quest would take. And equally enthralled for the hiatus I had negotiated with Pierre that would allow me and Annie a few months to settle into a small farm in Vermont.

But one could not stay forever, I knew. I was not of a mind to grow older in Iraq or among its neighbors. Much had changed since I had lain on that bed at the Best Western in Amman. Dishes were on almost every roof, cell phones had replaced HF, VHF, and SAT phones; Saddam had been tried and executed, the Internet had poked its way into hundreds of thousands of homes. Yet the roadside IEDs and the martyrs willing to explode themselves kept coming. Law and order was still tentative and would suffer from the departure of the American GIs – even as most Iraqis had become hostile to seeing the foreign uniform.

So, as the American Army prepared to leave, I announced my own intent to leave the region. The agency would find someone to replace me. Someone more malleable I was sure. Paul would have Iraq to himself. Together, we made the last trips down to South Central to receive the embraces, to sip the tea, and to be told how they were losing a father or grandfather, as the case may be, revealing again their needs for the patron – the hierarchy. We lay together on the floor, in the dark in their homes, where earlier we had eaten the plates of chicken and rice and flat bread together, all stretched out now, together, asleep till the roosters started crowing. And then we had been driven north by Tall Mohamed and been handed over to Qadir to bring us back into the Kurdish lands.

The last event was northeast of Khanaqin aside a creek deep in a ravine only a stone's throw from the Iranian border. They had fixed up a brazier and threw on dozens of shishes of chicken and lamb while a CD blared the Kurdish dancing music and a large circle of us came to life – men and women – raising the shoulders and feet in unison, following the lead of the sequined woman with the kerchief.

Later that night, for the first time inside Iraq, I had allowed myself to become drunk – to accept a bottle of whiskey from the Khanaqin gin mill and pour it down till I got very full of myself and spouted all and sundry before the Sudanese, the Serb, the Russian, and the Frenchman.

"Slum Gullion," I declared out of nowhere. "To get some slum," I had affirmed with a vigorous nod, "as in Steinbeck's Dubious Battle," I explained.

"That's what the reds in the striker's camp would say," I told them. "Get some slum. Aren't you drawn to the euphony? I mean slum is a good word, isn't it?" They were heartily entertained, not having ever seen me like that. Maybe some intimations when I had had too much coffee, but nothing to compare to this.

"And they all seem like tributaries." I charged on, undaunted. "Barely perceptible trickles...hidden under fallen leaves and rotting wood. Like capillaries to a brook when the snow melts to streams to rivers to the sea."

"So...don't you see," I declared, wild eyed. "To get some slum and you quickly get confused about governance...about why the reds failed with Utopias and Right Relations. About the relation of work to reward, the individual to community, the limits of ideals...nationalism, man's capacity for peace...violence as essential from atom to galaxy...according to Teller."

"And so...it is one more word which gets me to war. Trickles and then stream...into confusion."

"The book...the Irish lass in a dancehall had pronounced it 'bouk.'"

Yes, indeed, I had veered. Quite mad from the whiskey. I saw the perplexity on their faces. I paused to suck in mightily on my smoke.

"Later...an older woman," I continued. "God, she had called me on that...on new year's eve at the Gresham in Dublin. I mean our Kennedy had stayed there so that had caught me. The night before, across the sea, I swear, I could smell my ancestors in the coal smoke of Wales, holed up in a rented room by the port. The rude white boys there with curly hair and runny noses. I was blustering and drunk on Irish whiskey in the hall and pretending to be hot-blooded, so when she pressed into me on the dance floor, I looked for an excuse."

By now they were pretty much spellbound by this tirade from their boss. I suspect that none of them thought I had such stuff in me.

"The bouk used to be in a drawer next to my metal bed," I told them as I pointed up to the roof behind us. To what had been my old cinder block hut on the roof. "A bouk, a rowing machine, three days change of clothes, all from my son who has outgrown them. The high quality quite incongruous on me. Wouldn't you say?" Now moving my free hand across my body. "Speckled with basal cells," I mumbled, "and hobbled with bad knees." I patted one. "And a thin beard and my fingernails chewed up." I put my hand in front of each of them...with a can of Ifes beer in my other hand..."down by this here fountain which sputters along." I went on undeterred. "which like the drawer and my bed and the door and everything made in Iraq is, as we all know, poorly made and dying. One hard yank and my drawer will splinter. Chairs collapse when you sit in them; the windows rattle in the wind...the muezzins words are mangled by a faulty transmitter."

How I did go on that night.

And so, on September 15th, 2009, I was next to this failing fountain with my friends and the three wild dogs which had survived, looking through the chain link fence at me, their former provider, who gave them better than I ate: slumgullion.

And then, just as fast, I stopped, and we all just sat very silent and looked up at the stars and then across at the dogs.

Hash and greasy, as in easy, I thought. Old fried potatoes and vegetables cooked to exhaustion. Oh how I would marvel at those dogs...how they consumed the victuals I threw over or tore a cat apart...just tore it apart and swallowed it...crushed the bones in their jaws...that is...other than the dog named Drakoulis who had poked at a poisonous snake in his hole and just shrank before my eyes in froth and sweat.

Sitting there for the last time, silent amidst the dissonance of the Shia and Sunni mosques...watching the three male dogs try to kill each other...then hump each other...and then devour some scraps I threw over while I gulped down another beer and whiskey...just squeezed the tin can from the side and pushed the beer down the old gullet and then lay it on the ledge of the fountain next to my SAT phone, which could connect me to some unseen invention in orbit through the heavens...the same heavens the muezzins were trying to address.

And then my eyes dropped down to the perimeter wall around me and the watchmen outside and the Iraqi police and the stanchions against car bombs and Hamza with his wand, which probably was also defunct, to protect against a zealot blowing himself to pieces with shrapnel exploding all over the place, ripping through mud brick and flesh alike.

And so...right before me...and around me...my beer and slum...a lot to take in and each of it...a word put to it...led toward a confusion. The dogs killing and humping and then tails awaggin and purring at the chain link...and the suicide zealot and the muezzins' litany and the rowing machine and bouk and the Sudanese sensitive on one side and the quiet Parisian on the other and such another motley group elsewhere in other office locations. Yes, a word from any of them or just the sight of dogs or watchmen and you got stunned by where it led...the vision of George Bush...the vision behind words like open and pluralistic, democracy, open markets, evangelical empire...as they bump against tribe, Shia, Sunni, Kurd, Ayatollah, Saddam, Anfal, Najaf, Jew, Infidel Crusader, modernizer, The Avant Garde for Western Civ.

In the end, sitting there in Khanaqin, 4K from the Iranian border during a cold September night, a so-called humanitarian aid worker trudged off to bed, one last smoke before he pulled a dusty blanket, which Soriah never beat, over him.

The next morning, I had left early from Khanaqin for the Beechcraft up north that would fly me back to Amman.

Bye from Soriah – the hag draped in her black abaya with nine children and a dead husband. Swabbing the tiles by hand, bum up. Now sitting on a rusty gas canister, sucking on Pines in the shade of our tin roof. Chuckling at my Western antics, as I had blown her a kiss.

Tears from Solham – the plump cook, the great mass of bosom, the substantial backside, the hopeful smile, glass specs, the dirt under her nails – "a man without a wife is like a kitchen without a knife" on her Chinese apron – chicken, mutton or macaroni – chicken, mutton, or macaroni.

Goodbye Qadir – my ham-fisted friend who took me through the badlands, his magnificent grin. Like Soriah, he had humored me in my antics – often with the dogs. I was now beside the Land Cruiser telling him to watch over them. He had raised his hand and pulled his trigger finger. "No, no," I had laughed, "not that way." I recalled how, in a blink of an eye, he had plugged the sick dog with his AK and how we had stood over it, waiting, peering at it to die, so I could lift it up and put it in the plastic bag. "Gee," he had uttered – so long after it should have died.

For years now, back and forth across the fault lines, he tried to gauge my threshold. Two of his brothers now dead since we first met. We are very sad to leave each other, I thought, as Paul and I pushed out the gate.

Paul looked uncertain. We had been mates in the Levant for so long, it was hard to figure us oceans apart. He, the son of a Mexican immigrant with a father who had also served in Vietnam, the closest I had to TE, my summa cum laude wherever he walked, now taking the farewell drive with me – with me who had none of those attributes but who, after all, had taken the responsibility of mission and men for almost seven years in what was a defining moment for the West.

It was over. But in truth it was not. You can't just take off a coat and put on a new one. It stays with you. You have been in a wasteland where there was a lot of killing going on, and you have been there long enough for all the death to get into you. Most of us will need surcease; some of us will get it.

It will be the unsuspecting kindness rather than the perfunctory which will help. The fingertips on your brow, your shoulder, your arm. The kiss out of nowhere. The laughter at an inimitable foolishness. The towel held out as you emerge from the ocean at night.

I am now back in San Se clipping my toenails. And then the hair. Cleaning up and then sitting dazed on the corniche watching the parade of pedestrians in all their colorful variety and wondering how they do it, how they skate and amble and stroll and struggle along on spikes and sandals and flats and sneaks.

I am dazed by the parade. Beyond it are the waves coming

in off the dark and deadly Atlantic. Death stretching as far as I can see. How much kindness, I reflect, when the undertow has you or in the cold eye of a fish as you go down.

You desperately need the dreamless sleep. You will go nuts if you keep playing over the same stupid predicament – in this case, the road that cannot be found. Or the smell of the blood in my moustache that I cannot expunge – even after I cut away the skin from my lip. That is what Saddam left you. You, in your cinder block hooch on the roof with the inch and one half of mattress and the blind rowing after the muezzin blows you out of bed at 0430 hrs, with the psychos roaming the outskirts, hoping for a chance to saw off your head slowly – incurring the stench of blood in their moustache as well, no doubt, amidst the crowd of myriad forked tongues outside the perimeter.

Why does kindness play so big? How can a discernible kindness in San Se transport you to incomparable loveliness? Just the laughter, the fingers on the brow, the towel held out can make life worth living.

I mean it's not like a damn radiator that, when it gets corroded or clogged, you just flush out. With us, the walls of the veins or the arteries absorb it. They draw in the poison, become infused with it, all the way to the heart. So I cannot just flush myself of six years of abuse and sort of "head up" trot down the corniche. No.

Anyway and notwithstanding, I now have my dream for Vermont – since I must. I have even got to the point where I have graphed it. With a title on top such as the "road to health," lifted intact from one of our nutrition programs. Or rather simply, "The road back," since that allows for more interpretations.

I have discussed it. It, being 64. It will now take six months to get enough of the rot out to at least sleep well on occasion, to throw back a shot and have it hit and lift rather than the way it does now, which is barely a ripple in the sewer. To have the flesh resemble the mind. Sinewy and strung tight without any more of those little puddles of white fat on the gut. Maybe, if the conditions are right – around the oval at some college – I can do twenty-two for 5K.

So there would be a timeline across the top of the chart and down the side the first tentative goals for rowing or a swim across the lake and then maybe some fly along the shore and a few K's on my bike on the back roads, I think.

We'll see. Six months till I can do a 200 fly or a 20K cross country. Six months till I can sit on the stool at Frank's Bar and Grill and shoot back the distillate of the maguey weed or inhale a hallucinogen, which will get me away.

So, off to the hiatus in Vermont. After being hunted for years, standing in the wasteland, sucking down bad coffee and bad smokes, sleeping with an ear cocked, rolling on the tile with a poisoned gut.

Finally, they would fly me to HQ for the last download – along with a smattering of advocacy before persons of influence. Such meetings entailing the last of the alcohol from San Se to be drained from my head, finding a couple of shirts whose collars and cuffs were not frayed, putting a polish on the wingtips, getting a trim for the beard. And then to Europe – as an Avant Garde who had just been plucked out of the center of a global confrontation and put in the back row of a Boeing – soon to have some large fellow passenger compete with me for the armrest and the seat in front of me abruptly reclined on to my kneecaps.

Yes, I could strut before those assembled in Washington. I could bring a tear, provoke a gasp. They knew I was authentic. They could feel the war standing next to them. Successful men would look away; their wives would stroke my arm and try to commiserate.

My last encounter as a field hand with the so-called soil still on my shoes was with my friend in Congress, Representative Wolf, who, like me, went as far back as Vietnam. Just as I had arrived at his office, he was running out for a vote. "Come with me, and we'll talk on the way," he said. "I've just had four town meetings, Dave," he continued, "and they want us out. Completely out. No residuals. Tell me what do I say?"

One answers those types of queries with books, not short sentences on the fly. I think I disappointed him. I could only mutter, out of breath, "Long haul. You can't build 'open and pluralistic' on the fly. In any case, DOD was not the vehicle. With luck, there could be a facsimile by the time the oil runs out."

"So why do it? Do any of it?" he asked, as we stood before the chamber door. "What do I tell them?"

I remember feeling helpless.

He had to vote. Then he took my hand. "Thank you," he said. And turned into the chamber.

PART TWO

BRIDGING THE DIVIDE

Preface

Six months after the meeting at the Phoenicia, the first tranche of what would become two million US dollars was transferred to my bank. BtD (Bridging the Divide) was hatched. As it turned out, Pierre would never make a board meeting and would only visit Washington once. But nevertheless, he was always pleased to see me in Zahle, put me next to him at the Berdouni, and send me off with a bag of golden bracelets for my family. As for Nizar, as you will see, he had his angles. BtD was to manage all the details pertaining to his own quest for American citizenship as a newly vested CEO for "The Arab ICT Bureau in Washington." The organization was also to act as a subcontractor on any government grants we may receive, such revenues to pay for his rent, staff, and legal issues. Yes sir, I smiled, no flies on Nizar.

Except, that never happened. As it turned out, Pierre's association with BtD as a board member was to preclude any US government grants, and further, it was too late. I was now hell bent on reform. On cutting the faceless bureaucrats out of the equation and marrying up the energy and the aspirations of America – Wolfe's swarm – directly with their likenesses in God forsaken places. I could always drag up a Senator or two for Pierre if he ever dared Washington (about which I had some doubts), and as for Nizar, I quickly became too essential for what I felt was a photo increasingly coming into focus of him and his wife and boys putting some trans-Atlantic distance between them and Israeli F-16s – even as he faced the distinct possibility of getting his wings clipped by the more assiduous application of rules in America.

Compelling Idea, 2010

To begin with, there was this business of the compelling idea.
You must have it, among other assets, to be a success. To find a
market or to make a market – either way – what you pull up and
push out must arrest and then convert. It is one thing to holler
from the soapbox or over les pommes dauphinoise and quite
another to draw and inspire a crowd. So how does that cry to
battle come to market? At my advanced age, I wondered? Like
an asteroid crashing through the skull to splash in their collective
brain pans, I joked. Or, more likely, like a difficult trek along the
bell curve – those first linear excitations upward toward that high
plateau where growth induced complexity prevails and then,
inevitably, the acceleration of decay on the down slope. What
do I do, in search for the holler's articulation that can arrest and
convert? What can I retrieve as pertinent salvage as I approach
my own end, amidst the too crowded memories? Amidst the
humiliations, those moments of unforgettable pettiness or
perhaps those few unexpected flashes of loveliness?

Well, there was that picture in my mind of Ninos and his
mom in their second floor refuge, getting the feed together from
that heaven-pointed dish that could have put them both in prison,
had someone whispered. Or that girl who had flown from the
room and given me that eyeful of women who hours before had
marched the hot streets of Kut in black abayas, now wrapped in
their pink robes with their sparkling rainbow colored cells
watching Angelina – or the hilarious, half choking on his wine,
Nizar pronouncing the end of zealotry – or my great shame in
the Green Zone as I watched the foreman from Texas supervise a
squad of Iraqis raking the lawns – or that official arrogance of
presenting America, demanding that I risk my head traveling
across Bag so that they could put the tick in a box to certify the
monthly collaboration. I, who had willy nilly spilt blood for
Wolfe's America.

Those pullulations, now unfortunately somewhat south, in
the mid-Atlantic, sadly transmuted into a half million tapping
feet, tapping down the escalators, mute on the trains, staring
blankly into their iPhones, tapping up from the metro to their
government cubes to stare vacantly at another monitor, to
intermittently suck some water from a straw. An invasion of

millennial twits tweeting. A blight on what might have been a still groaning continent.

My terrible fault, I had settled amidst them. I had had Pierre's Senators on my mind and Nizar's mansion nearby and government reform. And to think I could have had a storefront in Union square, in lower Manhattan, but had ended instead in a brownstone off DuPont circle.

There was certainly some trepidation. That clammy feeling in the middle of the night, twisted up in your sheets, in and out of sleep, haunted in the recesses by faint past internal agreements made about that tightrope – the "incandescence short of the catheter" – as now applied to my lesser ambitions in DC as I sought to strip away the blasphemy of America's foreign relations with principal financing from a man who kept fast company with some of the world's worst tyrants, who happened to be from a small clan sandwiched between Hezbollah and Assad in these here post-9/11 days.

Given that America was now seeing a terrorist in every tube of toothpaste, that half million dollar transfer to my bank in Vermont – Beirut to Burlington – was to my ears ringing enough bells with the Feds to sound like a five alarm fire. I could read the headlines already: "Local Husband and Father Forsakes Noble Work in Renowned Charity to Represent Middle Eastern Crime Kingpin. Homeland Security and the Department of Treasury Issue Preliminary Warrants." The article would go on to reveal that when interviewed by a local reporter, the suspect had allowed that his benefactor had never been specific on the reason behind the sudden largesse, other than it was expected the transfers would serve to curry the favor of the American government toward Mr. Fattouche. The Vermont native then went on to state that so far the initial funds had been invested in forming a new corporation called Bridging the Divide, which had as its compelling idea the "disintermediation of Foreign Relations." Under further questioning by this reporter, the suspect started to ramble on about "the groaning continent" and "how it had become blanded over with millennial twits who had become, since the onset of postwar prosperity and fear, America's face to the world instead of those rightful multicolored, polyglot, pulsating pullulating swarms and their children."

Every big idea I had ever had – from pretending I was a secret disciple of Jesus at age six – to my East Asian venture into man's greatest winnower lasting no more than three months before I was lodged in a neuropsychiatric hospital – to my inability to ever reconcile my heart stricken romances before the yawning appetite – to going mad as I had sought His hem in Paris but instead had only got the rat's tail disappearing beneath the plinth – to my failed travel enterprise, which had decomposed the family – to lethal communication impasses with my beloved children and now to this. Another representation of my inability to imagine, to imagine myself in real circumstances.

But as the weeks went on, the Feds never called and the trepidation slowly receded. For sure, I thought, they were watching me, but for whatever reason they were not prepared to pounce. "Ruin" at my late age was to stay parked in the wings, it seemed, at least for the time being. In fact, it had always been in the wings for the likes of me. But, yet to impede me permanently.

Having been already warned countless times by those bystanders to my progress that "good ideas were a dime a dozen," I sought what I believed to be the foundations for disintermediation. Schumpeter's "Creative Destruction" and allied tracts, I concluded, were none other than the transformation I had witnessed as far back as the New York, New Haven, and Hartford Railroad when as a fugitive teenager, my eyes pressed against the filmy window as I rushed down the iron rails and saw city after city brought to its knees by the exodus to the suburbs. America was like that, I thought. It changed before your eyes with equal parts of dreams realized and the misery left in their wake. And then, later, during my first dive into the marketplace when I had to tried to take retail travel in Hartford by storm, there had been other specific intimations of disintermediation. "Barney," they called it so as to make it more user friendly. Hartford's first ATM machine. With such tentative appeal that early adopters would take five bucks out and then immediately go inside the bank to talk to a cashier and get her confirmation that all was well. It was simple in my mind. If you were in the middle and didn't add value, then you'd be gone before long. To do otherwise was pure sentimentality. And then, evident even from my far away homes in the Middle East, the Internet had taken those seeds of disintermediation and blown them sky high.

And so, here was the leap, perhaps the fatal leap. Absent the profit motive of a marketplace, even when clearly applicable to American values and interests, does disintermediation happen? Why would Americans let the United States government and the associated big charities take hundreds of billions of dollars from altruistic Americans and delegate the design and the spending of it overseas to those aforementioned twits alternately treading up and down the escalators in DC with their iPhones in one hand and their Big Gulp in another? Or to those same twits bunched together in triple perimeter fortresses overseas...when now they could rub the sleep out of their eyes, turn on the computer, chat online, and thus communicate with their likeness in Ghana for no cost and in so doing Bridge the Divide, melt the borders, which was at the heart of Right Relations? It was at this moment when I, David, imagined trumpets, notwithstanding some troubling and nagging recognition that governments and NGOs were often immune to the marketplace and that citizens might just be so constructed that they could well satisfy their altruistic instincts without ever needing to be assured of impact.

And so it went – these sessions within myself. Reading everything available, learning the vocabulary pertaining to the Internet and to web marketing, struggling with the critical ideas: does man make the market or does man find the market? Should I shell out money to West Coast gurus for an hour's time in their private incubators to bat down, if they could, my hypothesis, commission studies and business plans from renowned innovators, compete for seed monies from venture capitalists in SFO or NYC skyscrapers whose windows opened onto the limitless Pacific or Central Park? Should I plead my views on transforming foreign relations with thought leaders at Berkeley, NYU, or Columbia?

In the end, the savants took my money for their time. Pierre's money. And wished me well or they smiled and gave me that God awful pat on the back. But I could tell they never once caught on fire even as I sometimes shook before them with enthusiasm for this new disintermediated world without borders. I knew that they had no clue about that likeness in Ghana, and I suspected that while they found all this old man's newfound language on the World Wide Web charming, there had been a hell of a lot of water under the bridge since the ICT revolution has kicked off on the West Coast thirty years earlier.

Meanwhile, there was my benefactor whom I knew to be an illiterate in such matters and from whom I had received no response whatsoever to my several progress reports on the state of my thinking; and whom, as I roamed the innovation landscape from coast to coast, I knew to be making every preparation in the Bekaa or Nagorno-Karabakh or South Sudan to "fuck 'em."

A Logo and a Landing Site

Even so, as I got tucked into my cocoon in business class with a couple of flutes of champagne, I remained undaunted. I had my supporters from as far back as the smoking room at Suffield: "Whatever you can do, or dream, you can do, begin it. Boldness has genius, power, and magic in it. Begin it now." Further, I had some money despite the dramatic disconnect between my ambition and the donor lack of interest in such. Moreover, well before the Rockies, there was the pleasure of being master of one's ideas...of doodling on some legal pad the contours of your logo. "I mean," I was talking to myself (you see business class allows that), "even for the most 'off the grid' entrepreneur these days, eventually one needs an identifier beyond mere narrative to get in step with this new century inclination toward symbols eclipsing words or for some epiphanic flash for the eyeball on your website or in my case, something for the crown of my baseball cap. I mean shit...did the Apple make Steve Jobs or did Steve Jobs make the Apple? I mean cults are quite particular," I grinned, "another fruit may have achieved far less."

I already had paid for about thirty illustrations from a graphic designer in New York, and they all seemed dull. I had thought to crowd source it as was recommended in some of the literature on the subject, but I had never liked anything about crowds. In fact, I got vertigo if I stayed in a mall for more than forty-five minutes. And so it was, with all those postmodern designs still floating in my consciousness when I had thought to lift the flute to my lips while turning to reflect on the cloud cover at 30,000 feet. It was then at that instant that I had abruptly turned the opposite way – as in back to Homo Sapiens – two green banks and a slash of brown across it.

And then, of course, you did not exist if you didn't exist virtually. That made me laugh, loud enough to catch the attention of the man across the aisle. "Hmm," I allowed, coming as I had nonstop from my recuperation in Vermont. I wondered to what extent I had been virtual there. But I got it. Before BtD could exist really, I mused, it had to exist virtually. In fact, even when it had a street address and furniture against which you could bang your knee, its heart and soul would need to stay virtual. I rolled the cool flute across my forehead. "Well," I thought, "this could start to give one a headache," since I could now sniff both Plato and particle physics in the air when really all I could hope to fathom at that point related to whether I could be a pied piper for my demographic to some attractive site on the web that would hold their attention just long enough to effect a conversion.

Trouble being, I recollected, the only geeks I ever knew were either still buried in the likes of Rimbaud or laureates in classical Arabic. Not a soul spoke code or passed his days and nights in the back end of a computer. Trouble indeed since my business model was based on the inherent disruptions of ICT and my presentation as a disruptor clearly needed to be cutting edge. So I decided, as my plane now entered the night skies east of the Mississippi, I would do what well-heeled outsiders often do in such circumstances. I would invest in a blue chip.

Going to Market

The following week found me in the early morning with a cup of coffee in hand ascending Washington's Union Station, that great sandblasted monument to American Railroads, about to trundle north on Amtrak – thank God – to Wolfe's world – once again past the hollowed out cities. A proper break in the trousers, I affirmed, as I stood at the gate soon to descend to the tracks, a quarter inch of cuff showing beyond my ancient pinstripes, harkening way back to the first time when Henry had taken his mere boy to Hartford's prestigious clothier Stackpole, Moore, and Tryon. Now en route to Horn Group, founded and owned by Sabrina Horn and located impressively near Wall Street and as their website had also pronounced, bi-located with their San Francisco affiliate (off Market) where there was an image of redwood posts a foot square supporting a net of catwalks that encircled a flowering courtyard.

It was a complete bust. An expensive bust. That is, other than the wonderful office in SFO and the eager entry level staffers (BtD did not get Sabrina). As it turned out, no one could stay in the conversation with me for more than a minute once it had turned toward such keywords as Right Relations, Taking Down Big Charity (we don't want to be negative they counseled), disintermediation, and putting USAID down much as you would an old or crippled horse. They were all, by this time, fumbling with their pencils and urging me, "Why don't we start at the beginning?"

"Exactly," I had responded. "That's what I'm doing. If you don't understand the sickness, then you can't understand the cure, and then you can't understand BtD."

Over the weeks my patience wore thin. I told them that they were like someone cautioning Dr. Salk not to talk about paralysis as he tried to promote the vaccine. Their support staff was becoming fewer and younger. Ever fresh and ever "up," they remained ignorant of what was at stake. I had told them we were not selling toothpaste – that Horn could make a name for itself far beyond its imagination if it were to be seen as transformative in effecting Right Relations. I even went so far as to tell them about Michiko Ota and the water above. They listened appreciatively and would send me yet another screenshot indicating they were lost or I was...take your pick. Timelines were aborted. The much anticipated launch on the West Coast to which I would fly and which would, they said, attract a whole array of reporters and other assorted media reps was, in a word, pathetic. I had ended up nursing a cold coffee and watching a solitary apprentice try to assuage me. "We called them all," she sighed.

No reveling with doodles this time on the way back across the fruited plains. I blamed myself. I knew where the geeks hung out, where the folks who wanted to bend the technology toward social justice gathered – MIT, NYU, Berkeley – but let's face it, I didn't exactly have their numbers handy.

In the end, I refused to pay the last tranche of my bill to Horn and frankly believed I was being generous at that. There had been no dissembling on my part. I had explained the revolution from the start – the water below and the water above – albeit to some rather blank stares.

Sunderland

I was left with the only option left – to bring our need for media presence in-house. But Washington is pretty much a wasteland for what I wanted, yet I was still obliged to be there, given the sole requirement Pierre had made (to curry favor among Washington notables). And, of course, there was, hypothetically, the end game: that part where my virtual presence had so fired up my demographic that even a Congress as moribund as my own would act to take USAID down. The right because "no government should do what a citizen can" and the left because citizen engagement in Right Relations was its siren's call.

Thus I was torn – with the intellectual and spiritual capital I needed being four hours north by train, but constrained to earn my wages in our nation's capital. So aggrandized now since my Australian mother had pushed me up Pennsylvania Avenue in a perambulator on V-E Day. Never to my knowledge had the spoils of war been so great. Seemingly, those great evolutionary waves from across the Atlantic had peaked.

One would have to be hard-bitten not to appreciate Sunderland. A lane really between Brownstones with wrought iron gates and canopies of plane trees with a pocket park full of gaily dressed school children running their hearts out on the green at lunchtime. My office was well worn, full mostly of furniture that had been too heavy for previous occupants to move away, but accommodating for my need to slouch and reflect on a way forward. Behind me was an alcove looking out over the park. The trees kept it cool in the summer and the old steam radiators hissed through the winter providing an old-time warmth. On one side, there was the bullpen into which I had some IKEA wares delivered – stainless steel and vanilla colored plyboard – a playground for the imminent arrival of the ingénues who would come with lots of cushions and rugs, where they could jam on keyboards and try to be imaginative.

Aside this incubator, I had my conference room. Wainscoted, with a walnut table, and sepia photos on the wall from the turn of the century, depicting the ruling class back then.

All told, an appropriate nook for genesis despite the phlegmatic culture surrounding it.

I worked not far from the red line, which, when it was not down for as much maintenance as the unions could arrange, would take me direct to Northwest. Nights, after work, I would wait in the porcelain tunnel, listening to Janet from Homeland Security remind us through the intercom "to suspect every suspicious person around you and any suspicious move they might make." In any case, she had moving pictures of us all in case we decided not to take our nation's security seriously. Then Janet would be followed by another local voice warning us "not to eat cause if you spilled something it could turn our metro into other subways [not named] which had rats."

I knocked along till I rose up the escalators to Arch Stone, a great Mormon edifice with even more rules than the metro: all for my own good. A risk free, scandal free environment with such tidy apartments – all with perfect plumbing and climate control. Just what I had wanted – about as far removed from the room on the roof in Iraq as was humanly possible. The only possible diversion was a sports bar not far from the exit of the metro where I could rub shoulders with the same type of men who poured into stadiums each fall to jump and scream for Ohio State.

Workforce

I had never been much good at selecting staff since I believed that the only characteristic that counted was ardor and that the rest, the carefully modeled CVs and the poise before the interview, was all subterfuge. Back in the day – after my recovery from causalgia, when I had had a spell as an entrepreneur – I had scheduled interviews before the sun rose or even in the worst of weather. Of course, these could be faked as well, but what was a guy to do, short of imposing some sort of ordeal by fire?

I didn't have the network I had overseas. This was domestic, a very different arena. So this recruitment exercise ended up like throwing darts blindfolded. I figured a razor sharp intelligence would be nice and someone who fathomed the revolution afoot, but mostly, I wanted someone with a chip on her shoulders, someone who would stand at the barricades with relish. Angry.

And, who would take my telephone calls day and night.

In the end, I got a pale reflection of all that. I did not choose well or maybe there was no one to choose. Or, more probably, I chose as well as could be expected, but managed what I got poorly.

I got a high GPA girl who broadcast exclamation marks to beat the band, both oral and written. And who had such a spring in her step that she seemingly defied gravity, almost breathless in her excitement, but as the first few weeks unfolded, also evidently flawed by her overwhelming conviction that she must be well-rounded and, therefore, not available online during flute, jogging, neighborhood charity events, etc. Not, I suspected, solely for her own satisfaction, but as critical content for her CV as from day one she sought higher ground. Thus, my first BtDer – this slender girl with an abundance of wonderful ringlets, with extraordinary RPMs, but who, above all, would be well rounded. And, as I came to learn, who would also bounce into my office frequently, breathless about this or that peripheral discovery.

Then there was my foreigner. I mean if our name is Bridging the Divide, we needed an accent on our end of the phone. I had met her during an intervening assignment in Hanoi just prior to the Iraq job. She had come under the wing of the notorious American disruptor, Richard Falk, who did some visiting lectures there and who had stayed at a club where she had been waiting on tables. An oriental gamine with the sloe eyes – at the tables – but with hardwire running through her. One of the millions who had come to Hanoi from rural Vietnam, born during the great famine there and the war with China. They lived on scraps in a country only then beginning to adopt the "capitalist path to socialism."

Professor Falk had arranged for her to study at Santa Barbara and mind his house. She assumed him and his wife as her American family. She had long bony fingers that, even at the interview, she twisted as if she were trying to squeeze the last water from a dishrag. She, the CV said, had a degree in IT...and mon dieu...Richard Falk. If any of him had rubbed off, then there would be no issue "at the barricades." Just another alert for the feds to process alongside that of Pierre's dirty money. "If the Feds really did 'mix and match' data, they must be scratching their heads now," I laughed, in my swivel thinking chair.

But she had had no part in that wave that had washed over America off the north Atlantic as I was being pushed up Pennsylvania Avenue. We who work overseas, from missionary to cigarette wholesaler, we know. We are forever bemoaning the way the locals analyze and decide – how befuddled they are before the Western mind, no matter how hard they apply themselves or what natural and superior intelligence they have. They come out of a different stream; ignorant of how those tribes from Anatolia evolved "life-beating" ways of processing information and communicating. That was what the twisting of the dishrag was about. One does not just dive into the West fresh from millennia of different processes.

It was painful to watch her – courageous, always online, always there in the worst of snowstorms in her pink snowsuit, twisting those hands red while I explained, increasingly with less patience, that it was her job not mine to deal with the IT vendors. That work was what her CV indicated, "to be fluent with all that vocabulary so relevant to algorithms and servers and routers and bandwidth." But the vendors called me anyway, saying they could not understand her; "she's not logical," they complained. "I mean, shit fellow," I responded, "Professor Falk out of Princeton can understand her. What's your problem?"

Simultaneous with these goings on had been the arrival of the higher paid vendors, those who were essential to our survival in most ordered America. And these here types were worse than their blue-collared cousins, trying to scare me half to death by telling me all the rules and regs I was skirting and then sending me preposterous billing hours that could never be verified. And worse, they were in cahoots. The lawyers insisting on an intervention by the accountants and vice versa. All made much worse by their intimate knowledge of just how much money was flowing in from Pierre on a quarterly basis.

You get the picture: I was depleted from the battles with Horn on social and web marketing and from the various debates on the revolution with discerning apostates, and more recently from getting tied up like Gulliver with all the technicians. I was being forced to leave the wheelhouse of times past – so to speak – and spend more and more time in the engine room where I got frustrated with my own ignorance.

Imagine: this was the way I descended the escalator at night, listening to Janet and finding a seat amidst the twits, thirty minutes later, up the escalator and into the Giant supermarket where I would fill my backpack with edibles. I strolled the aisles as respite; a decompression amidst America's plenty. Even as I always bought the same items. Lugging the backpack like a donkey up a little hill, I finally settled down into my apartment where there was absolutely nothing extra – no plant or painting. So empty I could hear myself think.

Minimalist even within my fridge. A place for everything and everything had a place, with a carefully calibrated forty-eight hour turnover. Nothing got a chance for mold. I preferred it that way – just too many critical decisions to worry about the finer points of a menu.

And then finally, my work got switched off: a tumbler of scotch on my TV tray, some chunks of cheddar cheese, some saltines, then the cable news, and *Breaking Bad* or *Mad Men*...while I had my corned beef sandwich, a pickle, and some chips.

All to end by 10pm as I collapsed into a king size bed.

Not much spring in my step, those days. Even as I had already secured financing and a makeshift idea, the disinterest of the financier and the deafening silence of the experts as to the virtues of disintermediation were debilitating. Tied down by too much detail. Regaining the fat I had lost in Vermont – fat I could grab – and not yet seeing any eyeballs on the Beta version of my website, just put up by Horn.

I had known from the start that I needed to wage this war on multiple fronts and that the Internet was just one, albeit the most important. Still ahead stood the foundations that I now engaged in order to diversify funding, but more so to add sufficient credibility so as to quiet the "BtD who?" I was getting. In my dreams, I would respond, as casually as I could muster, "Well, Ford or Rockefeller or Google just bought in." And, even further, fantastically, deep down I toyed with the Trojan horse, "Yes sir, just striding into State/USAID and explaining the virtues of revolutionizing themselves. Something almost unprecedented for an American governmental agency in the history of the republic." "You can't kill them," a congressman had told me. "Once budgeted, they are bulletproof. Absent a 1929 depression, they just grow like topsy until they topple. Then like trees in a bog, they grow new roots and regenerate."

I persevered.

"And what about thought leaders?" I thought – such as those folks who discoursed on the future at such places as Davos and Aspen. If I could just get into the head of one such champion – ah the skies would open – guest lectures at Columbia – op-eds in the *New York Times*.

I surmised it was all a matter of statistics – a hundred op-ed submissions – a hundred grant applications. Eventually, someone would come calling. Finally, the ultimate frontline, right from *Mr. Smith Goes to Washington*. Yes. Congress...testimony yielding to bipartisan applause. "Yes," cried the Dems. An unengaged citizenry allows the abuse of power. "Yes," cried the GOP. Get our government out of the absurdity of developing foreign lands. I was feeling better after I had stretched out that thought...all the way to the cover of *Time*.

In that moment of reverie, I hired a familiar face: Penny. Someone older who would manage Ha and Ringlets, work on the designs for foundations, provide the particulars on why disintermediation was an historical certainty, and tell a radio station in Pittsburgh who Mr. D was and when he was available.

There she was. An ensemble of scribe, office manager, gatekeeper, secretary. Just release me, I prayed, from all the strings attached and find the research to support the unassailable intuition I bring to the effort.

But Penny was also someone I knew to be meek. Not especially indicated for the barricades. So...why in the hell? What happened to angry? Well, probably because these days I was valuing cooperative over tough. I was counting on her to be faithful to the enterprise to a fault. She had worked a few rungs beneath me in Iraq and done the trips into the badlands when asked. I never saw her without her laptop as an appendage – that and an apparent equivalent commitment to Strunk and White for which she reserved a disproportionate share of the zeal that might, in my eyes, have been put to better use at "the barricades."

Penny soon found a modest place to live, 450 feet squared in a colorless neighborhood at a good price, never spending a nickel she did not have to, and seemingly she never had to. A tentative good soul gathering the accoutrements of life, those foreign stamps for her passport. So, there she was, on the dot each morning, last to leave at night, my faithful sidekick, just approaching middle age with skin that had never suffered from too much weather, assigned to manage the Vietnamese and when possible the thin, well-rounded Graduate. "You don't have to do all these things yourself," I told her. "Just delegate what you can. Let Ringlets manage the eyeballs. Let Ha handle the vendors," I added, even as she constitutionally shrank from ordering anyone around and as her much younger colleagues took to heart the words I had said earlier about my open-door policy and walked right by her – one actually springing by her – the other keen to maintain access to me since any detachment from her work meant no continuation of her work visa, which meant back to Hanoi.

So that was the set-up just one year into my ambition. Legal now, officed now, staffed now, resided now, connected now, moneyed now, and depending on the day, armed with the most compelling of all ideas: Right Relations or as Michiko would say, "the water above."

Surcease

"Ah Surcease. Surcease, my good man," I muttered as I threw some laundry in my pack and headed for the farm. A flight from Reagan. An escape from the millennials, the exclamations and the tweets, and the mendacity of the fonctionnaires. But an escape, often troubled, in the first instance, by an uncertain departure: traffic held up by a cavalcade for a visiting dignitary, a mechanical failure within the aircraft, or by the immigrant behind the taxi wheel who did not know the way or whose GPS was down, leaving me sitting in a sweat that I would miss my flight. I felt a constant anxiety until the wheels were up, and the pilot came on to soothe me with an announcement of a direct flight into Burlington. Seemingly with no detours to Boston, Albany, or Hartford. No winds from Lake Champlain gusting over the limits, which would mean cardboard motels in other northern cities and erasing the hope of that night with Annie by the pond fire.

And then Annie was coming round the airport bend in the pick-up, the farmer incarnate, with the Schnauzer, Phil, always beside himself and yelping with joy, jumping around the cab with his stump wagging hysterically. Into the Northeast Kingdom far from the state's tax base farther south. Most of the people around these parts were poor white, all white, and nearly all poor...all the time. No, not the hollow cheeks and the limbs like vines. Rather, in the fading light with the cold descending, we would pass them, bulky in their plastic chairs between their trailers on the road that was taking us toward the dying dairy farms up close to the border with Quebec.

We made a right hand turn at the old barn that had begun to capitulate to the forces of gravity, past the silage fields, into the towering stands of Spruce, down a long dirt drive, and into the birches. I glimpsed the corrugated zinc roof, then the campfire flames blowing about in the wind off our lake where my Beiruti Hank had thrown on more logs.

Lickety split, I went up the staircase to shed the city wear for the long johns, the old army boots, the canvas pants, and army jacket. I joined Annie all bundled up with red cheeks, green wool mittens, and her pail full of vittles for the grill. Then

Annie first, unscrewed the Mason jar and took a gulp of tequila. A tradition I had told her for as long as we could handle it. Even deep into February when the snow banks around us were as high as the flames. Finally, bundling in our bed like the pilgrims I had recounted, in a cloud of homegrown as Bob Dylan and James Taylor laid us to sleep. All right in the world as the wind swirls and whistles around our thin walls.

When we had looked for a place to buy, we had just driven north in the aftermath of my work in the Middle East till we could get water of our own and a mortgage we could afford. And so we met the landowner, Violet, a tiny widow with small rooms and vinyl panels and midget toilets and a pond full of bullheads that she had been feeding for decades. "Just like Motel 6," I had said. And as for Violet, she didn't care what the market was and was not selling for one penny less than the "ask." "Anyway," she concluded. "This isn't my idea, it's my son who wants me out of here and into some damn rest home."

In the end, we succumbed to her price for fifty acres of forest and a three acre thirty-five foot deep, glacier gouged pond with nothing around the property boundaries except some pasture across the road and a struggling dairy farmer. And moose and coyotes and bear. Scat and tracks all over the place and once in a while real live ones just around a bend.

Manipulating the earth...blazing a trail around the property, up the knolls and through the swamp and across the creeks, lugging my Stihl and my bucket of essential tools. Much later, you could see me from the fire, evening coming down around me, about 100 yards off, leaving the forest now with my bucket and my saw, my beat up old army jacket, shredded and soiled, and my canvas pants all scarred with chainsaw mistakes. Slowly lowering myself by the fire, taking a shot from Annie. Holding out my bowl for her scoops of chili. Phil faithfully eating the scraps from my hand.

"Access," I would proclaim as I slumped down by the fire at sunset, bone tired. "If folks don't have access, then no one will learn what the forest has."

I filled a shed full of hand split wood and planted a thousand walnuts. Hank, Annie, and Alex were conspirators in the manipulation, all them red knuckled, pickaxing holes in spring for the seedlings or dragging in next year's firewood across the pond's ice in February.

Kept warm inside by a blazing firebox as well as by the drapes and carpets from our travels across the Maghreb – from the sandstorms in Kairouan to driving through the fogs in the Tchika pass in the High Atlas. From that birth of Hank in Hamra to Alex in Clinic Toufic. We were all bundled up in that kite of a house – just two by fours and vinyl. The wolf could indeed huff and puff and blow the house down.

I came back when I could, for the fires and the shots, for getting dog tired, deep in the forest, for bundling up under the blankets from the Maghreb – and in the spring to see the roofs repaired and the plumbing fixed and 200 more walnuts planted…thanks to Pierre.

Then with calluses and nicks from the saw blade and bruises from the hammer and aches in every joint, I had managed to insert myself into the plane back to the red line and the Arch Stone, and the surrounding bureaucracies.

The Arab Spring

It was a morning habit, along with the dregs of my morning coffee, to check the analytics, the views, and conversions for my compelling idea, as presented on the BtD website. To see into what distant corner of the world my idea had traveled and to determine if my latest post had caused a stir.

Concurrently, we were rolling up our sleeves and wading into what were called Value Propositions – basically, two to three thousand words explaining the virtues of BtD as an investment. Initially, there was some honest pick and shovel work, gathering appropriate data and applying nuance, but over time the dispatches got reduced to cut and paste of primary content and then broadcasting them to dozens of foundations with a tilt right or left depending on whether disintermediation was to be heralded as an antidote for big government or as an accelerator of citizen activism. Our vision could be played either way...and was. There were no scruples here. I would take money from the devil to redress the current danger. Perhaps already had.

So then, along with the morning analytics, there were the letters of response in a straw basket from the various foundations...both venerable institutions on the East Coast established in the main by men of industry who had wanted to assuage their sins before the Lord or by West Coast new tech tycoons who were getting closer to their legacy (those cemeteries of the hearts that would soon outlive them) and who had equally ruthless formative years.

From the dozens of grant applications we had submitted thus far at Sunderland, we did manage to get a few on the hook, so to speak, but none yet in the boat. I was learning just how tightly foundations are held. Often by families. And to what extent their donations are typically used to scratch some backs in recognition for some historical or current favor.

I was suspecting that merit was seldom the password; one needed an entry. Someone in the inner circle who will bring you past the gate. Otherwise, more often than not, it seemed that some intern opened your pitch and wrote you a kind rejection or might, under exceptional circumstances, send it upstairs to her boss with a forty word trailer, along with a bunch of others solicitations also ordained as problematic.

Then round about the time of BtD's anniversary, my office routines got swept away. Almost as fast as the gasoline had ignited on the body of Mohamed Bouzizi, I had become transfixed by Sidi Bouzid. And then quick as lightning on its heels, by Tahrir Square. Googly eyed, sitting behind that TV tray non-stop at Arch Stone, reeling off op-eds, chewing on a pizza late into the nights, taking a swig and rattling off blog posts, feeling redeemed about my prophecies of breaking borders with that lightning connection between Sidi Bouzid and the aspirations of young Arabs. I immediately rushed off to Dulles and grabbed a plane. In less than a day, I was inside Tahrir Square, hobnobbing with those who had been at the barricades. Catching the fever that I had last known at the Chicago convention in 1968 or way back when I was down in the smoking room at Suffield Academy with my Kerouac. Dancing on air, I was, amidst scores of uplifted working stiffs bringing their kids to Tahrir – getting a photo of their kids in Tahrir. When I asked them why, they told me, "So they can never forget. So my son does not see me cower before a cop again."

It was fever. Deep down I knew. When life seems better than it is. Before it reels back. I knew. Twelve years after Chicago, Reagan was in the White House, and I had fled to Paris with Annie and my dog-eared copy of "The Exiles Return."

Yes, Thermidor. The tromptromptromp of Thermidor as the fever recedes and life finds its own unfortunate equilibrium again – the cop and the cowering once again resurgent. And then the little people come crawling out of the woodwork. The pushback I was to get on the blogs: "You see, Arabs cannot do democracy." Multiplying each time as the hopes for Egypt and Syria and Tunisia were dashed consecutively.

"But from what I had read of the Directorate," I posted back, "if you project enough into the future from Thermidor, the trend also corrects to a slightly better place than we had before, notwithstanding all the intermittent bloodletting. The Arabs will have their laurels again on their own podiums. Perhaps not in my lifetime but maybe in yours and the Arab spring will have been an accelerator. Those photos at Tahrir of father and son, mother and daughter, tacked to some plaster wall in the home, will endure."

Afterward, still thrilled by a process still in progress, I went to Zahle to check in with my patron. And, of course, as was his habit, I got taken to the terraces by the Berdouni and was fed. Here my tales of the fever were summarily dismissed as childlike – equally dismissing the same movement not far from where we were dining, across the border in Daraa, south Syria, as well as my warnings that Pierre might get slammed himself given his business associations there.

Pierre had a limited definition for good. His mother was good, a Saint even. He was close to brother Moussa and to his son Elie whose leash would not be untied until Pierre was deep in his grave, which in that neighborhood could be any day. But Elie had no quarrel with him. He was soft and pleasing and trailed around like the cub follows the lion. The calculation, I supposed, was that Elie one day would graduate from his father's business on the frontiers to a more veneered livelihood as a mainstream rentier.

But outside that very tight circle, Pierre gave little quarter for good. Life was dog eat dog. To act differently was a dangerous indulgence.

The rest was as pleasant as it could be when the conversation is all one way and irrelevant to the money passing between us – mostly rants on the Shia influx in the Beka'a valley or on Iran and his disgust that America did not just use the arsenal it had. "You have to use a gun once in a while," he would tell me, "or nobody will believe it's loaded." And then he would smile as if "he oughta know," and I oughta know enough to heed him.

He sent me off with bracelets again for the family and silk ties for myself and while I demurred as much as possible, since they were all too gaudy for us, Pierre would have none of it.

But just before the car door closed on me and before the chauffeur could drive me back over the mountain to Beirut, Pierre let it drop that his Armenian pal, Serzh Sargsyan had seen no improvements in his access to United States government money ("millennium" funds blocked since 2009 by the US for election irregularities). Plunk. Just like that, dropped in my lap. It had been months earlier during one of my visits to Zahle when Pierre had whisked me along for 24 hours in his private jet to meet the president of Armenia with whom he was engaged with a massive makeover of Yerevan's city center and had told the president, as an aside but still within earshot, that "David would fix it."

My God, I had thought at the time, what other fantasies had Nizar told him? Now, with this nonsense reappearing in the back of Pierre's Mercedes, I asked myself: had Nizar been so blind to my position in life that he had mistaken the millions of US taxpayer grant money I spent – shackled as I was with its thousands of rules and regs hung around my neck – with my true worth? Did Nizar misunderstand the US so much as to confuse a step and fetch it with a mover and shaker – the Koch bros or a covert action by the White House, with a mere do-gooder? Wow, I thought, rolling down the western slope of the mountains toward Beirut and considering my sponsorship of this new green card holder, "You sure can take the immigrant out of the Levant," I was thinking, "but you can't take the Levant out of the immigrant." Nizar saw America as no more than deals: Watergate, Irangate, WMD, Gulf of Tonkin. Exclusively.

Alex Moves In

My son, Alex, was done with walking in his dad's footsteps, which had begun in 2007 when this 6'4" all American swimmer, fresh out of Berkeley, traveled to Helmand province to teach computer literacy to dirt farmers who were still dumbfounded by multiplication tables. Then on January 14, 2008, during a visit to Kabul, with his angel beside him, Alex had run right and not left inside the Serena Hotel and had slid under a desk in the business alcove and from a crack in the vanity panel had seen the Taliban repeatedly put bullets into a Norwegian colleague lying face down in the lobby before veering off toward the gym where they continued to kill.

Weeks later, he extracted to Peshmerga territory, North Iraq, where he worked in one of Nizar's emerging Internet cafes (financed by my agency) until, fed up with the contrived metrics, he shifted to a large IT company called Asia Cell where he helped them to know their market better through survey design.

So, not a geek and not yet an entrepreneur and not someone who would eat beans off the floor while he built a better mousetrap, Alex decided to try to sell his narrative to some distinguished MBA programs where for two years he could burrow into the language and the mechanics of international business and get a network before he got his hands dirty again in the marketplace. And so he moved into my apartment in Arch Stone to prepare his many propositions for acceptance and burn off all the accompanying angst each morning at 4am on the Potomac where he was the powerful stroke for a crew of eights.

We didn't see each other much. Alex was just coming back by the time I was boiling his eggs and went to bed not long after I had settled into the couch in the evenings to unwind.

On weekends, if there was a race, I would park myself on some vantage point along the shore with my binoculars and watch him compete as I had been doing since Alex was five and had won his first running and swimming races. Usually with me in the vicinity – always doing some middle aged equivalency – running in older categories, swimming in the public lanes, bicycling to rendezvous points after practices.

I had never yelled at meets nor chosen my son's endeavor. Rather, I was just always around, demonstrating my own resolve, my partnership, and in the end, and despite the shame of a father hanging near him, the boy had more than matched the father's resolve with magnificent results.

Now in Washington, I took precautions to keep my distance since Al's discomfort with my doting presence had naturally grown with age, suspicious now that when he was out on the water, his father would descend from his distant vantage points to the boathouse, checking times on the board and mingling vicariously with the other athletes. Clearly, Alex disliked me being still so close upon him, but equally he was reluctant to cast off the family infrastructure: those groceries hauled up by dad from the Giant supermarket to the apartment and the use of the company car to drive to practice.

And so, far from the Potomac, the father now worked out at night on the rowing machine in the basement of Arch Stone while pasting goals and times to the refrigerator. Willy nilly, we would share the rowing, the father hoped, as we had the running and swimming and biking of earlier years, even as my age made me a pathetic partner. The father rushing to the door that evening, to hear all about the day's race from his son, the stroke, arms out for the embrace, and having the son, in response, instead extend his finger toward a bit of ketchup on his shirt and shake his head.

And then there was the issue of how to describe him in 10,000 words for the MBA essays. Alex didn't do much free-style writing; he did analytics and concise text. So I offered some historical content that could, I hoped, stimulate his own submission. All true, nonfiction, but presuming some art. I had supplied background for the biographical essays to as far back as cycling over the Alps, as a ten-year-old, in the dead of winter. And then described the following spring careening down the slopes of Route Napoleon toward the Mediterranean.

Throwing our hands up as we had crossed the city limits of Antibes. Perhaps a bit more than the university could ever want. And Alex had confronted my approach with the instruction manual he had received from a preparatory course, indicating that I was not much help and my input would be of little value. Then, I watched him pour a scotch down. He put his face in mine with a volley of "prove it" when I tried to explain that I was just conversing about MBA's, not trying to prove a theorem. And then, Alex had his iPhone out, often to contradict my best guess with the facts.

The episode ended with me trailing off to bed while my beloved accused, "Don't want to know the truth? Do you? What's the matter, dad? Can't handle the truth?" Which, in retrospect, was probably one of the most truthful assessments of my life. I could not handle the truth; was, in fact, constitutionally unable to fathom the truth.

More often now such distress was compounded the following mornings. In frightful ways. Whereas I had always imagined the decay would be gradual, my body now seemed to be failing before my eyes, squinting still in the bathroom mirror at my ankle, at the swelling veins which would inevitably need to be ripped out. The docs had said they were leaking, aggravated by my intense rowing on the machine – those ungodly pools turning black under the skin.

USAID

As BtD moved toward its third year, the enterprise was coming to a head. Thus far I had been taking pot shots from the periphery. Those missives to the foundations, seemingly cries in the wilderness, the low circulation op-eds, and whatever modest radiation there was from the website, cumulatively, I feared, were a very small bother to the enemy.

And so one grey day in the winter of 2012, looking out onto the park across Sunderland from my alcove, I took a big breath in a sort of what the hell moment and decided to take the battle to the enemy's inner sanctum where, amidst an array of political appointments, resided one old friend. She was one of the NGO execs who had watched my work in Iraq from her desk in WDC where she had cultivated relations at the State Department and on Capitol Hill. In 2010, she jumped the fence to State and became someone the politicians could point to as NGO bred, albeit at some distance from where any rubber was hitting the road. Nevertheless, she could do "public poise and composure," and she knew who was on first in DC. She also had an adolescent's good looks and a young heart. There had been that defining moment between us on January 14, 2008, when she had rushed out after me from a conference in Amsterdam and onto the sidewalk where I was desperately trying to connect on the phone with Alex who had his phone cupped in his hand, whispering frantically, whispering goodbye, before his charge died as he was hidden under that desk in the Serena Hotel with his eyes on the legs of the killer.

Yes, I remembered. She had a good heart pumping beneath those ribs despite her infatuation with a place in the Washington firmament. She had had tears in her eyes for what I was going through.

And so I waited in her reception area with some cube dweller next to me who had just answered that he had served in Iraq – three months in fact, as it had leaked out – in the Green Zone. He allowed himself to tell me parenthetically about the incoming mortars. Three months, I knew, was the minimum to get the tick mark in his HR file for having served "above and beyond." No matter that it was in a cubicle no different from the one he inhabited now except for the fact that the steak and potatoes over there were deeply discounted. I said nothing, just nodded appreciatively at this type whom I knew to shit in his pants at the hint of any real "above and beyond."

And then Nancy had turned the corner in her Palestinian linens with the burnt orange piping and gave me a big Minnesota hug, for old times' sake. And then she was telling me that she had invited several others. Whereupon I had undoubtedly winced since I knew, alone, I could get in her head, but with the flat asses about, my pitch would be a nonstarter.

Moments later, with them seated in a circle around me, I was invited to launch, which I could do by heart with the one significant difference that this time I was daring USAID to do the unimaginable: to reform itself, to distribute its budget to American civil society. Real civil society, not just to those parasites from Big Charity, but rather to the women's rights group in Flatbush or to the Grange in Des Moines. And so went the discourse, with Nancy interrupting once in a while to smooth an edge or to make something more palatable in translation. Except for the one breakdown when the original fonctionnaire had begged to differ and had begun to reference his time in Iraq, causing me to instinctively speak over him and assert that he was never in Iraq. "Don't mistake that for Iraq," I had said and before I could pull the words back, the damage had been done. All of the phony narratives he took to bed with him each night now all publicly spoiled.

Not much later Nancy's secretary had stepped in to tell her that the Administrator needed to see her. Nancy had given me her hand and told all of them to stay where they were, to continue the interesting discussion. But as soon as she was out the door, there was a universal checking of watches. In disregard of Nancy's suggestion, they were soon floating out back into the hallways of State. In their eyes, she was little different than all political appointees, an outsider to disturb their well-padded life in the corridors until they rotated out – usually back to those private sector entities which clung to the government for sustenance.

It's like a morass, I considered, which, regardless of external interruptions, seeks and finds its own level. Despite quadrennial reviews and other such well publicized cosmetics, known among the field hands as "tinkering with the Titanic," it all sinks back to its old banks. "My God," I thought, as I pushed out past security and onto the pavement, "all you need is some sort of human instinct to tell vital from moribund." Walk into any USAID mission anywhere in the world and the moribund is thick as mud. "Principally," I was mumbling to myself in the cab, noting the driver's eyes catch me in my wrath, "because its hypothesis is no longer relevant, if it ever was. If the whole idea is all about changing their narrative to fit with ours, then God help us. Don't send the flatass I met in the reception. We are all damned if he is our narrative." At which point the driver turned slightly toward me and asked if "everything was okay." "Yeah, oh yeah, absolutely," I responded. "Just talking to myself."

That last guy out of the meeting seemed to pity me, I thought. "You know you're not going to win any friends here like that," he had said.

Pierre Arrives in DC

Slowly, in the aftermath of the "inner sanctum" event, and with other options being dimmed, I retracted more often into my own devised fanfare: the website and all its links. Alex intervened and redid it. "The better to capture you, my dear," we laughed. The visitors and the converted finally had an attractive web presence: stark images, soaring rhetoric, a call to arms. But still the demand side remained elusive. Finding those demographics in the first place. That was what Penny and Ringlets were supposed to do: get out there in the cyber universe and lead the citizens in while I did radio, TV, and print. Problem being, my problem, perhaps, but I didn't trust Ringlets enough to let her bat around the web as her chutzpah would dictate. I had told her that BtD's demographic was too old for that approach.

I told her I was not opposed to leaps of faith, per se, but there had to be some ground, somewhere, under one's feet. "Please remember," I had counseled for the nth time, "you are playing to married, married with child, 30 somethings, disposable income, who can find Liberia on a map. Not to 'anyone who signs in will get a chocolate.'"

"But my generation will create the buzz," she insisted.

"Your generation, no offense," I replied, "are charity butterflies, committed to a five buck donation for each pair of organic shoes they buy."

And then there was Penny, you remember, my ever-faithful sidekick who could trip over a twenty dollar bill and not think to pick it up.

"How about email blasts?" I asked.

"Oh no, I hate those," she said.

"But, hopefully for the last time," I scolded. "You are not typical of our market. It's not about what you like. It's about what our demographic likes."

"I don't see how anyone could like being interrupted all the time by obnoxious emails."

"You think our message is obnoxious?" I asked.

The following week, I asked her, my senior staffer, to take the girls to a mixer of sorts where a lot of advertising hotshots would be. "Just go there and mix and mingle. Find out what they would do to get eyeballs."

We all went, but after about an hour, she found me in my own particular circle and pulled me aside, the girls in tow. Arms akimbo: "Can we go now?"

"Did you tap into their minds...already?"

"Yes we tapped. We're not whores, you know."

Meanwhile, Ringlets and Ha were staring back at the table they had just left with some evident intent to return.

"Screw it," I told her. "Do what you want." I grabbed the waiter for more alcohol, and she escaped.

The next morning, hungover, I padded from my mattress to the bathroom, feeling strange in my feet, sort of like I had cardboard stuck to my soles. Bleary eyed, I turned on the light and looked at my weary face in the mirror and then instinctively down to the feet and was aghast. Somehow, overnight, they had transformed into summer squash, gross.

On Monday, I searched online for a doctor. Someone who had been to name schools and who had no reported malpractice pending and who could interview me, test me, and lay me out on the sheets for the first time since the trauma surrounding Chu Lai. I found someone and soon enough found myself gazing up into the glare with masked heads bobbing about and looking down on me like kitchen staff on a sink full of dishes. Emerging a few hours later with my leg stripped of veins and bandaged like a mummy – soon to have my legs elevated onto on my desk and straddling my computer and popping some pain killers while I tried to get lost in any emergent BtD fanfare.

One subsequent afternoon, I was jolted straight up by an email from Nizar who advised that after two years, Pierre was now coming to town. "Please arrange high level meetings."

"What is the message?" I replied. "Meetings to what end? They will certainly ask that, first thing."

"You know," Nizar replied, "Christians in Zahle."

"What about a back channel to Assad, given his murderous response to the Arab spring?" I inquired. But no sooner out of my mouth, I was thinking twice, given the reasons that such a channel existed in the first place.

So I scrambled, ungainly leg and all. In the end, DC being as blasé as it is, my requests on behalf of a billionaire – who as far as anyone had heard barely existed, being hidden as he was in those frontiers or entangled in the inscrutable confessional warfare of Lebanon – were met with a yawn. Thus I returned to the original notion of peddling something more enticing: "He can talk to Assad." Which, I knew to be treading on thin ice.

"I mean if you want access, you need to have something to sell," I told Nizar.

Thank God, I thought, for low hanging fruit; for those two congressmen who had visited me eight years previous in Kut: Wolf and Shays. They would see him – Wolf as an enduring incumbent and Shays deposed in 2008 now resurrected as the chair of the Federal Commission on Wartime Contracting. I also managed to get Pierre on the Assistant Secretary of State's agenda, given that he was one of the few who did actually know of him.

Not much of an all-star parade, but for Christians in Zahle, this was about all one could expect unless one was willing to pay for access. We would have had to set up an account with a PR firm, which I had dismissed out of hand given Pierre's usual comprehensive un-Christlike guidance when asked about Hezbollah in the Beka'a, "Fuck 'em."

And then on the eve of the event, there was another discombobulation. "Ahhh no," I screamed at the walls, alternately thrashing about furiously looking for it and then soon after for something to smash...like the TV table before me which my fist had just buckled in a heap onto the floor. It seemed I must have left the cap of one of my front teeth in my pizza and washed it down with a chaser of beer, and, worse, the first appointment on the Hill was long before any dentist could be had. I was beside myself, searching my brain for some ersatz solution, searching the cupboard for anything that I could shove in the gap...into the bathroom cabinets for anything paste like...a piece of chewing gum, even.

I left Arch Stone the next morning in pouring rain with only my collapsible umbrella for protection from the elements, hobbling down to the metro on my one good leg. I then made a similar wet trek through the elements downtown to the Mayflower where Pierre and Nizar and the limo were supposed to be waiting. Except Pierre had gone back to his room and would be late. I took advantage of the delay to hoist my soaking pant legs under the hand dryer in the men's lavatory – to the amusement of some other clients of the facility – hoping that the bulge from my leg bandages would be less apparent. All the while practicing little comments with my left hand curled in front of the gap in my teeth or otherwise mumbling through my lips.

I drew rather deep down at this point to find the wherewithal to get through the day in one piece.

In retrospect, I need not have been so scared. I should have known that folks like Wolf and Shays, in all likelihood, had to receive a dozen unusual characters a day, or they would not be in the business they were. Some of them even – over the course of the years – who arrived in clouds of talcum and cologne. They were patient as Pierre went through his diatribe about his confession facing extinction, which was duly translated by Nizar, and yes, thank God, Pierre had respected my advice, given sotto voce in the back of the limo, not to use his most colorful language in explaining the Shia incursions. He had responded, "okay, okay" as if to humor me...with a broad smile that said: "I was quite the ingénue, wasn't I?"

As it turned out, the enticing piece about citizen diplomacy – the Assad connection – never was broached. Pierre had vetoed it. He did not want that can of worms opened, not on Capitol Hill. Like millions skimmed off the hi-jacked telecom transactions in the Beka'a – a story already available on the back pages of the web.

There was lunch afterward, to which I had not been invited, strangely, for that had never happened before. I was instead dropped off at the office where I borrowed an iron from the concierge and tried to produce a crease and of course continued to practice my "hand over mouth" articulations.

State was last, and here there was less patience with odd characters and a knowledge, albeit through an American lens, of what went on in Zahle and that Pierre's brother, MP Nicholas, was on the wrong side of American support for The Future Party of Hariri. As a bad omen, Pierre and Nizar were left to cool their heels in the building's foyer for well past the appointed time – to the extent that I was getting nervous that Pierre who was not used to waiting, even before the hegemon, was going to get fed up and leave me there to explain my patron's absence.

As time wore on, Pierre and Nizar spent more time in Arabic, effectively leaving me on the edge of the conversation, hobbling over from time to time to the reception to inquire whether all was as could be expected.

Finally, an intern, very pert and tailored, appeared at the turnstile, and we were admitted – for a meeting with the Assistant Secretary's deputy since his boss "has been called away unexpectedly and conveys his regrets." Called away. "Perfect," I thought.

So, we met with the deputy who seemed less impressed than Pierre would have him be, concerning Pierre's assertion that he was representing Zahle, the largest Christian town in the Levant. Instead, the deputy veered right into the matter of America's unofficial support for Saad Hariri, implying that the Fattouches might well find it in their interest to get on board here. Which I could see, after the other indignities this billionaire had suffered in the building, was making him steam but, thankfully, instead of dealing with it the way he would with an unwelcome event in the quarry, he had managed to keep a lid on it even as the beads of sweat formed on his baldness. Still smiling, no longer the agreeable smile, but the smile that said, "If you only knew, mister. That Hariri man, Siniora…he never lifted a fucking finger to help us in the Beka'a."

As time wore on and as the dialogue continued to appear unsympathetic, almost mid-question, without any niceties,

Pierre rose and said "goodbye" to a rather disconcerted deputy, leaving me in his wake to lie about a plane to catch.

The intern immediately jumped to and took us back down past security.

It was at that moment – when we were leaving State and stepping out into the circular drive that in my relief that it was over, without significant disaster – I had sought to put my arm around Nizar who was aside Pierre and had felt Nizar duck away from my attempted embrace. Conspicuously. It was then that I believed I finally had the clarity I had been seeking for over two and a half years. Nizar's shenanigans now apparently had come to the point where they were at risk before Pierre's no-nonsense eye. Pocket change it may have been when measured against the half billion settlement on the quarry, but that part of the deal that had assumed turning US policy in Pierre's favor – absurd from the get go – was now fully in focus as such for Pierre. He knew damn well he had been humored in the first instance in Congress and interrogated in the second – and in both cases by people far removed from the world from whence he had emerged. Where violence was on his doorstep day and night. Not in the abstract but rather, not long ago, as in a sniper's bullet ripping through his left hand as he walked through town.

BtD Closes

Well, my leg healed, and the bones surfaced once again in the ankles. The swallowed cap on my tooth was replaced, and Alex had indeed helped make my compelling idea become a kaleidoscope on the screen before my eyes. Otherwise, not much had changed. I was still begging reluctant souls to see the light and getting in return: "You're right, David. USAID should be abolished, but no one here has the time or the inclination for that battle," as one progressive Senator had said. And then, alongside that, there was the growing confirmation of my suspicion that there could be no mainstream grant awards with Pierre on my Board of Directors, given his ill repute on the web. "Shit," I said, "he probably gets more eyeballs than BtD does."

So I languished like that for a couple of months, sticking my big toe into a few merger talks with other equally forlorn CEOs. Occasionally, I took the Acela north to finagle some Park Avenue visits with low level agents of Middle Eastern foundations or to sit and present before Corporate Social Responsibility types – the second bottom line, they called it – with my briefcase full of my best "value props," not unlike the Fuller brush man of my youth, trying to lay on the charm at the door. I made a speech here and there to a college crowd. Penning the occasional op-eds and as stated earlier, exploring every nook and cranny around my own website. All of it, as always, to support investments in disintermediation. To have America represented by activist Americans rather than the cube dweller I had met outside of Nancy's office.

It was somewhat of an anomaly, I had reflected one Sunday morning, laying about on my king size bed, that the compelling idea had seemingly received so little notoriety against expectations above ground, yet there could be a substrata whereby the taint of my published attacks on USAID/State and the expanding taint of Pierre on the web could circulate out of all proportion to the threat. Even allowing for a good measure of paranoia, there seemed to be an incontrovertible element of shunning. Email streams with notables abruptly halted. Appointments were postponed. Yes indeed, the landing site for BtD was certainly provocative, even disrespectable, as were the op-eds, but, I argued, didn't all of it ostensibly hearken to America's better values?

Not long afterward, about the same time crew had stopped, and Alex had been accepted at London Business School, I found myself one late afternoon, as if in a somersault, in the bathroom at Sunderland, trying to get my finger onto the prostate to stop the pain, lying there like that until I had heard the staff depart and then, stumbling back to my alcove where I had rifled through the online yellow pages desperate to discover where I could get probed professionally. "It is an emergency," I had told the answering service. Followed by a long plaintiff, "Please, Anytime. Tomorrow. Whenever." So I got one of those Medicare doctors down in the ghetto renowned for working off high volume. In his case, a credentialed doctor with a handlebar mustache who was immediately pronounced by Alex as "sketchy" – both him and the clinic I was soon to visit, conveniently located in a cul de sac in a suburban townhouse. All to end with the Trans Urethral Needle Ablation. And perhaps with the prospect of future "bundling" at risk.

Ages earlier, in our fever, I had told Annie to "burn bright" as I had proposed a life together and soon after celebrated our communion on the banks of my stream. But now the wages of burning bright were being paid. Now the moderates – the twits – would have the last laugh as they watched me struggle for a longer life, wishing I could at that moment trade a dozen brushes with war for a long spring day in Vermont. How could it be true? The awful sacrilege: the twits conscious of the better way. Those vapid moon faces peering over me as death approached, within the confines of all that I could afford – some run down VA hospital off an interstate.

One day, almost three years into the enterprise, I decided I would write Pierre. I would tell him that I could not take his money anymore. Just one more quarterly tranche to close properly, to release staff with proper notice, to pay vendors for what they had provided, to leave the web gracefully.

It was obvious now the project had been flawed fatally from the start. Any possible understanding between the sole investor and the BtD CEO had been so compromised by the Levantine and his connivances to have an impeccable American facilitate his green card at the same time he was promising sotto voce to Pierre that this wayward foot soldier for the avant garde could turn US policy in favor of Fattouche – when what was really going on was no more or less than a few discordant souls at BtD using Pierre's chump change from ill-gotten gains to scoop some rot out of America's overseas relations.

But more than that. I was wiser now and knew that one can't buy eyeballs, not in a sustaining way, and that what I had needed derived from the desperation of living off beans and sleeping on the floor – like the famous Woz in his garage. I had been allowed my cause by Pierre's money, but was too encumbered with declining energy levels and depleted brain cells and significant external interferences from my youth's original recklessness to attempt the mission again from scratch.

Pierre did not read emails, and God knows how Nizar would have translated it, so, in the end, I had sent my news to his son, Elie.

In sum, my resignation stated that I could not take his money anymore because I had never really known what Pierre had wanted despite a dedicated effort to ascertain such, so I had used my own judgment as to what I thought would be a credit to him. And then I had recited the latest cumulative analytics about conversions as a reflection of Right Relations. I told Pierre he could be proud of that – although it seemed that, finally, Pierre had little interest in Right Relations. I felt sorry.

A couple of days afterward, I called Pierre. I couldn't help myself. His English was normally very weak and often made incomprehensible with a jumbled up harangue on local issues close to his heart. I told him I had failed. "Best put it that way," I thought. I also encouraged him to read the email I had sent to his son. We had a bad connection. All I got was a faint, "I trust...ed (2 words) you," followed by some clatter and a dropped call.

Grim now, I had only the last quarterly tranche from Pierre left to close down BtD. Writing reference letters for the staff, I realized they all wanted to re-emerge as Washington twits within the existing "relief and development infrastructure," belying any original faith in the compelling idea or rather in me.

All of it ended in late 2012 with Alex and I packing up the car with what we needed to salvage (the financial records) and what we wanted to salvage (some sheets and towels from the apartment) and driving back to the farm one winter day. Three months later, the one still living and wonderful remnant – the kaleidoscopic website – was, to my grief, hacked and thus made inaccessible to viewers, first and foremost to me.

Yes, that image of polished black helmets row upon row against the chaotic aspiration of the street was now history.

BtD left no debt, mostly because I had taken no salary for most of the preceding months. Those beautiful images, described earlier, of Annie and me sitting around the leaping flames at sunset had now become the cold arctic winds rattling the walls and Annie's worried face as she declared distress before the most recent bank statements. We were once again broke, and I was older now. I counseled faith, but with my heretofore resilient good health depleted by recent events and with BtD as my last reference point, I was less confident. I could only respond that she would live in dignity and that we would not lose the farm.

PART THREE

The Last Stand

Haiti, November 2014

Preface

If you were to string my time in the Middle East together with that in Washington DC, and then with the twenty-two months in Haiti, I have been absent for most of a decade – drawn apart from my family because of the two different worlds we inhabited. While I sat waiting at dawn, cradling my coffee and smoke before pushing off into the badlands, Annie was bent over a frozen water pipe with a hairdryer in the dead of winter; while I was regaling an audience about disintermediation, she was watering the hundreds of walnuts – bucket by bucket. Differences that often were too great to bridge by that thin line of communication at night's end.

Haiti. Chosen because of a shared time zone with Vermont and direct flights from Port au Prince to Montreal and enough salary to pay the premiums on a Whole Life policy. So, I was definitely on the downward slope. An ignominious retreat, if you will, from the "captain in the swirl." Yet I was still short of the gummy old fart staring blankly at the tree line from the back porch.

I was a small boss now of a messy program, mop in hand, cleaning up after the UN. You read about us. In our prime stirring up movements; now stragglers. My body has started to ossify from sitting behind monitors too long, skin loose on the bone, ass sore from all that bumping around in the Mornes (foothills and mountains). Every so often, I made a muscle so as to confirm some residue of vitality. This ending, then, documents the last legs of an Avant Garde in late 2014.

Rosy Fingered Dawn

It's a routine, notwithstanding some variables, meant, as defined, to limit the options. A very tight, closed system, a careful conservation of energy. Beginning with rosy-fingered dawn and the crowing of the roosters outside the squatter shack below me, I then, perhaps, stretch the arms and legs, the vigor of which depends on how I fed myself the night before or the troubles I took to sleep with me. Then, I explore about the nightstand for my glasses, there among last night's book, a tin can with a butt in it, the base of the lamp, a pack of cigs, a disposable lighter, and my most valuable asset – the cell phone, telling me the pace at which I need to move for the next hour, and then soon after giving me a preview of what the world has in store for me. After a few minutes, I put it aside on the bed sheet. The thirteen pigeons outside my window pleading ever louder, for me.

I am off the bed. I make the short walk in the twilight to push the button to green on yesterday's coffee, now thick and potent from evaporation. Back to the dresser in the bedroom to get my pill. It's the pill that has allowed sufficient digestion since forty-seven years ago when a twisted piece of metal tore out a meter of bowel – part of that same incident that had crippled me for a couple of years with Causalgia. So, down the hatch with it, aided by a swig from a jug of juice and water. Toast in the toaster, tub of butter beside it, cereal in the bowl and now placed under the water cooler, advertised as potable through reverse osmosis. My daily gruel as I wait for the toast to pop, standing over it in my skivvies, bowl and spoon in hand. "Toast up, David," I still talk a lot to myself. Shave some butter onto its black surface, there to melt while I now move back to the one chair in my bedroom to spoon up the remaining cereal. Bowl into sink. Quick march into toilet where I activate the shower – three minutes it will take to get hot. Down the toast and then into and under the three shoots of water remaining in the old corroded head. Very quick and careful showers since October 16th, 2010, when the United Nations brought the cholera microbe to Haiti.

Then the preference is for short black cotton socks, given the "chaleur" and the welts it gives to aging Anglo Saxons. Over them, not less than khakis, of course, for "the Avant Garde of

Western Civ," together with the long sleeved cotton shirt rolled up to the knobby elbows.

Brush the almost absent hair and slip on the cowhide loafers. Grab the cell, the cigs, the empty can and slide them down the kitchen table. Then to the plastic container of Miguel rice, about turn, past the table, out the door, and onto the balcony overlooking the squatters hooch and now, twenty-two months into my assignment, crowded with frantic pigeons. I throw them a few handfuls and then retire the container to the top of the fridge. I pour the coffee, put the cell in my breast pocket, and in a kinda tricky maneuver carry the coffee, cigs, and can with one hand while I drag the kitchen chair outside with the other, placing my feet ever so carefully so as to avoid the pigeon muck all around me. Tin can now on the railing, alone now with my piping Rebo, thirteen beaks a pecking, and a panavista down the hills to the bay. This morning, I see, I have just enough time for one cup of coffee and two smokes. I also note that the newly born chick in the pot-plant is still alive.

Glorious

I, as a smaller personage, now lived much of what I had refused to accept in years past. Spools of concertina wire cemented onto the top of the cinder block walls around me. A guard with a sawed off shotgun who slept through his watch. And nowadays often hearing myself with a bored disdain as I made my increasingly stale advisories: "They don't understand," I said to those few remaining acquaintances I could collar. "They think the problems are bloated bellies and flies in the nostrils. But mostly the problems are these," I told them. "A young man in a uniform, salaried at bare survival, no schooling, three kids and two rooms in the bidonville. No 'upward' or 'out' for him or his like," I said. "No, there was only the web of his extended family to save him from collapse or a wild attempt to risk the sea for a clandestine entry into the great promise up north. Can break your heart," I told a thin coterie. The accident of birth was how I described it to them. The guard in his dead-end and my son Alex now on his way to graduation at London Business School.

Yesterday, I had given the guard some gaily colored cupcakes for his newest born. In return, the guard had showed me a dog-eared photo of his family.

Except that, alone at night, I often took it further. Where had my fortunate birth gotten me last night? The throbbing in that skein of veins around my skull, awakened by rising digestive acids from a subconscious entwining of logical frameworks with other current anxieties, fading, shifting and then reappearing. Goals, objectives, results, outputs, outcomes, indicators, and other diabolical development metrics squirming like worms in a can. All causing me to become too distraught around midnight. Strange, that what had served in Iraq to keep me sleepless – fear – was now transforming into hate. Wide awake, propped up on a pillow with a smoke lit and full of hate for those – my multiple bosses – who would tell me how I now must develop folks in God forsaken lands. That is to say – how to invest in the guard so that he could have what I now profited from. The guard who was just now crawling out of his watch-tower and waving good morning to me. Owing another day of pay, so to speak, to the kissing cousins of the aforementioned "development nits." Those would be the well credentialed "security nits" who stand arms akimbo, straddling the fear that is supposed to keep us all safe. In my particular case, to keep me as far removed from the Haitian people as possible, yet still technically in Haiti.

Eyes skyward, a sight quite brilliant enough – magnified by Rebo – to catapult me away from the pigeon muck and depression and arrest me, rejoicing, recalling what my mother had exclaimed on such mornings. "Glorious." Glorious blue skies, high above the smog hiding Port au Prince in the bay. Sipping my Rebo, improving my attitude by the sip, the immemorial pleasure of coffee and tobacco, the rat-a-tat-tat of the pigeons feeding and the barely audible yearning of the new chick in the pot plant. The sound of the squatter man below breaking rocks. All day lifting rocks from beside him and slamming his iron mallet into them to make filler for the walls of the grand house taking shape nearby, sitting on his pile of work not far from his tarp and tin shack, the scant shelter for him, his wife, three teenage daughters, and a little boy.

Manman nearby washing clothes in a plastic tub full of rainwater and then laying them out on a wall to catch the rising sun. The boy poking about for insects on the periphery of his father's rock pile. And the three daughters, buckets on head, in brilliant skimpy skirts, bringing the gravel and sand down the slope to the laborers. Occasionally stopping on the way back if the sound on the guard's radio so moved them to dance awhile with their shadows. Unconcerned with the old "blan" on the balcony who now is in the process of a last appreciation of the glorious sky before picking up his can and smokes and cup and pulling the chair after him back inside.

It was four steps up, off to the side of the kitchen table, to a unique little platform where the world came to me. Two monitors, a printer, scanner, UPS, keyboard, mice, a tangle of cables, and headsets. When I began in this business, I ran down the shattered streets of Beirut to drop off the mail pouch, usually with only seconds to spare. "The big dump," my colleague Tim had called it. A week's worth of mail with otherwise only the rare dash down to the Commodore to send or receive telexes. There had been no reliable landlines. You could pay someone at central to make you a priority or you could, as my organization had done, hire a disabled coffee boy to dial all day, repeating the number for hours with his finger until he would cry, "Mister David."

As I began the process to get online, I got waylaid, my attention drawn to a precious icon on my desktop. I was going back in my mind again – more often these days – recalling her. Yesterday, Annie had sent me the latest chapter for my memoir on Lebanon, a work in progress now for over thirty years. Like a dog with a bone, we agreed. Countless nights in lumpy and often unwashed beds across the span of a score of countries, propped up with my legal pad. At first, desultory. Attending to a bug bite, making some foolish doodle, taking a piss until I insisted I make a sentence. And that is how it always happened. Then another sentence, warning myself not ever to make any course corrections – just make sentences. And indeed, despite the varied circumstances, it was medicine for the spirit, the heart started pumping and the fingers started galloping without any concern

for any limits – neither punctuation nor grammar nor reason. I
got very excited even in those dreary rooms in God forsaken
places. Until the heart had done all it could and tailed off. At
which point, I flipped the switch, rolled over, and hoped for
sleep. Thousands of these pages over thirty years got stuffed in
my bags. Eventually to be removed when I finally made it home
and soon transcribed and packed in a suitcase for some future
editorial treatment. Which, fearing death more as I approached
seventy, that future had become now. Haiti – 2014.

And so, below, was the start of it, the icon that had pulled
me in on this glorious Haitian morning – the first such
transcriptions in 1981 and only now, as an old man, with the
clock running down, receiving some editorial scrutiny. It had
been in the middle of Lebanon's civil war, Annie waiting in
Suffield, several months pregnant.
Preceded, as you, my dear reader, may remember, by that
good Doctor Benjamin Whitcom who had rescued me from my
life in the basement at my parents' house. After which, I had left
Suffield for many years and had traveled to Africa for what I
called my "recuperative wanderings." Eventually quite wasted
from a host of intestinal diseases, I had returned home and
started a business that had soon become large – ungainly large.
Unbridled growth, thin-thin margins, taut nerves...till she, the
fundament and the firmament, had appeared in a tequila haze one
Friday night and I was spirited away, head spinning, to Paris to
do God's work by virtue of the ballpoint on the pad and the
indigo on the bond. Perchance to see His Hem. Wheels up it was
as the whole entangled enterprise crashed below us. Yes, her red
hair flaming alongside my child's passion to see His Hem...and
so yes, within a year I was becoming as mad as I had been at
neuropsychiatric and was again cradled into my parents' home as
the destruction we had fomented earlier circled us with a
vengeance...until, figuring on a last stand, I answered the ad in
the *New York Times* and upped and went to Beirut. To the civil
war in Lebanon – as a tiny piece of America's toehold in the
Middle East. In my case to dole out some surcease.

And so, my first scribbling as an Avant Garde began,

172

feeling that beyond my so-called charitable acts, there was a more ambitious notion worth transmitting.

The Avant Garde – Source and Origin, Lebanon, 1981

There it was, the fat manila envelope, sitting on her desk – her two very sculptured hands, glorified with a brilliant polish, protecting it. Now looking up at Tim and me then saying, "No, no, no. You can't see what's inside until Mr. Jack opens it first."

Wrapped up in her own conceit as she was, she risked, here, going too far. I mean these were war weary Americans suffering from too many incoming at night and muzzles in the face and trying to make our backs small. Inside that fat manila were undoubtedly letters – some affection from home that would be taken somewhere private, certainly not in front of my Lebanese assistant, George, to be read and re-read, probably each day until the next pouch arrived.

And there were these sculptured hands blocking the pouch and the pursed lips before our stare. Surely, I was hoping, she had to see that Tim was only one wrong word away from going crazy – his former sidekick not long buried – and that I was not too far behind him. Finally, his long, thin arms went skyward like a ref at a football game calling a touchdown, and they sort of paused up there, just under the ceiling fan, and now I saw fright in her eyes. Tim's hands fluttering up there and then, like a guillotine, they came down on the pouch, barely missing her hands, giving her barely a split second to snatch them away. And so now it was Tim's bony hands on the manila with him staring point blank at her and saying in a tremulous voice, "Don't fuck with me." And she pushed her chair back and emitted such a heartrending gasp that the staff now entering must have thought that Tim had exposed himself.

For an instant, action was suspended. It was a scene I won't forget. Tim still leaning over her desk with his hands on the pouch – she with her hand covering her mouth giving the appearance of a woman in shock – with the semi-circle of staff around us. And then she put both hands on her face and began sobbing. Before which, Tim remained unmoved. The staff still not budging. He ripped open the envelope, fished in, and brought out a few letters – took one himself, handed me a couple, and dropped the pouch on her desk. Then he walked out.

After a while George went over to her still sobbing, albeit less dramatically, and handed her a box of tissues. He said something to her in Arabic, and she responded with shaking hands as well as an extended outburst, interrupting this wail from time to time to quite carefully pronounce the word "fuck."

Then George put the box of tissues, now half consumed, beside her and left – the others taking his lead – with me abandoned – quite confused about my next step. I mean only a few minutes earlier I too had stood, looming before her. But as a new man, I certainly had no interest in getting on the wrong side of the gatekeeper, so to speak. But it was more than that. Anyone could see she was a poor show. A rather little person with a small life, punctuated each day for six years now by her daily course across the hazards of the green line. I gathered up the discarded tissues and put them in the trash. Then returned and put my hand on her shoulder. Her eyes were red, and her makeup had smeared. At that instant, looking up at me, she was very much the aging widow. She was telling me, almost in a whisper, "Jack will hear of this." Then she wiped her eyes and nodded as if in confirmation of what she was about to say. I leaned in. "Fuck," she said. "He used 'fuck' with me. No one can use 'fuck' with me."

A half hour on, Jack had yet to materialize, so I left early for lunch with the precious missives folded in my front pocket and headed toward, as far as I knew the only sanctuary left in Ras Beirut. A university green, unmarked as yet by craters or smashed walls, still somehow maintaining an aura of calm and deliberation.

So these are the precious missives we take away with us – as we hide from work and coworkers. Here there is no impatience for message. Rather, we prolong the savoring, the turnover of each word. The envelope develops increasingly worn folds as we return it to our pockets over the week, in the bed at night, on the pot at work.

But also, unfortunately, and notwithstanding the letter as affection, other news also got embedded there. Discordant news that amidst the affection could trouble us.

Annie explained that my father, Henry, was changed. Permanently – she wrote. "He hasn't shaved since you left for Lebanon and looks, I'm sorry to tell you this, like a bum. He has put a lawn chair in the driveway. At the end, near the road and sits there all day in the same Hawaiian shirt and shorts and waves at all the cars passing by. Not a normal wave, however. He stands up and bows with his arms outstretched like the movies have the slaves doing to Sultans. And," she went on, "he doesn't come in to pee. He just turns around and goes on the driveway with the stream running against his shoes and out onto the road. I mean, my love, I know how difficult it must be and we hear about it on television all the time but I guess I feel you should know about your father. It's not good, my love. Yesterday, Helen had to go out and get him to zip up his fly which he had forgotten to do and he called her a 'bitch.'"

I could imagine my Aussie mother, probably haunted by the advice, a generation back, from her mother about the bad sense, not to mention bad taste, to marry this 5'8" salesman from the Bronx. She, of Crosby shipping. She, of the great schooners that had plied the Pacific, marrying the boy, whose divorced mother made ends meet by clerking at the County Trust. She, who dressed for dinner; he, who pasted stamps of faraway places while his mother relieved her swelling feet in a tub of hot water.

I put the pages down. I imagined my mother as stoic. She would, I knew, not be ashamed. She had been brought up never to be ashamed. I could hear her. "No, of course not. He doesn't know what he's doing." And then, always, the assertion. "He was a good man, your father. He lived for you children."

She was, I believed, honorable. For better and worse, an unquestioning Victorian who was taking Henry's dishonorable ending as both painful and as a further affirmation of her own steadfastness.

Annie went on, writing on some practical matters. She was doing her best with the bills, but Henry was in another world and Helen, "frankly, doesn't have a clue." Annie went on to write, "The lawyer says, given Henry's condition, it is unlikely the courts would support action against him and Helen but technically or legally or whatever (he doesn't talk so as I can understand it all, my love) if the suppliers can't get everything from us, then they can go after officers – and as you know somewhere along the line Helen was made an officer.

"As for us, well I guess you know the worst. I call the lawyer – it seems like every other day – but it seems he's out most of the time or that he really wants to talk to you but I explained that those phones in Beirut are all out of order.

"Our house did finally get sold by the bank but it seems they took a big chunk of it so there isn't too much left over. The lawyer said he'd write you about this. And then I paid the lawyer with your Army disability check and we'll just keep handing this over to him, unless you say otherwise. And I guess that's about it. Your paycheck didn't get deposited yet so I called them at N.Y.C. They seem nice but still no deposit," and here she had put in a big exclamation mark.

"Don't worry about me and baby Hank. The doctor says we are both doing well. Of course I don't tell him that we are going to Lebanon soon. I don't really tell anyone since I've already had a couple of calls here – one from someone who used to work for you – who yelled at me and said she knew damn well that you and your sister had cooked this whole bankruptcy up just to make a bundle and that if she didn't get every cent coming to her she was going to the police. So you see my love I'm staying pretty mum about leaving.

"That's about it. I miss you so much with that war all around you and pray at night you will stay safe. We love you but I trust you know how to take care of yourself. You are so tough. The way you survived Vietnam and then those horrible hospitals and then Paris, I just know you will be OK.

"That really is all. Since I have to get to the post office before it closes so this can get to New York for the pouch. I love you so much and just don't want even one more little scar on you and will be there next to you the minute you tell me."

"It was the devil throughout," I thought. Like in Paris, I remembered – our favorite retreat at the time I was being nursed – that small park behind the Rodin museum. *Ugolino* was there and it always cast a spell on me. In the letter, I thought, there was a cannibalism going on. I mean it seemed as if each of us had sharp teeth buried into the next of kin.

I was where I had to be. Not exactly this war, but some rough equivalent. Another day or two under the willow would have meant both my mother and wife at my throat. Here, as related to them by local television, I was being heroic. Which is such a condemnation. I mean all that garbage after Vietnam – the various get well letters from third graders. The shit about "our boys in Vietnam" when over there we all knew that most of those "boys" were shoveling shit in some rear area or playing volleyball...or even the few who were really out there were either enthralled with the opportunity to kill some "dink" or doing everything possible to get released.

Anyway, if the news anchors said I was heroic then that was that. Christ.

Her letter certainly kept me longing to be the object of her adoration. She was, in her words, "always there for me." Alive still. Such thoughts kept me close company. The pages scattered next to me on the mattress while I blew smoke rings toward the ceiling. On the seat beside me at traffic jams. On my bench in the university grounds.

It wasn't a letter I could respond to quickly. I kept going over it and eventually got pen to paper, but only hours before our pouch went out. The response was, by then, necessarily short. I mean absent tracing my desire onto the page – à la Henry Miller – what else was there? Some small advice about dealing with the lawyer, which I knew to be futile given the distance between his wiles and her disposition. Some more threatening words for a situation that had so reduced my dad. A re-articulation of my several dreams for baby Hank.

And always scratching my head to put down something positive – seeds of hope – as Catholic Relief Services called their small investments in God-forsaken places. One such seed being the evident remission of the earlier madness associated with the "mad hunt in Paris for His Hem." No, thank God, it seemed from the instant that the creation of Baby Hank was confirmed, that particular devil had scampered off. So now I also mentioned that, along with my advices and threats and dreams.

As for her coming over, I wasn't ready for a decision. Dimmed as they sometimes were, hers were the only eyes and ears – the only faithful eyes and ears I should say – available to report in from that front. And then there was the issue of safety for a pregnant expat. I had nightmares about one of those sharp-shooters on the green line putting a round right through her belly. I suspected that for most American heads of household, this reality would not have even been discussed. But for me, for us – including Baby Hank – there was the contract for myth hanging over us. At the end of the day this pressure was and would be the compelling force. The ambition that refused "plain" work – and insisted on "heroic" instead.

And, to be specific, Myth now, maybe not this week, but soon, demanded they come to Lebanon. Baby Hank would not be born amidst the rather grimy story of family ruin in an American suburb. She would be born amidst war in the Holy Land. This was the understanding. This dramatic birth was to be the continuation of that brave, 5'8" salesman from the Bronx and his pursuit "down under" of his Helen – she, of Crosby shipping.

Scanning the Web

And so this long moment had produced a few precious reflections. Gazing up into the moving blades of the ceiling fan, I was out of Haiti and back to when Annie's and my future was born.

Resigned, I typed the passwords. There, past the first gate, the various devils were hovering. Putin, Clapper, Beck, and other frightening newsmakers who peddled fear of our extinction on this worldwide billboard – framed by preposterous breasts offering to teach you Spanish and handfuls of fatty tissue asking to be removed by some snake oil or another. All thrown my way by the unfathomable algorithms working relentlessly to raise my remaining hormones – to draw me in and "have me spend a little dime" to regain some youth.

Then, from front page to sports page, tentatively. I would circle around the site, knowing the news could bring me down. An almost impossible situation when the pennant began to appear on the horizon and the Giants were still in the thick of it. My inheritance. My dad dropping me at school on his way to work, chewing his fingernails as the West Coast ball scores came through to us on WTIC.

Next stop, my personal account. The subject lines of which I had been aware since the break of day. My son's and daughter's uneven march toward…I could never finish the thought. "Options" is what I had told Alex and Hank. "You'll have choices. Moonbeams home in a jar." I had repeated back in those wonderful early days. The nightly recitations, "In Xanadu did Kubla Khan" – and then the family striking up again to shout "would you like to swing on a star" – or with a great pause for emphasis – "would you rather be a mule?"

"He Haw," baby Hank would yell, scampering around the house. "He Haw. He Haw."

So, no mule. That had been decided by birth. Constitutionally incapable. But moonbeams? Well, I knew, no one had mentioned moonbeams in years. No one had held hands around the dinner table for grace since then either. Seemingly, I had spun a narrative that had not survived. Or maybe I thought, on a good day, it might still happen after my own demise. After all, I had bought them Giants jerseys for Christmas. I had reminded Hank of her "Black Cars and Mad Rivers" – her first great poem. And I still talked to Al about "going for the wall" – those last five meters of the 200 butterfly when his child's heart had been ready to explode through his ribcage.

I continued to peruse my personal account. I was learning to shut my trap these days and persist, hoping vaguely for a belated payback. A plot in the heart of those I left behind. I remembered better each day how I had not given my own father the time of day – not even at the funeral – but how now Henry was getting into my heart more and more each minute. His soul – what I could make of it – was causing what, I guessed, people called love.

It made a little ping – the business account – each time a new mail flew in. HQ was stirring. What I had seen at dawn was multiplying. Nothing from friends this morning. In actual fact, I had no definition for friends. I had people I had traveled with, eminently replaceable with the next traveler who happened to sit next to me on the train. A cast of characters in a potpourri of events.

The dread was growing. There would be no more diversions after the last lick at Annie's photos from the farm. Photos of the alternative. The trails, the pond, the walnuts, the black cherries, in various stages of death and rebirth, along with assorted tales from her of life in the Northeast Kingdom of Vermont. I guessed better health lay up there. Principally with a splitting maul and a pickaxe, blueberry pancakes and meat grilling over the fire on the banks of the pond. And an occasional deep sleep in sheets washed in well water from 150 feet underground.

Big breath. Click on the business account. Scan the table for significant incoming. This process was my current humiliation. The vocabulary of giving. So false, I would think. The sentiment, the act, all reeking of asymmetrical relations. By now, thirty-five years in the trade, I knew most people gave because they needed to for their own well-being far more than in response to the need demanding it on the receiving end. Or if it was some government insistence on charity, it was no doubt doing it, as Colin Powell said famously, as a force multiplier. Hard for any man worth his salt, I had concluded, to earn his money from this business.

But, it had gotten us around the world, Annie, Hank and Alex. A constant shower of learning, wandering amidst the diversity of humankind and rubbing shoulders with my ilk, "the have-nots" as we were called. A dirt floor, a shack, a glass of sludge, a smoke. A pale suburbanite making company with every creature on earth, most in some approximation of a hovel. And my work, all salaried. And all salaried tax free.

I saw now on the screen that I was invited to a meeting. A conference, a reunion, a workshop, you name it. Ardent young expatriates in therapy, it seemed. Working themselves up to some righteous position on this or that issue of injustice – but equally, these days, I bemoaned, ardent about work/life balance, meaning weekends on the beach. Part and parcel, I was informed, of the professionalization of the industry.

So I persisted. Twice their age. Sat ramrod stiff, the old loquacity now in check, realizing that very few had any interest in a presence from the past. Contra-indicated for their therapy. I felt like they were the pigeons on my balcony, pecking like mad, and I was just sitting in a cloud thinking of the farm and how to pay for it. Soon I would be crisscrossing the great swarms of the city – Wolfe's pullulations – with a smartphone and a little plastic briefcase. Sales and Marketing, I called it – no different from Henry – as I pushed out in search for a piece of the action.

Density

Like a lot of kids, I had been drawn to the dynamics of centripetal and centrifugal since the time we would windmill buckets of water in the summertime – long before I had sought to figure it out. "It" being that sashaying between the grave and the fugitive, as I had first described it when curled up on my pillow on a hardwood floor in an attic near Metro Cadet with my paramour nearby as succor – soon to embark on my treacherous endeavor. She did, after a while, leave me for consultations back home and by the time she returned, I was quite nuts, pretty much petrified, staring blankly at the pool in Concorde with the only consolation for my pain being that I had discovered a vérité, as I had confided to my love: That the fugitive and grave were not antagonistic, as I had thought, but rather they were made from the same stuff. Indistinguishable. Much later – in fact just a few months ago, here in Port au Prince – I had this vérité corroborated during one of my bedtime strolls with one of my favorite authors, Dr. Frank Close. A learned physicist who had chosen to educate folks like me with his primers on the Void. Which, by my reckoning, was where those who presumed to develop others should begin. A Quixotic notion, if there ever was one, I chuckled, as I picked up my plastic briefcase and descended to Jean Claude and the pickup that would soon release me from my cage, an expression Jean Claude found quite amusing, and out into the swarm. The swarm, I reconsidered, as Jean Claude took the truck through its gears. Wolfe's pullulations. Those millions of souls streaming on pavements, on subterranean trains, tramping across the Brooklyn Bridge. And the anthropologists' assertions that such densities were essential for cultural dominance and that instigators from Henry Ford to Thomas Edison radiated from that. So I had my old face pressed against the windowpane trying to fathom this tropical swarm. Four million now in Port au Prince. A different can of worms from Wolfe's – those sepias I had seen of New York's streets 100 years ago. Sure, the multitudes were here. But languorous by comparison, selling goods off almost no margins. A tinker's pushcart in New York 100 years ago, in Haiti meant most often sitting all day behind a small pile of mangoes surrounded by all the colors of the rainbow – not the great greys of Northern cities. There was, of course, the constant equivalent hunt for a penny, the cheap death, the vermin, the epidemic, whirling your business in a bag and flinging it to where it no longer had any association with you. A helio, they called it here. And the hogs, groping in the rubbish. But no chill wind from the Hudson across Manhattan to the East River. Rather, suffocating, thick air. A dust bowl, the cinderblock and zinc stretching up the barren hills upon which the sky cracking thunderstorms descended and would flush anything not tied down into the bay. The elites just hung up there above the zinc line in their splendiferous circumstances, a cool passion fruit cocktail in hand, a million flickering candles beneath them at dusk.

Down there, I knew, it was anything goes. Not even the veneer of the Irish cop. Warrens of dark folk in dark circumstances. Those 200,000 were crushed by the tremblement de terre on January 12, 2010. Mornings, these perishables emerge, more often these days marching against the President with only America's occupation force, MINUSTAH, holding the line. Circumspect as well at Kanaval and Ra Ra when great flamboyant, voodoo laced, Dahomey sourced, vibrant, liquored up citizens dance by.

No. I gazed down the road at a thousand vendors on their tiny margins. Not NYC, but centripetal nonetheless. The countryside was emptying out, pouring into these dark circumstances. Could creation and productivity alight from this? Alight from the anthropologists' "density." Even as it differs so from Wolfe's streams of grey souls that threatened at the time to tear the very system down by cold design and cold will as a prelude to re-creation. No record of that here, I mused. Here, it was rather like watching oil dance in a frying pan: erratic, hot as hell. A chronic molecular disturbance.

"One hour," I told Jean Claude as I left for the container. Temporary housing since the earthquake, for the Government's Minister of Health.

Ministry of Health

This here container was all quite anomalous. In the so-called "less developed countries," hierarchs tend to dote on imperial trappings. Massive desks (often on raised platforms), a bell or buzzer for immediate service, one or two televisions that broadcast uninterrupted during any and all audiences, a sycophant who comes and goes, whispering confidences in the Minister's ear or placing a document before him for his purview and approval. While you, as supplicant or solicitor, persist with your request for a permission – typically to provide charity to those downtrodden within the Minister's jurisdiction.

So, I climbed the wooden stoop and proceeded down an aisle past the secretaries and their miniature desks all pressed together in a row against the side of the windowless container and waited, chatting with this last secretary who had the designated authority to allow further access. Soon enough, she got the call and a laissez passer was given. Now, I passed through a metal door behind her into an equally narrow container at a right angle to the one I was in, past a metal frame bookcase, a silver plated tea set and onto a rather plump Administrative Assistant, compressed behind her desk. Above her stared the likeness of the President and on her right, another door, presumably to the Minister's office. A smart phone in her ear and a tablet on her desk. Three collapsible chairs, one of which I took. I perused my own incoming. She finished. I began tapping out my three fingered responses, glancing over from time to time to smile. She was pressing her hand over her hair, stretched tightly back to a black bun about the size of a pin cushion, smiling back. I kept tapping. She took another call. Something to do with lunch.

"Sorry," she said, "that was the First Lady."

Then came my inkling...then the shame gathering fast

within me. Some quick thinking too about extrication. I started to tiptoe into it without the usual exaggerated address. She was looking amused. Screw it, I told myself and took the leap, "I thought you were the Minister's secretary. I feel like such a dope."

"Well, what can I do for you, David?" she asked, looking for all the world like a turtle, settling back, bemused, and retracting her head. So I showered her with "Madame Ministers" and got my questions asked for which I got pleasant but non-committal answers – and as the subsequent days rolled on, no answers to my emails, which concerned an all-expenses paid junket to Los Angeles for her and her coterie as keynoters before the Hollywood crowd on the urgency of an American donation for the 8000 dead and 800,000 infected from Cholera. An opportunity, I learned later through subsequent visits and emails that would be postponed indefinitely since as President Martelly's team knew well: Cholera is bad for business, specifically tourism, and "open for business" was the very shaky platform on which they all stood.

So there she was. The face of all that clogged the system. Madame Eboutillage. Sitting in her makeshift circumstances until the US government had finished the new digs appropriate for a Minister. Health, with a pitiful share of the national budget, a raging epidemic (brought there by the UN) and every Tom/Dick/Harry international charity crying out sanctimoniously about the absence of public funds ever getting past her desk for impoverished health centers across the country, or for critical medicines for the victims of cholera, or simply elbow grease and cleanser in all the catchment hospitals while the elites above the zinc line, they alleged, crowded around the Minister for the inevitable emoluments. And she hollering back, in full-page announcements in *Le Nouvelliste*, about the countless cadavers of projects begun back in the days after the earthquake when Tom, Dick, and Harry's hands were flush with cash. When Haiti had been a proving ground for any project a lame brain US citizen or celebrity could concoct without even the courtesy of informing her. Now, she was proclaiming they would be taxed. Taxed until they left Haiti.

Next Stop...Customs

I had begun my effort for duty free imports a week before with my first elucidation on the correlation of "dignity," for adolescent boys who had so recently seen their parents crushed like so many eggshells, to my T-shirts now sitting in a dusty depot in demurrage. Picture me here leaning forward for emphasis, "while they may bed down on canvas cots and clean themselves with poisoned water, I have never met a Haitian adolescent yet who did not prize looking smart. No," I continued, "not a penny to their name and bereft of parents, but God forbid a ragged shirt or, for that matter, stepping out without an aura of bootlegged l'eau de toilette." At which point, Monsieur Labonté slowly rubbed his eyeballs, and when he removed his hand from his face, it was as if to say, "Spare me. Please." And then the grin as if between friends who were both in on a joke.

So Monsieur Labonté was a "gro moun" in the local parlance. In mine, "the lanky pitcher who knew the game." "You again," he had laughed each time I had broken past his gatekeepers with a new development in the case – yet again another revised airway bill, held on high.

Monsieur Labonté. Impeccable cuffs, a gold adornment on his wrist, yet seemingly above the fray, even though I could not imagine that airport customs was not enmeshed with temptations. I sensed he was quite entertained by my old white man's insistence that there must be a way. With my being careful never to suggest the actual fastest way since I knew that any chips I had in the game were laughable. And would a man of such easy humor ever dare to do covert business with an international "benevolent" who claimed right on his side in all such matters?

So anyway...what was the game we shared? Here it is:

The manufacturer has an overstock of T-shirts and would like a tax write-off. So it values them at full market price and donates them to a charity. The enterprise gets good publicity as a "caring" organization. Or "giving back to those in need" as they like to say. And a dollar for dollar tax exemption.

The airline then accepts them and puts them on a plane, which has empty space in the hold. They also value that space at market rates and then claim that as a tax exemption – while they also advertise their good deed among the public.

The charity then accepts the T-shirts because they can be included in their annual report as "overseas relief" and thus added to their bottom line as "program value." This process serves to reduce the ratio of admin to program costs, which is measured by industry watch-groups and subsequently allows the charity to allege that it spends less than 10% of its donations on administration costs. "90% of all you give goes to the needy overseas," they proclaim on their website.

One fine day, the goods arrive in the airport depot in some God forsaken country, which, in turn, taxes them; in many cases, at the same rates as if they were commercial imports. The charity pays the tax and assigns that cost as "program costs" as well. Some charities that have no spare cash try to negotiate the tax downward. Thus the tale of my adventure above. The trick here is that the local government has you "coming and going" since if you dig in too hard and too long during the negotiations for the best price/tax, you will exceed your free storage limits (usually twenty days) accorded the airline cargo. After twenty days in Haiti, the daily rate is 300 dollars a day.

If and when you liberate the cargo, you offer it to the orphanage, which may find it "inappropriate" (such as one delivery I received of sports bras to the Shia heartland in Iraq) or the wrong sizes (such as a container of American men's large footwear to Vietnam). Thus the option for our orphanage: to ignore the agreement with the donor and sell the T-shirts in the local market and use the cash for what God only knows – antibiotics or crucifixes.

Needless to say, I could have avoided all this venality by simply using a fraction of the money spent on import taxes to teach computer literacy for the kids in this impoverished orphanage.

On this particular day, Monsieur Labonté and I had managed to push the ball forward. He would apply a different tax rate to the T-shirts. "But please get me another airway bill which calls them something else. Textiles are our biggest export here;

you don't want to take away jobs from Haitian workers, do you David?"

"But these are free," I argued. "The orphans wouldn't have them at all if they had to pay."

I had begun to leave and Monsieur Labonté, now beside me, ever so slightly nudged me toward the door. "Bring me the new airway bill and I'll see what I can do." The game was starting to get tiring for both of us.

So I had traipsed across a lot toward the pickup parked down the road and sought a dirt path across a berm to reach it. There were, typically, a dozen women there in the shade selling chewing gum, fruit, aspirins, soda. As was my habit, when I met the elites, I had on my Ferragamo shoes – the soft leather, metal buckle, long toed court jester sort, which were distasteful to me who was from birth very understated but who was even more tied to Christmas presents from my children. I went up the berm, plastic briefcase hanging from my shoulder, through the women, when my toe got caught and propelled me downward. In a split second, I caught myself just inches from the ground in a push-up position. I held steady in that position and peered beneath me...to see four rusty ends of re-rod secured vertically in some concrete under the ground and not an inch from my chest. I was holding the position straight and true. I felt damn proud. A lesser old man would have been impaled. I pushed up and got my feet under me and stood up triumphant. No dust to dust off. I looked over at the vendors. Nothing. No expression. Not even the delightful Haitian smile.

By now, the sun had already passed its meridian.

Travels with the Half Pint

A half pint. That is what the boys in Suffield would have called Jean Claude. Despite some arrested growth and the associated ribbing, half pints, you see, fit in. They can turn on a dime, scamper up trees, low crawl under fences, and squeeze through half open windows. Somehow, despite some side-splitting outrage or another, they don't get caught. On January 12th in 2010, the earthquake had crushed his wife to death. To my eyes

– and I spent more time with Jean Claude than any other person outside his family – he seemed to have absorbed the death and moved on. He now had five living children, from seven to seventeen, and a new wife, not much older than seventeen, shorter than he was and like many Haitian city women, already with the urban curse of incipient adipose. As of last week, Jean Claude had the equivalent of fifty cents to his name.

When I would leave my various meetings, there was no "snap to it" from Jean Claude. In fact, I often had to call him on the cell phone to find him. If I did see his truck, Jean Claude appeared to have left the cab. Fact was, as I learned later, he was curled in a bundle on the front seat with his earphones plugged in, listening to Real Madrid. I had given up months ago. It was obvious. He was in some kind of football stupor day and night. I no longer bothered to ask him to quit, even as we were driving. I knew that while it probably had no basis in fact, Real Madrid might be considered by some as salve for post-earthquake trauma.

The other consideration I had given was to stop instructing him on safe driving (Jean Claude always gave a huge berth to oncoming traffic even as he spared pedestrians by only inches).

"Jean Claude, we can't kill people," I said.

"They shouldn't be on the road," he replied.

"But there is no sidewalk," I explained.

"Nope," he said...meaning the end of the discussion.

Of course, assuming a certain liberal thoughtfulness on such things, I later agreed with myself that Jean Claude must have his own narrative and that, here, there were slim pickings indeed – especially if you took away the presumption of his preeminent role as driver.

Jean Claude had, I am guessing, about 200 words of French. And I had about the same amount of Creole, so we had a thin band for dialogue. It didn't much matter. After months together, we had established our dozen jokes, and we just kept repeating them, never less funny. The landlord's men who were often not available to turn on the electricity or jump start the water were always, as they asserted, "aux toilettes" at the time they were needed. Thus provoking my comment that whenever someone who was supposed to be someplace, but wasn't, "Must be aux toilettes." Jean Claude knew it was coming and got a good laugh out of it. Then there was the employee who never answered her phone and gave me sufficient worry to ask Jean Claude to go to her home. "What if she is dead?" I asked before my driver's disbelief. Well, of course, it turned out she had only misplaced her phone, yet again, and so now, as we were tooling around Port au Prince...and I could not get through to someone, anyone, on my cell, Jean Claude would smile and say, "Peut-etre elle est morte."

Other intimacies as well – our little contest to depress our door locks when we were starting to move into some tough neighborhoods. Our mutual appreciation for danger across this city of four million became almost identical. Individual "wins" were by a matter of fractions of seconds. Or our mutual exclamation each time we passed a bank, "Les Gangstas."

Of course, hanging over it all, always hanging over it all, was the "accident of birth." That, when I had done my very small part in reducing cholera, I was going back to my farm in Vermont, and my half pint friend would be left with his fifty cents, a large network of drivers – in and out of work – and, in all likelihood, some small revenue from his children, as they came of age. I told him to forget about NGOs – that their heyday had come and gone – but that if Haiti ever managed to stumble through the next elections, I expected plenty of diaspora money to wash up on its shores. Much of it for the gangstas. "But hell, even they need drivers," I joked. Jean Claude had looked at me and frowned.

"Nope," he said.

So, stuttering up the hill through the mess of vehicles and across roads that I was likening to those I had banged over in the African hinterlands in the early 1970s and now with the chronic throb in my upper left molar increasingly aggravated, I began a look out for some kind of dentist who looked legit – when serendipitously Jean Claude spotted a storefront ahead with two larger than life photos of Hillary. Before and after. With "before" as some ragged likeness taken by a wire service of her in a candid moment and the "after," a State Department stock photo that adorned the embassies around the world. Above them both was a huge needle about to pierce the crow's feet of a young woman's face. "Botox," it proclaimed. "Erases wrinkles." Then over to the side of this display was a huge enameled tooth atop a long brazen screw. "Implants. Same day. German trained surgeon. Dr. Dieudonné. Berlin, Paris, New York."

Meanwhile, stuck in traffic and still looking at Hillary up the street, I was recollecting the forty-eight hours just a few years back when I was closeted in a cinder block chamber with a horrific abscess during a string of Shia holy days until rosy fingered dawn had finally brought Ali, the dentist, to my cell and who with a great splatter of blood and pus finally had tooth and root out in his pliers, held up before my face as if he had just captured Satan himself by the tail while I had slumped down in "born again" gratification, pounding my heart vehemently with my fist, as faithful Shias do.

I signaled Jean Claude to stop. With a full calendar of official holidays ahead that would close down many profitable Haitian activities, I thought it sage to inquire. I rang the buzzer and could see through the iron grates the receptionist move toward me.

"Are you open?"

"Yes," she answered. "You are here to make an appointment?" And around her were the various loafers all glued to the TV and the Western daytime drama – the fog-like inculcation of "spills and chills and soft porn from America." "I just need a business card," I told her, "so if I have an emergency over the weekend, then I could call."

"Well, you need to see Dr. Dieudonné." Then she led me down a dark, unclean hall and into the doctor's office, which was not much different than the waiting room with another group of loafers watching the same programs, including several piled onto the dentist chairs themselves whom the rather rumpled doctor now shooed away. But I was already raising my hand in a signal to stop, knowing full well where my line in the sand was drawn and that I was not getting buckled into that contraption under any circumstances other than what had befallen me in Kut. I explained I was a visitor to this fair city and as good sense would dictate, being aged and all, I wanted the dentist's card in my hip pocket should I fall prey to an emergency. "Could I please have his business card and would he really answer if I called?"

"Absolutely," the dentist said, scrounging around for a rather uncrisp card as I reaffirmed my need.

"Even at midnight? Even on a Sunday?"

"Absolutely," he replied, smiling as if both parties knew that his response reflected current intent rather than future certainty, the doctor being quite sure of the extraordinary circumstances surrounding this old Blan, which would cause him to have a Haitian rummaging around in his mouth. "You know, at my age, I just think it wise to have your card."

And then Dr. Dieudonné said something about age I couldn't understand, but got the loafers snickering.

Back in the car, I got to reflecting on all the waiting rooms across the span of Port au Prince that had a TV and a ceiling fan and where loafers passed the day, their lives. Sort of indistinguishable pockets. No matter − a center for Botox and oral surgery or a room at customs where you watched your dossier, slow as molasses, circulate from hand to hand, some glued to the screen, others in a lively dispute, others eating their meal from a Styrofoam container.

But...and here was the difference. Again, there was a "but" for me − who had also been subjected to the clean and orderly and unrumpled and always crisp, back in the "world." The unrumpled lawyer who had fleeced me and my Annie when, in the throes of romance, we had burned our bridges as we had taken a fast plane for Paris. Or the doctors in the VA in Richmond who went into my gut for "an exploratory" and left with a meter of bowel in their slippery hands and then hid the results of the ensuing investigatory panel of peers from my poor eyes and clean got away with it − in perpetuity − while I suffered the humiliation of streaming liquid shit for several years till some drug company finally came up with the appropriate pill.

Not to mention, all the crisp and unrumpled folks who had sent the likes of me to Vietnam in the first place. Similarly, "unrumpled and crisp" was that shining northern city on the hill when it slammed the door shut on the liberation of the slaves in Haiti in 1804 fearing a pervasive contagion of black freedom moving inexorably north to ruin the unprecedented profits of

King Cotton from Boston to New Orleans.

And then, in a snap, I got jolted back to the "here and now" as Jean Claude had hit another pothole. Yep, a sharp shot from that molar – via the eyeball – to the cranium. "Gawd," I moaned. Would Dieudonné be there for me – in the middle of the night – if there was to be a hemorrhage? All my experience in this part of the world told me, he would. He and his assortment of utensils. That is... if his phone worked.

A quick stop at my bakery where I always bought two baguettes. Never three and never one and thus was soon known as Monsieur D'habitude by the counter girls. And I always dropped some gourdes in their tip bottle – thoroughly against my principles, but always in keeping with my indulgence to appreciate the momentary joy I gave Haiti's "generation next," all arrayed in their pink get-ups and flashing smiles.

This afternoon, I broke my regularity and bought a cake for Director Labonté at Customs. "Thank you for the gymnastics," I had instructed to be written in purple icing, a reference to the Director's last comment on what it had taken to get me "a good price for the orphans."

Back up the ascent to the cage where the accumulated emails awaited me, of which I already had a glimpse from the small screen on my smart phone. Among them, more guidance on increasing the line items for HQ costs within the budget for the hurricane response proposal I was crafting – and also amidst them, I had noticed, an additional aggravation from the global security team, parked quite securely, thank you, in the Maryland suburbs, wanting to know the places I frequented – to assure the organization that the risks were tolerable. "Not just for the agency," they quickly added, "but for you, as well, David."

Fucking parasites, I had muttered as I climbed the steps to my office. "Sucking up all they can out of fear."

Flies Batting around the Temple

Negative energy, I recalled later, now strapped in behind my monitor. It only serves to whittle away body and mind, killing cells faster than you can create them, especially given an aging wellspring. So, for some many months now, I had tried not to engage. A tricky maneuver since such an approach could either put me on the high road or bottle up the angst till it swilled like acid in my gut. Tricky also in the sense of knowing how well my detachment would serve to placate or when it would enrage the clerks at HQ still further. Was this just the devil "pride" at play? A renegade temperament? Perhaps, but the larger part was the righteousness of the charge against these so-called professionals ensconced in the heart of these mega-charities surrounding CEOs who had never worked a project from start to finish overseas in their lives and who were easily convinced by the coterie that they were the last line of defense in assuring that precarious equilibrium of "Mission/Men" in those distant "God Forsaken" lands where the corporate flag was planted. Patent nonsense, I knew – since nothing happened as planned in such countries from the minute you unbuckled your belt in economy and took your pack from the overhead and left the confines of the West's magnificent flying machine. Yes – to squeeze any good out of the charity's presumption, one had to find ways around American strictures, so as to invest in homegrown ambitions, unregulated or not, which with time and some luck might slowly emerge from a landscape of weeds into something vital that actually had a shot in that unforgiving race for the sky.

What now was today's doozie? That the new intern...if she ever were to find herself in a bad situation, they counseled, was to immediately call the security stiff in Maryland. Which, of course, produced the resounding guffaw in the field. "And then what?" they laughed. "Send in a special ops team to pluck her out of some seedy bar where she had gotten in over her head?" Or what was it yesterday? That we should establish a baseline with twenty-three performance criteria for government health centers that to date were unable to find ways to pay their staff. Or the day before, some other "green eye shade" had calculated that we had overspent $13.67 for two thousand pencils we had purchased for our training program – even as whole containers of antibiotics had been lost in the bush to spoil when the HQ Emergency Response Team had barreled across the Dominican border into Haiti during the first response to the earthquake

...cameras rolling for the News at Six.

Of course, this aforementioned represented just the clutter in the inbox. The flies batting about my temple. The essential arguments were far more troubling. They involved Right Relations between Americans and other peoples. Is America simply more inhabited terrain or an exceptional idea?

It was during those halcyon days back in 1961 when the presumption of overseas development went big time. When JFK had captured the enthusiasm for broadcasting the American story with citizens emerging from colonial empires or contesting the dictatorship of the proletariat. Back then, there was a sense of America as a global idea, struggling within an America as archetypical hegemon. Where was the meeting place to be for both its values and interests, seemingly in opposition, for hard power and soft power? And who manages this? Makes each decision? Who can develop the foreigners who have no historical references for what the Yankees preach? Who can get 1000 tons of American flour through the port of Tangiers without half of it being summarily labeled as unfit by some sad assed official at the port...so that within days the import is crowding the shelves in the souk and killing demand for local grains? Who can squeeze out a little bit of transformation for the oppressed when the mechanism at hand – USAID – went from new model car to rusted out rattletrap before the turn of the century? Whom do they send? Well, the answer is: they sent folks like me. Cannon fodder for official America's notions of exceptionalism.

So where was the egress for the likes of me? I was now seen in equal parts as a nuisance. Except sometimes among the few, the very wet behind the ears, who might, out of unbridled curiosity, still spark. They might, did sometimes, sit at my knee. But for the rest, the convicted, USAID and the mega charities, I was becoming more trouble than I was worth.

Cheating the System

I had begun cheating the system for the greater good since the day I had arrived in Beirut in 1981. Not only bending the budget for better cause but also slipping my thoughts out to distant media outlets for pseudonymous distribution.

So now, while I, hypocrite, curried favor as a Sales and Marketing Representative, replete with his plastic satchel, for a charity in Haiti so as, in the immediate, to acquire a piece of the resilience pie – a so-called potential grant now valued at ten million dollars – I secretly relieved myself of my more precious thoughts as follows.

Starvin' Marvin Op-Ed

Late last fall, I was sitting outside in our farmyard in Vermont, just south of the Canadian border. My wife and I were remarking on the influx of the Common Red Poll, a bird not often seen in such numbers where we live. Upon further investigation, it seems that what had been a rather mild drought for us had been more profound and enduring, deeper into Quebec. There had not been enough seed to sustain the population up there.

"Influencing the Narrative"

That same fall, inside our home, on our monitors, I had noticed two other related phenomenon gaining momentum. The first pertained to "resilience," a new branding effort by the principal Western purveyors of foreign assistance, meant to rally consensus among the liberal democracies that humanitarian interventions must henceforth shift from the West doing what it perceives to be necessary for desperate communities abroad, toward insisting that the local communities fare for themselves in times of distress. Here is what Helen Clark – the head of the United Nations Development Program (UNDP) – said in April 2012:

> "At UNDP, we see development challenges in the 21st century as different in nature, scale, and scope from those of the past. If our world is to be one in which poverty is eradicated, and inequality reduced; and where growth is inclusive and production and

consumption do not break planetary boundaries; and if we are to be effective in combating the effects of climate change; we need to look beyond our traditional interventionist logic to harness the agency of people, their communities, and institutions. It is this logic which has led UNDP to encapsulate its mission statement in the simple phrase: Empowered Lives, Resilient Nations. This speaks to both means and ends. Empowered people can build resilient nations."

And then, later that same year, I surfed upon the figure of "Starvin' Marvin" and Michael Huemer, a philosopher at the University of Colorado. Now, I believed, I was getting closer, much closer to Right Relations as they apply, in this instance, to refugees. Read on for an excerpt from Huemer:

"[Marvin] is very hungry and is trying to travel to the marketplace to buy some food. Another person, Sam (Sam has a large number of nephews and nieces, so we'll call him Uncle Sam), decides to stop Marvin from going to the marketplace using coercion. He goes down there with his M16 and blocks the road. As a result, Marvin can't trade for food and, as a result, he starves. So then the question is, did Sam kill Marvin? Did he violate his rights? Almost anyone would say yes, Sam acted wrongly. In fact, if Marvin died as a result, then Sam killed him. It wouldn't be that Sam failed to help Marvin. No, he actively intervened...This is analogous to the US government's immigration policy. There are people who want to trade in our marketplace, in this case the labor market, and the government effectively prevents them from doing that, through use of force."

Refugees and Borders

So we get to borders, to boundaries, to walls and fences – and the savants of Western development are telling the poor and oppressed to "hang in there." To take a lickin' and keep on tickin' because in forty years they may have glimmers of good governance, in fifty years they may contribute to the prevailing global sciences, and in sixty years "you may see less of your topsoil flow into the sea around you."

Meanwhile, the West, which drew your borders for you ages ago, stops you – the refugee – from invigorating its own lands, then parks you in squalid camps at the borders, interdicts you at sea, and throws you a bone. The West tells you to be resilient, while all of preceding history indicates that resilience means migration – for man and beast. Meaning, not accepting life within those borders. Meaning, flying to opportunity.

And meaning, speaking now as an American, the recipient hegemon is equally denied enrichment by the new blood which has always been at the heart of the advancement of its Bill of Rights and open, prosperous markets.

And finally, meaning that the creation of Diasporas, which provide far more investments and knowledge transfers to those left behind than any overseas aid endeavor with its accompanying rhetoric, is equally thwarted.

Refugees are created by untenable circumstances within boundaries created for them by the West, created to the West's own detriment and to the enduring plight of those living in God forsaken places.

One morning in Haiti, I had a discussion about resilience with an unemployed, ambitious young man. I asked him what resilience meant to him. He answered quickly, "Miami." Not unlike those Common Redpolls flying into our farm last fall, he would go where there was seed to eat – would, if it were not for the United States Coast Guard standing ready to turn him back.

I was always a bit nervous with my duplicity, chewing my nails after I clicked send. Because at the heart of it was the humiliation of a sixty-nine-year-old man whose peers had mostly retired to the porch with their lemonade, but who still needed an income. Being "corrected" daily by apparatchiks who had spent a small fraction of time compared to him as either "Captains in the Swirl" or in more stable times like a dog with a bone, trying to figure out the development conundrums. Licking my wounds these days instead of walking away because, truth be told and hypocrisy revealed, I could not stand the thought of my family living in a post-David era without dignity, without the farm and without the wherewithal to keep the wolves at bay. I knew the wolves far better now than when I was younger; the wolves were both sharp fanged and ubiquitous – and seldom appeared as wolves.

It was all actuarial, I concluded. Quit now and live those remaining days on the farm counting on an early death, seamlessly coincidental with the onset of widow's insurance or accept these degrading circumstances longer as a hedge against the costs of a longer life.

Mont Joli

So when I had enough finally of the keyboard or there was no more incoming worth my time, I sometimes descended from my platform, usually in the late afternoon, for better ground.

It is a tall rather awkward wooden frame at Mont Joli with lattice embellishments and shingled spires poking into the branches of the divine Mapous, surrounded by coconut palms, jacarandas, figs, and mangoes with an understory of wild flowers and long grasses. One sits on a veranda speaking French to French women who, like me, love to enthuse and exaggerate while sipping demitasses of Belgian coffee. And then – sweet Lord – the afternoon rain sweeps down on the tin roof, and from time to time I hear the mangoes dropping. And you may as well be reclining in Elysium notwithstanding that the specifics of the discussion centered on the donors' new love child, called Resilience, and how that was now, in the donors' view, the cure for what ails Haiti. And how the proposition was such nonsense, but, nevertheless, how might they, the NGO reps on that veranda, get a piece of the resilience pie. And sometimes, they just shook their heads, at the absurdities in which they were swimming.

This was, in fact, the sole virtue to emerge from the months of NGO confabs. Benjamin and his veranda, my last stop on many such afternoons. The irrepressible socialist son of a famous Belgian Philosopher, a long drink of water with a black curly mop. Extraordinarily kind to his elder allowing me to take him under my wing as concerns the history of the trade's current presumptions, but reluctant nevertheless to forsake the egalitarian argument during our many debates.

Undeterred, and jacked on caffeine, to their great amusement, I would stream. Pointedly trying to upend their belief in idyllic end states. These few French loved it. This old American up on his stump.

"First off, friends...let me say...I am still struggling with this notion of happiness and have thus far come to no permanent resting place.

"Thomas Wolfe wrote a short story called 'The Far And The Near' about a woman who for twenty-plus years went to her porch in North Carolina at the same time each afternoon to wave to the engineer of the daily train passing by. Finally, one day, the engineer retired and went to visit her. There was mutual repulsion.

"I have known it myself, standing in the corridor, head stretched out the window of the hurtling train as it rushed through the night...across Russia...across Europe...and down the rails where they existed in Africa. Exhilarated with the movement and once there, quickly depressed with the destination.

"I think that so much of individual happiness is caused by the prospect of movement toward a destination – and the movement itself – and not the destination, which has its own disappointment or destruction sown deep within it, whether that destination be a new flat screen TV or a revolutionary cause.

"So, the calculation is: 'aspiring to move' triggers 'movement,' which triggers 'arrival at a destination,' which triggers 'discontent,' which triggers 'aspiration to move.'

"It seems as if this is the natural state for vigorous human beings. And even if one is not vigorous – rather tied up in bed in a neuropsychiatric ward – one travels. One gets the Demerol and one travels avoiding the arrival at a destination as long as possible. Or, similarly, as an old man within dusted off memories – revised.

"War, of course, is the great explosion of this amalgamated movement and the great vacuum after it is spent.

"Now...the collective:

"The most stable society is the one in which The Pursuit of Happiness (note: the founding fathers did not say happiness itself) is ubiquitous. Meaning, among the mass who aspire, most can move toward that aspiration – even as that eventual destination is a dead end. When that possibility of movement becomes suffocated by some dark and heavy hand – whether that be the nomenclature of the USSR or the 'virtual eviscerations and sedations' now so prevalent in our nation – a society dies. There was a thousand times more life in the slums of NYC or Naples than in the dead cities I wandered through in the 1970s: Moscow, Vladivostok, Warsaw. Fraught as Naples or Harlem was with tragedy and inequities, they were alive with movement. So I have come to realize our happiness as humans is not about end states. It is rather about allowing for ubiquitous flesh and blood motion, often dangerous, toward a multiplicity of destinations – most of which disappoint.

"As Wolfe said: 'The old hunger for voyages fed at his heart...to go alone...into strange cities; to meet strange people and to pass again before they could know him; to wander, like his own legend, across the earth – it seemed to him there could be no better thing than that.'"

They actually clapped, these French, followed by a din of dispute and exclamations while I, quite spent, would just lean back in my wicker chair and let French – its music – float around me, mixed as it was with the intermittent sweeps of rain and the occasional thud of ripe mangoes.

And so I took my leave from my tropical refuge, out the creaking Iron Gate and now looking every which way for signs of Jean Claude...wondering still about movement, which had so defined my times. And whether the same rules apply as those times evolve from that great industrial reality with its fecundating densities – the slather on the muscles glowing before the furnace – to the delicate fingertips firing through that skein of synapses to cerebral catchments...googly eyed...a rocketing distance toward a different prototype of man...a non-moving version or rather only moving in the mind. Now in some intermediate stage – living on the small screen with their lips fastened around a plastic straw attached to a big gulp.

Day's End

Back in Beirut in 1982, before Annie and baby Hank had taken the last flight out, on the heels of the Israeli bombing just down the coast, as discussed earlier, it had been the weekly pouch that carried the private thoughts and emotions across the divide. Letters taken off to some makeshift sanctuary where they were quietly absorbed word for word.

But the gestation of the new information and communication technologies was both quick and transformative. New sociologies sprang up. In 1991, after Desert Storm, my colleagues and I had trucked in a sat phone to Baghdad, as large as a full-sized Samsonite, which took the better part of a day to install on the roof of the Al Rasheed Hotel. By the time I had returned for another tour in 2003, I had held the sat phone in the palm of my hand as Annie and I were sharing our news nightly by email. Soon to be replaced by VOIP.

Now, at 6pm, most nights, we were Skyping, from the cage to the farm. About such phenomena as the departure of the geese from our pond or a sighting of the Bluegills in the marsh, the giant pileated woodpecker digging a hole in the poplars big enough for your fist, a very large bear paw in the mud down by Hank's Convenience Trail, and most often the great and hazardous adventure with the Eastern Black Walnut. Planted absolutely as far north and with as few growing days (143) as any cockeyed gambler would dare. I just smiled and said, "Climate change. These trees are on the right side of history." A thousand of them. A monoculture. And my folly was becoming Hank's folly as she toiled in late October on her knees with frozen fingers...or Alex's folly as he had rushed to the rescue during a gale last July when the winds had bent a quarter of the saplings over so far that their canopies were flush with the ground...lifting them back up to the vertical and tying them taut to stakes...or Annie's, all the dry summer long while I was gone filling the 250 gallon tub and giving them all "a good drink" as she would say. A thousand trees and all from our own muscle. Holes dug, mulched, staked, watered, insects picked off by hand, pruned...the growing boles stroked with my affection. Even a graduation for the first trees to break 6' BHD (breast high diameter), ceremoniously casting down extra potash on their drip line as due recognition. I had made a graduation speech alongside the laureates, encouraging them mightily to weather the trials and tribulations that would surely come their way. So...we chatted nightly:

"No movement on the row of seeds I planted," she said.

"Well, unless you planted dead seeds, they'll rise. Give them some more hot weather," I answered.

"Maybe I should have planted them deeper."

"Absolutely not," I replied. "Squirrels don't plant them deeper. I mean in Ohio, Annie, they just drop them and cover them with cow plop."

Or discussing a fatality among the six-year-olds:

"All the leaves just turned black in 24 hours. I have no idea why."

"A real puzzle," I responded or "puzzlement" when I was trying to sound like an old timer.

"All I can think of is that an animal pissed on it...like a deer," she said.

"Musta been something with an awful lot of piss," I rejoined.

"Yeah, I suppose. Disease would take longer."

"Or maybe its taproot hit a shelf," I offered.

"But twenty-four hours?"

And then three weeks later – still on the subject of the fatality:

"There are two shoots coming up from the base."

"Excellent."

"I was just going to spade it up. We'll have to thin them someday, anyway."

"No," I insisted. "Maybe the root is OK. The root is the thing." I went on, "If that is still alive, we can still get a tree."

"But it'll be a runt, not good for anything except firewood."

"Please. Don't mark it off yet. There are just too many variables. For all we know, it may turn out magnificent."

"David," she objected, "they're not humans. They're only there for the sawmill. Right? That's what you always said. America's most precious hardwood. 5k a piece for a 14' trunk, 30" DBH. And now you want to nurse the runt back to life, and I'm the one who has to cart all the water to it all summer long."

"Maybe, some potash," I said.

So, emerging anger. Time to sign off. Cause it could become brooding and hang over us for days or longer. Compounded. And I knew it was no longer about trees. But about how one took life – as a dreamer or not. Annie, once eager and spellbound by the prospects of "burning bright," as I had initially exclaimed before the leaping flames on the bank of my old mountain stream, was now more realistic about what life could offer. A root would grow a good tree or not – in the face of my "a root, damn it, will produce a great tree."

Then proceeded the evening equivalent of the morning routine. *Le Nouvelliste* spread out on the kitchen table. Two bottles of beer (Prestige – je suis fier de ma bière) next to the headlines, a Chinese plate, a knife, a baguette, a chunk of cheddar, a tub of butter. All set for a slow read through the political debate, the police blotter, the sprinkling of human interest stories, and, of course, the recurrent scourge: this week – Chikungunya. It was as I had told Annie on Skype: "Think of Haiti as a person with no immune system. It does not matter what hits it. Malaria, HIV/AIDS, cholera, the winter floods, they all ravage Haiti." Then, typically, a mango, peeled and eaten over the sink to avoid a sticky mess. A sliver of meat cooked in the frying pan and then back to the table. October 24th, 2014, and May 14th, 2016. That was when the latest chapters of Haiti were scheduled to be told. Free and fair elections. Parliament first and then the presidency. There was no precedent for free and fair and no reason to expect more now. Open the second bottle, fork the meat from frying pan to plate, a squirt of ketchup for taste, and then the ensuing workout to grind the flesh sufficiently, so I could wash it down the old gullet. Dishes in the sink, rinsed free of residue, leftovers in the fridge, lights off, gas burner off, and then the quick shuffle to the bed. Prop up the pillows and then the exquisite gratification of the reflective smoke. "Another day, another dollar," I told myself. I wished I were in Ukraine. Haiti, I deemed, to be no more than 100 or 200 years of malignant US public policy. Ukraine, I repeated. Now that could get my juices flowing. Reborn Russian nationalism. Nuclear tipped, no less. The EU disparate as always about its resolve. NATO toe to toe with the Kremlin. And once again the enlightenment trying to hold its own against the bored boy in the back of the class.

And then my long arm reached for my "bouk." Tilt the lampshade for maximum light and then open the bookmark to: Leptons and Quarks and Bosons in particular, a dissertation where my comprehension hovered around 10% but still, I drove on... And when I felt that the rather small sponge I had inherited was filled to the point where even the 10% was unattainable, I put it aside and grabbed Huck, where my comprehension soared to 100%, and I was soon gliding down the Mississippi, naked as the day I was born, on the raft with Huck and Jim, smoking a corn cob pipe and spinning yarns to kingdom come. Till my eyelids began to droop, and I had to put the story aside, placing my glasses and phone on the nightstand. I then clicked off the light, rolled left toward the window where the pigeons roosted, and wished myself a "good night," hoping the meat would settle well and that I would not wake up till dawn.

Haitian Roosters

I had grown up flying. Beginning in 1950 as a five-year-old. Back and forth from New York to Sydney, sometimes alone. "Boy 9 tells Doublets about Travel Down Under" was the headline in the White Plains newspaper. Bygone days those were when one flew in the weather. Not over it or around it. Beautiful stews and plenty of vomit bags. I was, this morning, at Guy Mallory, a small air station adjacent to the larger international airport, Toussaint Louverture, waiting for the flagship of Tortug'Air, a Let L-410MU, to carry me up north. An old Soviet box like contraption, which definitely flew through weather. Buffeting around, not much above the subsistence farms and barren slopes, wingtips skirting the ramparts of King Christophe's Citadel.

Still, after all these years, I felt exhilarated, from the moment I left the terminal and walked across the tarmac to the ladder that took me into the somewhat rickety interior of the box and soon after into a slow separation from the ground and into the long curve over the surf.

At Cap Haitian, I had gone straight through the airport from Tarmac to Latteau, the driver, in less than two minutes. We then fell into excited talk about how we each were doing. A year and a half ago, it had just been the two of us who had explored the backwaters of Le Grand Nord on weekends, poking our noses wherever I thought I could learn something. A Hounfour here, a Clarin-still there, a dilapidated health center, a gaily-colored peasant's hut. I still called it "Mucking About," a necessary precursor for a good idea in a strange context, seldom practiced these days by the trade's new professionals. "Value added" had been my more formal guide. No other health NGOs in these mountains. More impoverished than the rest of Haiti. In fact, the majority were still in the Lakou's where they had fled 200 years ago. "Isolé and Negligé" was my first proposition to donors. It was now more than a year since I had moved my "Noyau Dur" (key staff) from their disgrace in PaP, casting off, as I did, all the ne'er-do-wells and those too fatally afflicted by the "attitudes and comportment" of the previous expats. Those who, in the months after the earthquake, had become notorious for their lifestyle in the luxurious and gated community of Belleville, far, far from the rubble below and where they made every effort to decompress from their purported day job of "saving lives." Though, as a subsequent analyst explained, "there weren't a whole lot of metrics to support that claim." Mostly, there were docs shuttling from the US to repair some casualties and then skedaddle back to the world before the stitches were out. Cameras rolling. The larger aid community had come to call the Belleville experience "Miami Vice" with varying degrees of affection and disdain.

So, it had been an effort for me to move the organizational culture from Miami Vice to the new T-shirts that proclaimed "Shock and Awe." Shock that they pushed off each morning at 8am. And awe that they did not get back from the Mornes till sunset. Further, to move the culture from the incestuous hub-bub of PaP to "Isolé and Negligé." From white man managed to all Haitian run. My primary role becoming – aside from Sales and Marketing in PAP – to keep HQ from screwing the transformation up with those 100 weekly electronic intrusions, most of which were about securing yet another signature on yet another document that no one read, confirming to the compliance department, for example, that no terrorist was selling us toilet paper or that every hour of every day had been assigned a cost center.

MMU's, they were called. Mobile Medical Units. A driver, a doctor, a nurse and a hygienist with boxes of medicine and disinfectant, all in a four-wheel vehicle. Out from the coast and into the Mornes. Now proud. Step aside and let us show you how it's done. "It" being the war on cholera. "Cholera Fighters" stenciled alongside "Shock and Awe" on their T-shirts. I loved those guys. Plying the Mornes...going the last kilometers to the village by foot, lugging their knapsacks full of medicine, fording swollen streams and torrents of rain, shivering, slipping, and sliding up the muddy trails, bellowing out their messages about cholera prevention with their megaphones and tending to the desiccated old folk with intravenous solution. Quite apart from what one hopes to do, I had long ago forgotten there was any difference between their black and my white. And the way they strutted...coming home like roosters past the Ministry of Health MMU, which hadn't fired a piston in a week. "Out sick." "No fuel." "In meetings."

Annie, who had done this work in Nabatieh, Lebanon, during the 2006 war, and I had often discussed this at our nightly fire by the pond. It was all so sadly ephemeral. A memory for these roosters for a lifetime. But, around them – in the Mornes – all those "generation next" in their spanking clean school uniforms and bright bows in their hair, treading the dirt roads in these Mornes to remote schools where they were learning almost nothing and those with any gumption soon would fly the coop for the cities on the coast. There was almost no topsoil left and would take hundreds of years to restore it. The "still" owner still crushed the cane for Clarin with a long pole handle and one gear the way it had been done under Toussaint Louverture, and they still made planks from what remaining hardwood there was with the log on two sawhorses and a man below in a pit and a man on top pulling an old rip saw up and down. "A flash in the pan" was how I was thinking of myself as I took my usual seat for dinner alone at the Hotel Roi Christophe.

It seemed to be an old plantation home with cobble stones running up to a veranda shaded by a gigantic Mapou tree, which given its girth (6' DBH), must have been there since Toussaint Louverture. A planter's carriage was parked beneath it and other paraphernalia of the times was scattered about, rusting gracefully in the shade. Cannon balls, Chaudières, chains — lots of chains. Inside from the veranda stood a field-stone courtyard and a fountain surrounded by sleeping chambers under a roof of red tiles. The veranda and the courtyard both gave way to a dining room through ceiling to floor arcades. Their mahogany shutters — thick hand cut planks tied across by wrought iron sashes — fastened now against a whitewashed stone wall, opened the tables to the palms and tropical flowers outdoors.

I was the first to arrive and took my place near the kitchen, directly under one of the old-fashioned ceiling fans. I ran my hands over the linen for the feel of it and then lowered my nose almost to the petals of the gardenia before settling in my straight chair. I was quite thoroughly paralyzed there in the amber coming off the candles scattered about the walls in iron sconces. Ramrod straight, I was, imagining the planter life. Back when they provided fully half of France's GDP on the backs of their imported slaves. Such had been the growing popular demand for sweetness in the old world. I tried to imagine the conversations had in that room on the eve of the revolt, which would end with all those white settlers cut to pieces. Hacked to death by machete, still the common sidearm for all those peasants still up there in the Mornes. "Spaghetti," I told the waitress. "Comme D'habitude," she smiled. "Bien Entendu." Together with one glass of red wine and one glass of water, which I would pour into my wine at appropriate intervals. Imagining a little more with each sip, interrupted only by the beep of my phone, indicating "incoming," unlikely now that most of my various HQ's had gone home for the day. I held the gardenia to my nose and saw what a colleague had sent. Quite abruptly, my laughter burst into the calm. My plane...or rather my type of plane....the LET 410 MU had had an accident three years earlier.

"On August 25, 2010," the report read, "an L-410 crashed with twenty fatalities in Bandundu, Democratic Republic of the Congo. According to the sole survivor, the crash was caused by a stampede of passengers after a crocodile escaped from a bag in the cabin. The crocodile itself survived the crash, but was killed by rescuers."

And then just as fast, the mood began to turn melancholy. Forsaking my team of roosters here was treachery. So perfect for Haiti. Just another white man who had jumped in and sold them a bill of goods. I knew that in a month, at most, they would be picked apart by the compliance types in HQ. I knew it took a weathered old American like me who knew how to tangle these twits up in their own rules and regs. "Think about it," I was talking to myself in the middle of this empty room – "a Haitian with all his miserable history is just now alerted that his headquarters in the center of America is calling...so he runs around like the chicken with no head, trying to serve, which is an endless and useless task...and with time he will be brought to tears or rebellion. And if HQ decides to replace a white with white, what are the odds that my replacement would not be all puffed up about being a boss (since no one else would have made him a boss back in the world). And it would soon have him allowing himself the accoutrements of 'boss.' Meaning – the driver waiting outside in his car, way into the night, while the boss has a few more for the road."

So how long before the team melts down? Goes back to a Ministry for a lifetime sinecure and a fat ass. In any case, it was certainly the end of "Shock and Awe." I could already see the look on their faces when I told them I was going back to Vermont. Not hostile. Not "take your Shock and Awe and shove it blan." Rather – a resignation – "well, have a good trip."

Chikungunya beeped on my phone. There she was Minister Guillaume, meeting the press. In French. Telling them that the Ministry was preparing a vast campaign. Fumigating all through selected slums and "what's more" free Paracetamol at your nearest health center. "Good thing," I thought. "That 90% of the people who could benefit from what she was promising never heard her speech – or, if they had, would not have understood the language. Free Paracetamol at the nearest center. Lady, in case you haven't noticed, this is not Connecticut. Most of your health centers have no medicines of any kind." And she just kept rolling on...never interrupted for a second by that reality.

And now I watched the mosquito circle in the candlelight before me. I would have to sleep under the sheets tonight. That was exactly what I did not need. Only a month before I left for the world. High fever, excruciating headaches, and swollen joints. For old people, Minister Guillaume had declared, it could even be fatal.

"Enough of the worry," I counseled. The spaghetti had arrived, and I now offered myself another rather large slug of wine and quickly returned to my imaginings of the planter's life just before it had been extinguished...

ABOUT THE AUTHOR

David Holdridge served in the Vietnam War in 1969 as an infantry platoon leader outside of Chu Lai. He was wounded and spent eighteen months getting repaired at various hospitals in the United States, culminating with operations at Hartford Hospital in Connecticut where neurosurgeon, Dr. Benjamin Whitcomb managed to free him from his trauma.

Subsequently, he spent thirty-five years working with humanitarian organizations amidst populations suffering from war, exploitation, and impoverishment, including assignments in West Africa, the Middle East, and Asia. From 2010 to 2012, he directed an advocacy effort in Washington D.C., which argued for significant transformation of the current systems and approaches of American assistance abroad.

Currently, he lives on a tree farm in Vermont with his wife, Annie. His daughter Hank was born in Beirut; his son, Alex, in Tunis. He is the recipient of Prize Americana in 2015 for his memoir, *The Avant Garde of Western Civ*. He is currently working on a book describing the beginnings of the counter culture revolution in 1962. Visit his website at http://www.avantgardeofwesternciv.com.

ACKOWLEDGMENTS

Benjamin Whitcomb...whose hand and scalpel got me past Vietnam

Michiko Ota...who lifted many of us up to a place from which we are yet to descend

Zevart Nadjarian....Godmother to my Beiruti, Hank

Ruth Andersen...always "sister Roo" in the great midway

Andy Lowe...who was there for Al, when I was away

Sameer Farhan, Ahmed Jabbar, Tall Mohamad, and Ahmed Qadir...who, on various occasions, saved my life

Paul Butler...the Arabist at whose knee I sat

Albana Sala...the best Avant Garde we had

Jim White...who managed to manage me

Karen Saba...a comrade with cerebral palsy who walked the talk in Iraq for three years

Shapol A. Abdullah...the chief of staff in Sulaymaniah

Efanor Nore, Fritz Jean, and Lucito Jeannis...who schooled me on the Haitian dynamic

Phil Karber...the first outsider to tell me I should write

Leslie Kreiner Wilson...who worked hard to make this narrative sensible and who, along the way, gave me an education

Printed in the USA
CPSIA information can be obtained
at www.ICGtesting.com
CBHW031028270124
3795CB00005B/244

9 780996 777919